"I FIRST HEAR[...]
TELEPHONE, A [...]
IF I WOULD TA[...]
SHE WAS WRIT[...]
YES: I WANTED TO HEAR THE VOICE
AGAIN. I LOVED ITS SOUND, BRIGHT AND
QUICK, EDGED WITH A HINT OF MYSTERY,
A STRONG VOICE. BUT I HAD NO IDEA
HOW STRONG IT WOULD PROVE TO BE."
—from the Foreword
by Josephine Humphreys,
author of *Rich in Love*

"An elegant, finished book by a writer who may
have begun as an amateur but grew into an
artist. . . . This is the kind of black speech that
Faulkner smuggled across the color line and got a
Nobel Prize for."   —*New York* magazine

"A testimony to the human spirit with all the
urgency of a page-turning bestselling novel."
—*North Jersey Herald & News*

"Ruthie Bolton restores meaning to the word
true. . . . *Gal* is the record of a woman who
survived hell—barely . . . it indelibly captures a
particular time and place . . . it illuminates the
common humanity, or inhumanity, of which we
are capable . . . it deals unflinchingly with issues of
male and female, African American and white,
power and dependence, but somehow it overturns
every cliché and affirms the power of good in the
face of bad . . . it is a rare achievement that
succeeds brilliantly."   —*Los Angeles Times*

g a l
a true life

---

ruthie bolton

AN ONYX BOOK

ONYX
Published by the Penguin Group
Penguin Books USA Inc., 375 Hudson Street,
New York, New York 10014, U.S.A.
Penguin Books Ltd, 27 Wrights Lane,
London W8 5TZ, England
Penguin Books Australia Ltd, Ringwood,
Victoria, Australia
Penguin Books Canada Ltd, 10 Alcorn Avenue,
Toronto, Ontario, Canada M4V 3B2
Penguin Books (N.Z.) Ltd, 182–190 Wairau Road,
Auckland 10, New Zealand

Penguin Books Ltd, Registered Offices:
Harmondsworth, Middlesex, England

Published by Onyx, an imprint of Dutton Signet,
a division of Penguin Books USA Inc. This is an authorized reprint of a
hardcover edition published by Harcourt Brace & Company. For
information address Harcourt Brace & Company, 6277 Sea Harbor Drive,
Orlando, Florida 32887-6777.

First Onyx Printing, October, 1995
10 9 8 7 6 5 4 3 2 1

I dedicate this book to the Lord above,
my five children, my husband;
Jo Humphreys, Harriet Wasserman,
and Cork Smith.

foreword

ruthie bolton and I call the same place home: Charleston and its islands, some of which are bodies of land surrounded by water and some of which are clusters of people divided by less bridgeable things. We were both born and raised here, and live not ten minutes apart, but we never met until the summer of 1993.

I first heard her voice over the telephone, a young woman asking if I would take a look at the book she was writing. Right away I said yes, for a reason I knew was odd: I wanted to hear the voice again. I loved its sound, bright and quick, edged with a hint of mystery, a strong voice. But I had no idea how strong it would prove to be.

Her manuscript was handwritten on notebook paper, fifty-eight pages bound in a red folder her daughter had brought from school, labeled "Parent Handbook." It outlined the extraordinary events of Ruthie's childhood—but she was having trouble saying the things she really wanted to say. Every writer knows how the very act of putting words on paper seems to spoil the original reality of the story; the mechanics somehow interfere with the telling, and what we want to say is seldom what gets written.

So she decided to try another way of telling, the way southern stories are best told: out loud, teller-to-listener. We agreed to meet twice a week, and between sessions I would transcribe the tapes and type up the chapters.

As *Gal* was being told, I was fortunate enough to be its audience. But I knew that Ruthie wasn't telling the story for me or even to me. I was only a witness and a secretary, while Ruthie was *in* it, seeing it, making it happen again. She recalled tiny details and actual conversations from her earliest years. While she spoke she moved around the room, took the voices of different characters, acted their parts, and cried and laughed. And she never hesitated. She told the story of *Gal* straight through to its remarkable and inspiring end, then later went back to fill in some gaps and expand some scenes.

Gal is a gift to us all.

—*Josephine Humphreys*
Charleston, South Carolina
January 1994

"Ruthie Bolton" is a pseudonym. The names of all the people and many of the places in this narrative have also been changed. The author has chosen this method in order to spare her children, her family, and her friends any pain or embarrassment. In every other respect, the words and events in *Gal* represent the author's true life.

chapter one

now, all the streets are paved. But before Hungry Neck was like it is now, the house that we're in wasn't there. It was off of Rifle Range Road as you're going around that curve. It was a white house, it was a white cedar house—and it was a *showcase* house. People could walk in to see how that house would look, if they wanted one like it. The floors were all wood, and the siding was cedar, it was that very strong cedar wood.

What happened, my grandfather Clovis Fleetwood, who was a cook on a ship, got stationed here in Charleston. He married my grandma—she was from Hungry Neck and already had my mother before she met him—and then they had three daughters more. He went and he saw that showcase house and wanted to buy it, but they told him that he would have to get it moved—it couldn't stay where it was at. He knew there was some lots for sale just below there, in Hungry Neck, so he bought a lot, and he bought the house, and they moved it. The streets were all nothing but dirt, they didn't even have no street signs or anything like that. Most of the houses were old, but little by little, new houses was being built.

At first we didn't have hardly any neighbors except a old lady behind us called Miss Coralie, and one man across the street. His name was Mr. Buzz. He had a horse and a old buggy and a house—it was a house that nobody would even think that somebody lived there. He sold beer, liquor, cigarettes, candy—you name it. My grandmother and grandfather got to know him very well, knew that he was very old, and they felt like giving him meals and stuff because nobody would come and feed him. So as we grew up we would take breakfast, lunch, and dinner to him and also give him water because he didn't have any water in the house, didn't even have a bathroom in the house.

My grandfather decided that he was going to let this man babysit us. My grandmama, she was home, but Mr. Buzz would mind us when she would go places. He was a nice man, but he kept a lot of traffic in and out of his place. You would find drunk mens, drunk ladies there. We would steal his candy when he wasn't looking, and he would take us riding in the buggy, with the horse, up and down all the dirt roads in Hungry Neck. Only once we rode out on the main road, Rifle Range, and that was paved. But we didn't go but a short distance. Just to the big curve and the sign that said Mount Pleasant.

And finally the horse broke his leg. And broke something else on it, so they had to shoot it. It was during the fall, the leaves were yellow and brown. Some of the leaves were on the ground. I was standing there. Mr. Buzz took a rifle, shot him right in the head, and the horse fell down. There were six or seven mens, the drunks that always come out there, and they buried that horse right there in the backyard. They did it just to get a bottle of drink afterwards. A brown pretty horse with a cream-colored tail.

I was four then—knotty head, raggy shoes, dirty clothes, snotty nose. They called me Gal, because of one time I wandered past the yard and my grandfather hollered "Get that gal out the street" and they called me Gal all the time after that.

I was born January 6, 1961, when my mother was thirteen. She couldn't take care of me, so my grandmother took me. I didn't have any sisters, but since I was given to my grandmother, I considered myself at that time one of her daughters. I knew we were aunts and niece, but we were like sisters—Naomi, Kitty, Florence, and me. I had three brothers, but I never knew them. Every time my mother did get pregnant, she would give the kids away. She never kept nobody, she just gave them away. Why, I don't know. Maybe she just didn't want to be bothered with any kids. Or she couldn't handle them.

I never really knew where she was. Only a few times, she lived in the house with us, but when I did see her in the house, she was always being beaten by my granddaddy.

She was in the band at Mount Pleasant High School, she played the drums. One day she came home out of school. I was in the kitchen eating, and I heard somebody come in the door. And when I looked, it was her. She had on the band blues, blue-and-white with a gold trimming in it. I heard the bus pull off. She came down the hallway, because she slept in the last bedroom. She took off her clothes. And then I heard the yelling from my grandfather.

I got up from the table, and my grandmama she grabbed me as I was coming down the hall. She caught me, and when I was trying to peep around her—there was two twin beds in that last bedroom—I saw my grandfather had a belt and my mother was jumping from one bed to the other trying not to get beat.

She ran past us and out the house and I didn't see her no more that day. Late that night we had a phone call from Miss Coralie. She said that my mother was there, and she was afraid to come home. When my grandfather found out that she was there, he went out the back door.

My mother heard him coming, so she ran on to a lady house name Miss Furber. She was a old lady that had cancer and had both her legs cut off, she was in a wheelchair, and she was blind. But she could tell what money she give you—one, five, twenty—it's a feel that she had. My mother stayed there awhile. She moved in there with Miss Furber, and she end up dating one of Miss Furber's sons. But then all of a sudden she just left town. Disappeared. Nobody didn't know where she was at. We got a phone call saying she might be in Philadelphia.

I don't know how many years went by— could have been one, two—but we had gotten a dog. He was a collie and we named him Lassie because he looked just like Lassie. And we heard a screaming. I don't know if it was day, night, or what, but I remember the screaming. *Yelling.* The dog was barking, and then I remember seeing that the dog had someone hand in his mouth, just pulling, tearing it apart, and then I saw it was my mother. She had come home to see me.

They had to take her to the hospital to take care of her.

The next day my grandfather took Lassie, and we all got into the car. It was a white Chevrolet—he always bought a Chevrolet, never no other model car. And we took the dog somewhere into the north area and let him out on the railroad track. Just let him go. When we drove away, it was getting dark, and the dog was standing on the track looking at us. He tried to follow the car.

That night my mother told me, "I'm only going to stay here for about a week. I won't stay longer because I just came to see you."

But a guy came over to the house—his name was Marlon Taylor. She had probably had a fling with him before she even left Charleston. I'm not certain. He came to the house and Daddy wasn't home (Granddaddy, but I called him Daddy). There was a little red chair that was always passed down to the next daughter—it was my mother's chair first, and then it went down through all the sisters until it came to me—and I remember that red chair right there just before you walk into the dining area, and I was sitting in it, and my mother was against the wall with this man, kissing and rocking, I mean they were just going crazy. And I sat there and I watched that. Then he took her chest out. I mean I watched this thing. They were kissing and kissing. And I remember walking up to him, and I said, "Marlon," I said, "are you my daddy?"

And he never answered. He never answered. But he didn't stay that long. He left.

That night my mother went into the bathroom. I don't know why but I said, "Mama, can I come in the bathroom with you?" And she said yeah. I just wanted to be with her. And then I asked her can I suck her chest and she told me no, I couldn't do it.

She said, "Gal, I'm going to leave in a couple of days, but I'll be back."

And I remember crying and crying and begging her please don't go, and I said, "Can I go with you?" and she said, "I can't let you go with me." And she left two days later. But she said, "I will come back."

THAT SUMMER, my grandfather went out to sea. And when September came, my grandma said, "Gal, you know you got to start Head Start so I bought you these clothes. 'Cause you know your mama don't send you any money." She said, "Clovis send money here," and I said okay. And she said, "I'm going to have to iron you something. You can go ahead on and lie on the bed for a while."

But I didn't go to sleep. I was peeping at her, watching her. The ironing board that we had—we still have it today—is a wooden old ironing board. I was peeping at her and making her think I was sleeping, but I wasn't.

She had four gold teeth in her mouth. Two up top on each side. She was a lady that you thought she was a white woman but she was not. Her mother probably or somebody in her family was white. She was just as bright, with pretty curly silky hair. Everybody liked her. I mean everybody liked Ruth. They named me after her. Her name was Ruth Homer Fleetwood. And I was Ruthie.

I fell asleep watching her iron me a new blue dress for school.

In the morning she woke me up out of her bed. "Come on, you got to get up before the bus come and pick you up."

I put on the blue dress. Grandmama fix my

hair. I knew I was getting ready for something, but I didn't know really what it was. And then came a knock on the door.

I never seen a car pull in. It was just the knock. My grandmother answered the door.

"Gal, your mama here!" And right then I knew I wasn't going to go to school.

When she come, she always have a pocketbook, and two luggage in her hand. And it made me think she was going to stay. And I remember going through that luggage, searching through it, looking for things. Just want to see what she got. And see if she had something for me.

And I told my grandmama, I said, "I'm not going to go to school because I want to stay with Mama."

"No, you got to go to school, Gal, you got to go to school."

Mama said, "Oh, can't she stay home and play with me?"

Grandmama said all right. So I didn't go to the first day of school—I stayed home. I asked my mama, I said, "Mama, can I go away with you this time?" and she said no.

And she said, "Anyway, I need to let you know something."

I asked her what it was.

She said, "I'm blind in one of my eyes."

"No, you're not."

She said, "Yeah, I am."

I said, "No, you're not!" and I started jumping up and down. I said, "Can you see me?"

She said, "Yeah, but let me cover my eye."

I was just jumping up and down and waving my hands, I was doing some of everything, and I said, "Can you see me?"

And she said, "No, I can't see you at all."

"Yeah, you can."

"I can't see you, Gal."

She took her hand off that eye and put it on the other eye. I waved one arm, and she told me exactly what I was doing.

"How did you get like that?" I asked her.

"A man that I dated knocked me in the eye."

And I said, "Mama, you know that man you was talking to named Marlon?" I said, "He came by."

"Well, I'm not going to see him, I'm going to leave and go back. I just came back to see you, because I remember you crying from last time. And I brought you a present."

"What is it?"

She said, "Go outside and look by the back room."

That's where we had our washing machine and our freezer. When I went out, there was a pink bike with white stripes. I couldn't believe she had bought me that bike. I rode that bike and I rode that bike and I *rode* that bike that day, and I rode that bike so much until I couldn't even stop. I fell off right in the front of the Wickers' house and skinned my knees so badly that I couldn't even walk. It was bleeding, the meat was hanging out, and I was screaming and crying. They didn't take me to the doctor, they just threw alcohol on it. Later on that day I told Mama that I did feel better.

Right across from us, catty-corner, there was no house there, there was nothing but plum bushes. I told Mama me and Naomi was going to go get some plums. She said, "Well, you better watch out for them snakes out there."

I said, "Yeah I'm watching for the snakes."

But when we went out there we decided that we didn't want to get plums again, we wanted to go taste those red things on the cactus because they looked real good. So instead of us going where we said we was going, we ended up going where something else looked good.

We pulled the red fruit off and we et it, and the next thing we know our tongue was hanging out of our mouth—because the fruit was full of stickers. And we went home with our mouth, and they had to pick all that stuff off of our tongue, and Mama said, "Gal, didn't I tell you to stay from over there?"

Daddy wasn't there because he was out to sea somewhere, and then we snuck later on that day to the plum bush anyway to get plums. Somehow when I was getting plums a thorn stuck straight in the corner of my eye. I ran home and it was bleeding so bad and Mama said oh jesus christ and I was crying, crying,

crying. They took that out but I never went to the doctor.

My grandmother was a really nice lady, she never got mad at me, but she used to fuss at me a little—and she said, "Gal, you know your mama's leaving, and you're acting crazy, getting yourself all hurt up."

I said, "Mama, don't go, don't go." Kept crying. But she left anyway. I thought she left to go to Philadelphia, but she didn't. She only left to meet mens or whatever.

The next day my grandfather was home. He came home. And when he pulled up, he had a white Chevrolet. He said, "Gal! Naomi!"

We said, "Sir?"

He said, "Get out there and clean that car."

Naomi said, "I'm going to clean out the front seat."

I said, "No, you ain't. I'm going to clean out the front seat. You can clean out the backseat."

She said, "I'm going to clean out the front seat because the money's always in the front seat."

That's where, you know, when you sit in the front seat the mens' change falls out.

So we was fussing about that, and I didn't know that my mother was still in town. I saw a person walking up to the door and it was her, and I ran around the front where she was at and I said, "Mama, why didn't you tell me you was coming?—I thought you was leaving."

"No, I'm not going. I'm going to stay a couple more days."

"Mama, Naomi won't let me clean out the front seat."

She said, "Go ahead on and clean out the car, because you know Daddy told you to, and you know how he can be."

So I went back to the car. Naomi was already in the front seat and we started fighting. We started fighting, fighting. She spotted a can in the car. She hit me in the eye with the can, on the side of my eye, and I ran in the house bleeding. "Mama, she chop me with a can!"

Then I stopped. I saw that luggage on her bed.

"Mama, you *are* leaving again?"

"Yeah, this time I am going to go, and I'm going to be gone a long time."

"But look here at my eye where the thorn stuck. And my knee is still hurting me some."

"I'm sorry, Gal, but don't worry, I will be back. You go wait outside in the yard."

And then that man came. Marlon.

He said, "Gal! Your mama home?"

And I said, "Yeah, Mama home but Daddy in there."

And then my grandfather and my grandmother they went out, and they took me with them. I don't remember where we went to, but when we came back my mother was already gone. She had left and gone.

THE MAN THAT live in front of us, Mr. Buzz, the old man, he had a path that you could walk through his yard all the way to the next street to the store called Joe Mink. Miss Sadie and Joe Mink. That place is still sitting today as they left it when they died. It's a two-story house with a store in it, and that building is still sitting there today on Nebo Street. We would go there because Daddy had a credit there. We would go buy baloney, these big long baloneys, and they slice it up and they wrap it in white paper. We'd get baloney or salami or liquor or whatever Daddy wanted to credit. We'd give Miss Sadie the list. Up on the counter they always had these pickles, these sausage, these cookies, these candy—and they had a bubble-gum machine. We used to put a penny in, Naomi and me, to see if we could get the lucky ball. It was black with white specks. If you get that one, you can change it in for twenty-five cents, or whatever's worth twenty-five cents.

We would always lie and tell Miss Sadie that Daddy or Mama had said to get something else that wasn't on the list. They knew that the cookies were a lie, but we would lie anyway, but they'd give it to us anyway.

And we would walk that path—and sometimes we would *run* it, because it's bushes, all high—not knowing whether or not there were snakes in there. And coming back to Mr. Buzz house, there was a hogpen he had that was always stink, and his doodle house there. And the mulberry tree was right by it, and that mulberry tree would always grow. It would grow real good.

Daddy would always send us there so Miss Sadie and her husband, Mr. Joe Mink, got to knowing us real well, so when Daddy would go out to sea they would still give us credit to get things. Mama (my grandmama, I call her Mama too), she would always tell me to go on over there and get this and that and whatever. And eventually she started hanging out there. She started hanging out there with mens and having a good time. The mens in Hungry Neck really liked her a lot. And she messed around—she probably did—and we knew it, but we didn't care. She was happy when she was there. Joe Mink had a back room for grown-ups only, with a pool table, and they would cook back there. And she would always have a little drink. And you could hear them laughing. She would tell me and Naomi to sit on the back step, and they would give us a bag of sugar cookies while she was in there with her friends. These were the real sugar cookies. And they would slice up that long baloney real thick, and give it to us. That was the only place she ever went to, never anywhere else. She was still in the neighborhood. She never went out of Hungry Neck. Because she couldn't drive anyway, she never had a license. A car was there, but she never drove it.

She would go to Joe Mink place but she wouldn't stay that long, she would come back. She always cooked and cleaned and made sure we were satisfied. She was a housewife, taking good care of us and the house, making sure we were happy. She sent us to Sunday School every Sunday, to Second Zion right there in Hungry Neck.

But when Daddy would come home, somebody out there was telling him that she was going back and forth to Joe Mink store.

MY GRANDMOTHER talked a lot, but she never told us anything about her childhood.

One day, she had on this real pretty dress. She was lying on the bed, but on the tip end, not the whole way in the bed. She didn't even take her shoes off. I peep around the corner to see if she was sleeping. I was easing in there on my hands and knees, and when I got to her, I reach and lift up her skirt, and I peep under her dress. She caught me.

"Gal, what are you doing?"

"I wasn't doing nothing."

She told somebody that I was peeping underneath her dress. And why I did, I don't know. I just had to look. That was strange. I had to look underneath her dress, I don't know why. What was I looking for?

The last time my real mama came home, I remember, she took me outside, and I was sitting with her on the back step. It was late in the afternoon, and she had on blue jeans. I said, "Mama, can I go and get some candy from the store?" She said, "Yeah, go ahead on." She gave me some money, and I had it in a bag.

"And buy me some squirrel nut," she said.

I bought me a bag of this candy called Mary Janes, and I bought her the squirrel nut, this little small candy you chew and it has little nuts in it. I bought her the squirrel nuts and I bought me the Mary Janes because the Mary Janes had a little girl on it—a yellow wrapper with red around it, and in the middle, peanut butter. I came home with that bag of candy and I gave her hers. We were sitting on the step. She ate a squirrel nut, and she was looking at the Mary Janes.

She said, "What did you get for you?"

"I got me some Mary Janes."

"Let me try one of those." So I gave it to her and she said, "Can I have yours? Whyn't you have these squirrel nuts and let me have that?"

And I said, "No, these are mine, Mama."

"Well, then, let me give you some money and you go back to the store and get some more of the yellow kind."

So I was going back to the store through Mr. Buzz's. All you do is cross in the front of our house, and go through Mr. Buzz's. (You would never know it today. Right now it's bushes, the house is fell today, from Hurricane Hugo—it's flat. The house is still there but it's flat.) Went there, had to go through the little gate, and as I was going through, I thought I heard something but I wasn't certain. I ran through there, and I went in the store. There was a bunch of guys that I knew, Wallace Plunket and some other little guys, and they said, "Hey, Gal, how you doing, you old knotty head little Gal." Always called me that, called me Big Eyes, and called me other names.

As I was going back through the path, I looked up and I said, "I better get me some of these bullets before they all go." These are not really bullets for a gun, they're like a grape but we call them bullets—they are green, they got that tough green skin. The vine was growing right by the path in Mr. Buzz yard. I pulled it down, pulled it down, put a lot in my bag.

I heard something again, but I didn't run this time—I started walking slow.

Somebody just grabbed me and pulled me back hard. It was Wallace Plunket.

"I want some of your pussy. Give me some."

He was rocking, you know, but my clothes were still on me. I was crying and I was kicking, I was fighting, and I said, "Wallace, don't do it, don't do it," and I could feel his thing on my butt, but he didn't never pull my pants down. He just wanted to rock on me. He said, "Give me some, give me some, Chick told me you gave him some at the hogpen."

"I never gave him none, Wallace!"

He said, "Give me some, Gal, I want some of you."

I said, "Let me go!" and I scuffled away.

I was dirty up when I got home, and Mama said, "What happened to you?"

"Wallace tried to get me, Mama, going through the path."

"I'm going to call his mama and tell on him."

I said, "No, don't call because Wallace might beat me up later! Please don't call!"

I gave her that candy, and she said, "Oh," she said, "I am so happy, I didn't know that they got this kind of candy. I never saw it before."

I said, "Me either, but they had a lot more of that than they had the squirrel nut."

LATER ON, Daddy and Mama came back home—that's Granddaddy and Grandmama— and Daddy wanted to fight and beat my mama again, I don't know why, just beat her again, and she said she is never ever ever coming back. She told me she was never ever coming back.

She said, "It's not you, Gal—but I am just never ever coming back."

And that time she did left, and I never seen her again.

MY GRANDMOTHER was crying and crying, crying and crying. "Oh, Clovis, why you run her away, Clovis? Clovis, why you run her away?"

He said, "She ain't nothing but a damn whore anyway. All these men coming here, every time coming to see her, and hell, Gal don't even know who her damn daddy is. Gal's calling Marlon her daddy. You don't even know who your own daddy is, do you?"

I said, "No, sir. I don't know who my daddy is." And I was starting to cry, but I didn't want him to see that.

And Grandmama said, "Clovis, when you going to go back out to sea?"

He didn't answer. He looked at her, his look. He said, "Ruth, I been hearing a lot of stuff about you. All these mens, these drunk mens, you been out there in the damn street—you're nothing but a goddamn whore yourself. That's all you is, nothing but a goddamn whore."

"Clovis, you know I ain't no whore."

Florence and all of us were listening to all that conversation, and stuff going on. And Grandmama had a scare to her face. She left out of the house. She went to Joe Mink store, and she went drinking. And when she came back, she was drunk.

And he was drunk.

Me and Naomi slept in the last bedroom where the two twin beds at. In the room before that, two twin antique beds—and those antique beds are still there today, and they are beautiful beds—Florence and Kitty slept in those two beds. But, I don't know why, that night me and Naomi slept with them. I was in the bed with Florence, and Naomi was in the bed with Kitty. And we heard a noise outside, and we all were really frightened. We were really really really frightened.

And all I know is the front door opened, and we heard the door open, and we heard them coming down the hall, you could hear the footsteps coming, and she say, "Oh, Clovis—oh, Clovis," and then he say, "You see where your kids are now?"—and he dragged her to the door, slammed her face into the door—"You see where your kids are now, and you in the damn street out there, you with all these mens, you see where your kids are now, girl?"

She said, "Oh, Clovis, don't hit me no more."

And we were just watching, because he turned the light on. Florence was covering up her head, because she didn't want to see, and she was just shaking in the bed, and I could feel her toes hitting against me, and she said, "Daddy, please don't hit mama no more, don't hit her."

But he grabbed Mama and he dragged her outside, and we got up and we looked out the window. He knocked her down, and you could tell he was looking for something, and all he spotted was the water hose. The green water hose.

And he unloosed it and he grabbed her and he put it round her neck, *twisted* it, and he dragged her in the house, all the way in the house with it, and she was suffering, and she was trying to get away, he was choking her with the hose, and we was standing right there, he saw us watching him, and he grabbed her and he threw her in the bathtub.

I ran in there and I said, "Mama, Mama, are you all right?" But she couldn't move. And when we looked, she had already shitted up her clothes.

And he acted like it was just nothing, like it was nothing going on at all.

She stayed in that tub all damn night long. He didn't even touch her, didn't call the doctor, didn't do anything. I thought she was dead.

The next day her brother came. Her brother live on Edisto Island. He came over and she was still in that tub, and her brother went crazy and started fighting with Daddy, and the next thing we know some of her people from Red Top came up, and people from Baltimore, Maryland, came down, and then she had to go into the hospital.

Ten days later when she came back, we didn't even know that was her. Daddy had beat her so bad. And they had cut all her hair off her head, she didn't have no hair on her head—she was bald-headed. She couldn't even go to the bathroom. We had to pull her up, she couldn't make it to the bathroom, from the damage that he had done to her. We would always be sitting by her and she would say, "Gal, I got to go to the bathroom," but we were little, and we couldn't hardly pull her up. By the time we'd pull her up, she'd be already peed up her clothes.

And Daddy was still beating this damn lady. He was still beating her up.

And she was pregnant. He went back out to sea, and when he came back she was big, but still weak and still hurting. Her relatives and friends all hated him, they didn't want anything to do with him. But I didn't like those men. One of them—he was in the service, too, and one of his hands didn't have no fingers on it—he would come to see her, but when he come in the house he would grab us and kiss us and put his tongue down our mouth. He would do all that, and Daddy and them seen that, my grandmama seen that, but they let it happen. He would feel us and touch us.

When Mama had the baby, that was Sylvie. After three days Daddy called his sister in Mississippi, Aunt Beezy, to come pick up Sylvie because Mama was too sick to take care of her. We all had to get in the car and go. Mama didn't come with us because she was too sick to travel, but he took us with him. We met Aunt Beezy halfway, in Macon, Georgia.

Aunt Beezy was a big fat heavy lady with chest down to here, and Uncle Oscar, Daddy's brother, was there too—and they took that baby. They took Sylvie, and we came back to Charleston. But no more than six months later, Mama was pregnant again, with Evelyn. Every time Daddy came home from sea, she would get pregnant. She had a child three years straight. After Evelyn was born, Daddy called Beezy again and said, "Ruth had another baby, could you keep this one here for me too?" We had to meet them in Macon again. Within six months, she was pregnant again with the last child, Pamela. Aunt Beezy agreed to keep all these babies. She never signed any papers to adopt the kids, but she kept them because she had no children of her own.

After the last child, Mama was still sick, she was very sick. She got a little bit better, but that pretty hair she had, it looked like it was never going to come back.

But he still hit her and hurt her. We were too small to try and stop him. We'd just go in our room, and hear her screaming and knocking the walls. Then a fall to the floor. He'd go back to sea, and Mama, who loved us very much, would never tell us nothing. She would go to Joe Mink's, maybe run into her old friends, and act like nothing had happen.

She was strong, but the time was coming for her soon.

Daddy was still going back and forth out to sea, and when he finally came back again about six months later, he came back the same way. He didn't change, he didn't change at all. Came back with the same thing—"You whore, you in the damn street"—and this and that.

And she said, "Clovis, I ain't doing that, I ain't doing that."

We were in the bed, and all I remember is we heard a glass break. I don't know if she broke it first or he did. But she told him she would kill him if he hit her again. We heard the scuffle in there. We heard the table fall down, and we were crying in the bed, crying and shaking, and we ran up the hallway and we were peeping around the door, and we saw—we remember we saw—how he grabbed the glass and he pulled it down her arm, a long deep cut in her arm. But that didn't do him no damn good, he beat her for worse, he beat her all in the head, and she was on the floor, she was on the floor, there was blood, blood, and were just too scared, anybody to do anything. And Florence was just so frightened, so frightened.

I don't know who called, but she end up in the hospital.

And—she didn't live long after that. She died.

HER FAMILY and some of her friends came to Daddy and told him that they hated him because he killed her. To this day they have never cared about him. They would come, every blue moon, to see us. But when that one man came he would kiss us and put his tongue in our mouth.

After she died, Daddy started taking us down to the end of Hungry Neck to this place they used to call Crabnet Beach, but now today somebody bought that land and made big houses, with a security gate. Back then, you could walk right down to the water. He'd take us for us to go on all the swings and the sliding board while he'd go walk that little boardwalk and go on inside there in the sweet shop and drink with the mens. We'd go every day, and we'd stay all day long. We would eat there because they'd give us pickled pig feet. And they had the best hot dogs, those red hot dogs, real red. We'd be there from morning to night, and he'd be drunk, and he'd call us, say "Gal, come here. Tell these mens here, tell them who's the boss here. I'm the boss here."

I would say "Yes, sir."

And he would say "Tell them what you could do for me. Tell them that you get my clothes for me, you comb my hair, I don't even make my own bath water. When I call Gal, Gal be here in a split second, don't you, Gal?"

And I say, "Yes, sir."

"I can send Gal to the store anytime, Gal is back within five minutes. If I send Naomi to the store, hell, she is gone all damn day long, somebody got to go and look for her."

But that was true of me. If he send me to the store, I would *run* to the store. I was afraid to be gone long.

And the mens he was hanging with while we were going back and forth to Crabnet Beach—I don't know if this man was kin to us or not, but Daddy asked him to take us home, and he would be home in a few. And the man said okay. Everybody got in the backseat except me, I got in the front seat. There was a lady sitting beside me, and I didn't know who this lady was. But I remember, while I was sitting in the car, I reached over and I grabbed that man's dick. I did. And I grabbed it and I squeezed it. He was a light-skinned handsome man, and he just looked at me and he smiled. And since he smiled, I squeezed it again. The man and the lady laughed.

The next morning, Daddy said, "Gal, Kitty, Naomi, Florence, y'all come on in here. See, I can't take care of y'all, cause I gotta be y'all mama and y'all daddy. Your mama gone, and Gal mama, she ain't never coming back 'cause, hell, she don't want her, that's why she left from here. I called Beezy and ask Beezy can she keep y'all for me. You ain't going to be down there long, I'll come to get you."

And we was wondering, *Mississippi, where is that? What's that like?*

chapter two

a week later, we packed up a little bit of clothes that we had, and we got into that white Chevrolet, and we drove to Shootamile, Mississippi. It was a twelve-hour drive, but seem like we got there within a hour because Daddy drove like a fool, not stopping even to eat. He was always the lead car. And when we got there, as we were getting into Aunt Beezy neighborhood, it was all dirt, dirt road. Looked like everybody lived on a pasture or something, everybody had two or three acres of land.

Aunt Beezy house was a gray-looking wooden house with a porch on it in the back and the front, and she had a *big* pasture. When we got out of the car and we looked, we said, "Wow, look at all that land back there." She had it all fenced off.

She said, "Heeey there, Clovis"—that's how she talked, high and squeaky—"Heey, Clovis, I haven't seen you in a long time."

"Zee"—that's what he called her—"Hey, Zee,

I told you I'd bring these children on down here."

"Well, Clovis, they ain't nothing wrong with that, I'll keep 'em. I'll keep 'em. They ain't nobody here but me and Captain." Captain was her husband, and he worked on the railroad. She did have the other girls, but they were smaller than we were.

Daddy said, "Well, Zee, I can't stay, I just came to bring them children, and I'll send you some money to take care of 'em."

"Okay, Clovis."

After he left, she said, "Captain on the railroad, y'all, but he'll be home in a few weeks. Y'all go take a look around."

We walked and looked. We walked down a little trail, and we came to a well. It was a bucket on it and a rope. We took it loose just to see. We looked down in it, and we could see our face in the water. We spit in there.

"Aaayah, don't spit in there," she yelled. "That's the water y'all got to drink." And we didn't know no better, we spit in the water. There was an outhouse there. Then you walk about twenty feet, you go through the gate— and the pasture! I swear to God, it was so green, and so big—it must have been about five to six acres. They own all that land because Captain's father bought about a hundred acres of land and divided it up between the kids. He had enough to share with all of the kids, didn't leave anybody out.

We walked on in. There was a bunch of cows and goats and pigs and chickens, everything. We walked so far down in there, until Aunt Beezy hollered, "Y'all children come on in here now and eat your dinner."

We went in there and we sat on the floor. We et. Pig feet with collard greens and corn bread, and I swear to God, it was good. Real good.

She said we had to go and get some water to take a bath. But we didn't take a bath inside, we didn't have a real tub; we had this round tub. We would have to sit in there and pour the water, and everybody have to take turns dumping the water out, dumping the water out.

"Y'all children hurry up now and get to bed, cause y'all got a lot of work to do here in the morning. Got to go get them cows, got to feed them pig, got to feed them chicken, got to milk them goat, and you got to churn some milk."

Every day we did that. Get up in the morning, go find the pigs or cow that got out. She said you call them and say "Yo pig, yo pig," and when you call them they think it's time to eat. We squeeze the goat and squeeze the milk down into this black heavy bucket with a churner in it. You had to keep churning it, that milk, to make it thick.

Kitty and Naomi was out there feeding the cows and goats, and Pam and Evelyn and Sylvie was sweeping off the porch and emptying the stink bucket that we used at night. Aunt Beezy said, "Gal, go on up there and help Florence milk that cow." Florence never wanted to milk the cow, because when you sat there the cow tail would slap you on the side of the head.

Florence said, "Gal, I ain't milking no cow. Here, you milk the cow."

I said, "Florence, don't tell Aunt Beezy, but let me taste that." I licked my tongue on its chest.

She said, "You nasty self, girl."

"But Florence, it taste *sweet*!" And it was warm.

THERE WAS some children live nearby us on another dirt road. Their names were Ivory, Lucille, Randall, Wilbur, and Tit, so many people with different names. We were new to the town so everybody wanted to see us. And they came over, they was curious, wanting to see us. Florence and Kitty started liking Randall and Wilbur, and they started messing around behind the well. But I didn't.

Aunt Beezy didn't work, at all. She wore a housedress—a big old dress, with no bra, no nothing, not even no drawers on—sitting there in the house. But one morning Aunt Beezy looked different. We was wondering why she put on a bra and clothes, because she never did. And we couldn't figure out why she was so dress up that day.

Captain was coming home.

And the house was spick and span clean.

And when Captain came home, he was dressed just like a railroad man. The hat was striped, the overall was striped, and he had on a blue shirt. Oh, that man had love us to death. It's because he didn't have any children of his own, at all. Oh, man, he played with us, he played with us, he *played* with us. He used to get on the floor and ride us around like a horse. But he would keep on his railroad clothes and those big shoes, and one by one bump us like he was a horse and we were on a saddle. But Captain never stayed long, because he always got to go back to the railroad. He be gone for months, then come back.

Aunt Beezy started selling some beer and liquor and candy and everything. This man, we called him Mr. Slide, he would sit outside and every day we would see him, and he would have a little small knife and he would peel a onion and he would eat that onion raw like he was eating a apple or something sweet.

Tit and them, they had earrings in their ears. And we didn't have none. So I said, "Aunt Beezy," I said, "can we get earrings in our ears?" And she say, "Well, you know how Clovis is. I don't know."

The next morning we got up and we went and stood by the stove, because we had no central air or heat or anything like that. We had to put wood in the stove and go down the hallway and try to get warm up in the morning, and put a pan on top of the stove so the water can heat up so we can wash off. And she said, "Gal, put that pan on there. You need two of them thing

up there 'cause I'm going to pierce y'all ears."
And we started jumping up and down; we
couldn't wait to get our ears pierced.

So she told me to sit down on the floor. I sat
down on the floor. She had hot water in a pan
and a needle with thread in it and a match. She
lit the tip of that needle and she stuck that thing
in my ear, and I screamed so loud, boy, I tell
you, I screamed. And she pull that thread
through—it was hurting, and I said "I don't
want the other one did" because I was so
scared. I went half of the day, but she did it
eventually by the end of the day and got the
other one pierced. That day, looked like my ears
was *big*, oh man. But she put peroxide on it and
Vaseline, and kept pulling the string, pulling the
string through so the string wouldn't get hard
and stuck.

Naomi and them saying "I ain't going to get
my ears pierced, not me, I ain't going to get my
ears pierced." So I was the only one got my ears
pierced. When Randall and Ivory and them
came over, they saw I had my ears pierced. The
string was so long it looked like earrings hanging down.

So Aunt Beezy said, "I know y'all out there
messing with them boys doing all them fresh
stuff."

I said, "Aunt Beezy, not me, I ain't doing
nothing like that."

* * *

WE DIDN'T have a phone in the house, but we got the news one day that Captain got killed. On the railroad track. He slipped and fell and got his arms and legs caught up into the train.

Aunt Beezy went berserk, crazy, throwing her arms up—"Captain gone, Captain gone"—and we started crying, got crazy ourselves. Somehow Daddy got the message back here in Charleston, so he figured that she would send us back. But she didn't do it. She decided that she couldn't live in that house anymore—she would move on some more land that her family owned, to move closer by her brother Oscar.

So we told all the neighbors, we're leaving, we going to move somewhere else. The day before we left, we told Mr. Slide, we said, "Well, we moving, we going to move somewhere else now."

"Yeah, y'all little damn bad children, y'all going to go somewhere else and mess up now," he said. "But I guess we'll miss you."

It was hard for us to get the pigs and cows in these trucks. We had to chase them and chase them, we fall in the mud, and I was afraid of some of the animals. But we manage to get all of them in there. So we pack up, went.

All around Aunt Beezy house, it's all dirt road, and these hills was so high. She would drive over the hills so high until when we go over, feel like our stomach go up, feel like it's going to come out. As we going, we shrieking in the car and she saying "Ooooh, we going on another curve now!" I mean she was just going, just screaming over those hills. We had a nice time, you know, moving.

Where we move at, the house was bigger than what we had before. It was a wood house, white with red trimming, bathroom outside. Behind the bathroom was a chicken coop out there. And about a hundred feet away, the other side of the land, her brother Oscar lived there, and, oh God, he lived on so much land. And farther on down, on the same dirt road, Oscar's daughter Claudette and Claudette's husband, Jokey, lived in a brick house. Next to that brick house was a old wood house that her brother son, Clovis— name was Clovis also—lived there with his wife, Minnie.

Aunt Beezy say, "Y'all, you know we ain't got no running water here. You got to go down to Oscar house when we need some."

She didn't even have to talk loud, the little valley where we lived at was so echoey. "Oscar?"—she'd call, and he could hear it— "Oscar? I'm sending them children down to come get some water." We had the buckets. I was kind of scared to go down there because his sons liked us, but we were cousin. And when we went down there to pump the water, you had to take water to pour it in there to get the water going, and keep on, keep on, keep on, and it was so cold your hands be freezing, you be pumping and pumping, your rear end going up and down—it take a long time, and as we doing that, they be behind us sticking us in the butt and touching us. But we are kind of liking it, you know, playing.

So—got the water, and Uncle Oscar wife, Iris, say, "Hey, Clovis ain't come to see y'all children yet?"

"No, ma'am."

"Y'all come on down here. I ain't seen y'all in a long time, come on down here and eat some of this corn bread and stuff that I cook."

And we say, "Okay, we got to go tell Aunt Beezy." And we was running with the water, I mean we was *running*, to get back. So we took the water, but we had to keep fulling up so many things, to get enough water, and we full up the tub. She had a tub in this house but it was never connected up with anything, nothing.

That day we went to Iris house was the first time I have ever seen white corn bread. It was white and hard and thick and dry. But it was good. And Iris girls, Laura and Baby, and all of us, we became good friends. We were their cousins, but we became closer to them, and we'd hang out with them. We never really hardly had any clothes, we kept wearing the same clothes over and over again, but our cousins would give us some and continue to come to see us every day. Every day we'd talk. Everybody was so excited to see us because we were still the new people in town.

And Aunt Beezy met a man. Name Rider. He was a tall nice-looking man, and he started bringing mens to the house. She started selling the same things all over again, and we would steal her cookies or candy, whatever we could steal. We snuck liquor, we snuck her snuff. She dipped snuff. She kept her old bucket next to her chair—she could sit and spit right in there. It was awful, it was like slime, but she'd call us to dump it out.

And the tall man had really like Aunt Beezy, which I don't know what for because she was big and fat and never wear a bra. But she started looking better, you know. She started looking good.

And she said, "Gal, Naomi, Florence, Kitty, Pam, Evelyn, Sylvie—when I call y'all to tell y'all to get something for Beezy, y'all get it for me 'cause I can't move."

And we said, "Aunt Beezy, we don't know where your stuff at."

"Go look behind my bed and go in there. And if I ever catch a man past this hallway here, y'all in trouble."

So she show us where all her liquor, beer, and everything was at. We snuck and drunk some. Then our cousins would come there. They were older than we were, but they liked us. One name was Robert, he really really liked Gal—he really like me—and I liked him too.

One day he thought Aunt Beezy had had too much to drink. So he came back in our room. Aunt Beezy was sitting in her chair, and he thought he had sneaked past her—but she saw

him. And he came on back, and he started
touching on my chest, and I let him touch me—
and she said, "Oh, Robert. If you don't bring
your skinny butt from down that hall, I'm sure
going to tell Oscar."

"Oh, Auntie, you know that ain't me. You
know I won't do nothing like that."

"You leave them girls alone back there."

So he came on out. She called us and told us
to come on in there so she could see us. She
wanted one of us to light one of the stoves.
Kitty lit it, and I went to try and sneak into the
freezer because I wanted something sweet to
eat. But Aunt Beezy had put a lock on the
freezer to keep us from getting anything.

Aunt Beezy said, "All y'all want to do is mess
with boys and eat my food. I'm going to tell you
one thing. In the morning, we got a crop to do."

That next morning we plant seed. We don't
know what kind of seed it was. But, we planted.
We planted and we planted—just little seeds in
dirt—the long, long rows in the field beside the
house. After we planted, the cow break loose,
and the pigs break loose, we didn't know where
they were at. We went down to Uncle Oscar
house. "Yo pig! Yo pig!" Just calling. Wouldn't
come. Wouldn't come.

Then we went up on the high hill that they
got, where you could see the pretty water coming down. Just coming down. The water was
so pretty, and I reached down, and I said
"Florence"—and this is my exact words what I

told her—"Damn," I said, "this water sure feel good," I said, "but how in the hell do it taste?" Florence and them laughed and laughed at me, because I was so little, six years old, and to be talking that way.

Eventually we found all of the animals except a couple, eventually they came home. And after we found half of them except three, Aunt Beezy said, "When it gets dark I want y'all to get a flashlight and we going in the henhouse." I was wondering why we going in the henhouse. So we got the flashlight and it got dark, and I said, "Aunt Beezy, what are we going to do?"

She said, "Only way to catch a chicken, you got to get him in the dark and blind him with a flashlight. That way he can't see you." Went in there, among all the chicken, and she grab one, she had him by the neck. And she *wrung* that thing. She wrung his neck. Then she sat him on a old wood stump. She chop his head off. Then, had to pull all the feathers off. She fried that chicken. That chicken was delicious. That chicken was *good*.

She said a man was coming over that same night to bring some squirrel. I never et squirrel before. When he brought them in, their heads were down swinging, they were all limp and dead and furry. But she took each one, and she would cut around its neck and we would hold the head and she would *peel* the skin back. That's just how it came off, it came off just like nothing. Like magic. She cooked that and we ate all that.

Aunt Beezy complained, but she made sure we always had a full stomach. She made the best corn bread, and collards from the field, with pig feet mixed in. And rice pudding, she made that too. But she said, "Clovis ain't sending no money here. I ain't got no money. And y'all children eat more than I don't know what. I can't afford to feed you." But she wasn't really buying meat because we were killing the animals that we had there.

When she cut the tongue out of the pig mouth, she would boil it and let it cool off in a pan with vinegar. And the next day when she get the knife, the tongue was easy to slice. She'd slice it up and give it to us. But the ears were always tough, and hairy. Sometimes she would make hog-head cheese out of the pig tongue and the ears, and then some of the facial part, and could have been some of the brains, liver, we didn't know what all. She would put some red pepper and bell pepper in it, too, chop it all up, and then shape it like a square, and wrap it up and let it get cold. When she unwrap it, it was rubbery like Jell-O. It was good, we et it. Hog-head cheese was the best thing going on.

And then, those seeds that we didn't know what they were, they started to sprout. First a little bit of green, and then the plants taking shape. And it came up to be cucumbers, watermelon, corn, squash, okra, collards, everything! Things that looked better than in the stores today. It was a surprise to me when they came up like that. And I thought it was so pretty, so pretty.

All of us had to work in the fields, picking for a farmer, because Daddy wouldn't send money for us. Aunt Beezy would always drive us to the fields, and we never had tooken any food with us because there was a house close by the field that sell candy, cookies, honey buns, even bread and meat. We would get something to eat there, but we always took the water with us, in a big glass jug with a cork.

We first started off picking lima beans, and we pick all day long, all day long. Every day, sunup to sundown, out in that big old field. There was lots of people out there, even Mexican, some of every kind, picking, picking. And then we started picking tomatoes, and after that we started picking cotton. I hated picking cotton. That stuff would get in my eyes and burn.

There was a little shed out there that we could use the bathroom in. And we had to walk about a mile to the truck where they weighed your pickings in a sack, and after that they put your money inside of a brown envelope. Once we got that brown envelope we ran to the car because Aunt Beezy would be sitting in the car waiting for us to bring the money to her. And she'd give us all the change in there. She'd take all the green out.

But she wouldn't take Florence's or Kitty's because they were older than we were. They would give her what they wanted to give her.

And we'd go to the little store in town. The soda machine was always outside, and you could see the bottles through the glass door. Most likely I would get a honey bun or a Rock and Roll for five cents and a Coke for fifteen cents. That's all the money she would give us. She would take the rest of the money and use it to buy liquor and cigarettes to sell to mens on the side. The house was always full of mens. We were small, but we knew what was going on, knew they was coming to buy that stuff. Some of the mens even tried to talk to us.

But our cousins were coming up to the house, too—Robert, Eugene, Laura, Baby—they would come and hang out, and we played the radio.

It was coming time for us to go to school. We thought Daddy was going to come to get us, but he didn't. He called Aunt Beezy and told her that he want us to stay down there and got to school.

We had to walk down a long clay road. The sand was clay, it was that clay sand. Walk about a mile and a half and then go around the curve. We would pass the white church, and the Powell house, and then we got out on the main highway, and we'd stand out there waiting for the bus. It was cold then. It was getting cold. Before we could even reach the highway our hands were like frozen ice.

Mrs. Powell would come outside and say "Y'all want to come in the house and get warm?" and we would tell her yeah. I remember I went and put my hand over that stove she had, and I thought my hand was coming off. It hurt worse after I warmed it up, it hurt so bad I was crying, and Mrs. Powell told me never to do that again.

This fat girl name Johnette, I never did like her. On the bus she would always want to sit in my seat or in the seat behind me, and I didn't like her sitting by me.

We came home one day on the bus, and she said, "Move over."

I said, "I'm not going to move over." I was on the tip end of the seat.

"Move over," she said.

"I'm not going to move over."

She raised her arm. She had a pencil, and she stuck it into my hand. I felt the blood coming out.

The bus driver stopped the bus, and he said, "What's wrong?"

"She stabbed me in the hand!"

"I can't let you off here—you got to wait until you get home."

So when we got off the bus, I ran up the hill, ran around the curve and down the dirt road. I cried to Aunt Beezy, "Johnette stabbed me with a pencil." They took forever to take me to the doctor, but they took me. My hand was big and swollen. The doctor said, "I can't find anything in your hand at all." But I knew a pencil lead was in there—the swelling was still there, and I felt a lump in it. But they just let that pass. The doctor said, "Let it rot in your hand." That's what he told me. And the mark is right here now, still on my hand.

I never messed with Johnette again because I knew that she would hurt me. But in school I had a couple of friends. I remember one girl named Tisha Franklin and a nice handsome little guy name Skeet Burns. He was bowlegged. And there was three other girls I used to hang with. Between lunch and recess, a lady would always bring a ice-cream cart in the room, and if you had money you could go and buy a ice cream off there. I would always have a little money because we was working in the fields.

Tisha Franklin wanted to be the boss. She would tell us what to do and we would listen to what she said. When one of us would get mad with her, somebody else would have to be the boss and say "Don't talk with her today" or "You give me your money"—this and that. I couldn't wait till it was my turn to be the boss. When it was, I learned that I could make people do what I said. And Johnette—I made sure that nobody played with her for a long time.

It was coming up towards Christmas. Uncle Oscar had already called Daddy and told Daddy that he need to come and check on us because we were being bad and doing all kinds of things, and Aunt Beezy had a bunch of mens coming in there, and us girls in there the whole time, going to bed around three or four o'clock in the morning. Uncle Oscar knew Daddy was coming, but we didn't know.

He came. It was getting dark, and we were in the kitchen. When he came through that door, all he did was look. Then he picked up a broom. And he started beating Florence and beating Kitty, calling them a bunch of names. He beat them and beat them. He broke the broom on Florence.

Aunt Beezy said, "Clovis, don't do that, don't do that."

"Zee, leave me alone."

She was mad, but she didn't jump in to stop him. He didn't hit me and Naomi. Uncle Oscar was telling him how Florence and Kitty was always with this bunch of mens, and that was true, they were dating some guys. Daddy left that same night. He just came and beat them and left.

Kitty was talking to a guy name Henry Granger, and Florence was talking to a guy name Earl Mason, and they wanted to know how Daddy found out that they were seeing them. Uncle Oscar told Aunt Beezy that he told.

So Daddy told Aunt Beezy that he was coming back the next time to get all of us and take us back home. She said, "Well, Clovis, if you take some of the kids, won't you leave some with me?" He said he was going to leave the three youngest. He was taking me, Florence, Kitty, and Naomi.

We didn't get a chance to finish school. He came before that time. He came and he got us, and he didn't even make one stop coming back from Mississippi to Charleston.

chapter three

when we got home, the house was a total wreck. A mess. Dishes was in there and mold was on them, just like he had never done anything at all. It didn't smell like a home.

He told us that the next morning he want us up early in the morning—Kitty and Naomi to get up first to cook us breakfast, and then the next morning me and Florence would get up. We would have to take turns. We would get up at six o'clock in the morning, put the water on, fix his coffee, then start the breakfast off. He had one of those folding tables leaning on the wall in his room—we would open that up and put it by the bed. Then bring his breakfast, wake him up, get his work clothes, have his shoes sitting in the living room, get him some socks, get him some underwear, get his glasses. Everything.

So he left to go to work in the morning. We ate breakfast and started cleaning up, because he said when he come back home he want the papers pick up down in the yard, he want the trash burnt—and he say he want the house spick and span, he want the floors buff, and then when he get home he want the dinner cooked. And that happened the next day after we came from Mississippi. We took all the papers and trash and burnt it, dug a hole in the yard, and burnt it. We cleaned and we cleaned, and I mean the house was spotless, *spotless*, when he came home.

We didn't know that when he walk in the door he wanted us there. When he sat down to the table, we didn't know that he wanted us to take off his shoes, take off his socks, have his food sitting on the table, have his glasses there, have any kind of mail sitting right there for him. So when he came in, he said, "Gal, Naomi, Florence, Kitty, where is the food? Where's the mail? Where's my glasses? Gal, take off my shoes. Naomi, unloose my shirt."

We didn't know that he wanted anything like that. So Kitty and Florence fix his dinner, put it on the table, and I be taking off his shoes and socks, Naomi unloose his shirt, take his shirt off, we run and got his glasses, put his glasses on the table, run and check the mailbox, put the mail on the table, and after that he called us to come and clean up his mess off the table, his plate and stuff, and take it in there. He don't want the plate to sit there on the table even one minute, after he's done with it.

"Y'all ain't eat yet?"

"No, we ain't eat yet."

So Florence fixed all our food and put it on

the table. And we was hoping that he would get up from the table, because we didn't want him sitting there while we were eating. He got up and sat on the blue couch, and as we were eating, he was sitting there looking in our mouth. I was scared to even eat. I didn't want to eat all my food, and Florence and them didn't want to eat all theirs either, so when he got up and went into the bathroom, we scrape all our food real quick in a plate for the dog.

He came back in there, and he said, "Who put all of this food in this plate on this counter?"

"Everybody put their food in there."

That man carefully got that plate of food, that we all had scraped in there, and he made us go in that slop and eat that food. We had no choice. We et it.

He said, "Gal, come here and change this station."

I'm standing there. I'm changing the station. And the TV blur a little bit.

"Turn that knob."

I stand there the whole time, while he watch his shows. Switching, turning, fixing the TV. The whole, whole, whole time.

"Tell Naomi to run me some bath water. Tell Kitty to get me some underclothes. Get my clothes ready for the next day's work. Make sure you got my glasses sitting on the table and make sure you got my lunch ready for tomorrow. And Florence, in the morning I want you to shave me and pull the gray out my head."

All this was happening so fast—the second day that we were there.

WHEN HE WENT to work, Rhoda and Carmen Wicker came over to the house, knocked on the door. They said, "We just came to see y'all, because we hadn't seen y'all in so long."

We decided to go outside because we was afraid to let them stay in the house. We didn't know if someone was going to tell Daddy that someone was in the house. And we was standing right in the front, by the door, and I was laughing, and Carmen she said, "Oh, look at Gal. Gal's face is so smooth, and her teeth are so white and so pretty." First time anybody ever told me I was pretty. They wanted to touch my skin, on my face and arms. And she said, "Listen, Rhoda, listen to the way they talk. You hear how they talk, girl?" We had this accent, it was a accent that we had from Mississippi.

Mrs. Wicker called Carmen and Rhoda. Their real mother, Miss Wilhelmina, wasn't living in the same house, they were living with their grandparents. So she called them home to do some kind of work. Florence told us, "Y'all better get this house together before Daddy come, because y'all know."

When he came home that day we had already cook some sauerkraut and pig feet and rice. We just boiled the pig feet, and you had to let it boil for a long time, and throw the kraut in the pot.

It was sour to me, but I always et it. I had no choice but to eat it.

When Daddy came home, soon as he sat to the table, he didn't even have to call me. *Bam*, I was taking off his shoes. These shoes that he would wear were black steel-toed shoes. They were black and they were steel-toed.

And I have never seen a man feet look like that before. Round the toenails of his toe was a white powdery stuff, it was cakey. There was white in the crease of his feet on the side. The bottom of his feet wasn't like a palm of your hand. It looked dingy.

"Daddy, you got all this white stuff on your feet."

He said, "After I take a bath tonight I want you to take a knife and scrape all that stuff off my feet when I get out of the tub."

Kitty was laughing in the kitchen, saying, "Gal got to scrape Daddy's feet tonight now."

We ate that sauerkraut and did the work that we would normally do, and he kept up the same calling us *constantly*. He took the bath that night, and he told me to go in the kitchen and get a butter knife.

He sat down on his bed and stuck one feet out at the time, and I remember scraping all that old dead skin. I had a rag beside me and I keep wiping the knife.

I said, "Oh, Daddy, you got a lot of stuff on your feet."

"Well, you keep on scraping till you get it all off."

I mean, I was scraping and scraping and scraping.

"Daddy, I got it all off that feet."

"Well, get the other feet."

Did the other feet.

Naomi and them was laughing, say, "Oh, Daddy going to call me to do his feet."

Next thing we know, he call Naomi. "Naomi, get the comb and grease."

We got the comb and grease.

"Now, I want you to part my hair little by little and scratch the dandruff out and then put some grease on it."

So we did that.

That same night, he said, "Gal, when you was doing my toe, do it look like one of my toenails got a ingrown toenail?"

I said, "No, sir."

"Well, get the clippers and clip my toenails."

I almost clipped one of his toenails off. I said to myself, "I hope he don't call me no more."

He got a call from a lady, Miss Mamie Nightlaw. She live on James Island. As he was talking to her on the phone, we figured that he wasn't going to bother us no more, so I stopped doing his toenails. Naomi stop doing his hair and ease out of the room. Well, after he get off the phone, he call us right back in the room again to finish up.

I told him that I was finished. Naomi was still

doing his hair. Then he said, "That's enough for now." And he said, "Y'all go in there and get that TV and bring it in here." We had to go inside the living room, get the TV, bring the TV, sit it on his dresser, then stand there like a zombie and keep switching and turning and fixing the aerial.

Then we finally got to get in our beds. And lay in bed—*Bam*, he call again. "Gal, come change the station. I don't want to see that."

Did that. Went back in the bed.

The phone rang.

"Naomi, come answer the phone." I mean, the phone is right there by his nightstand. He just don't want to answer the phone.

WE GOT STARTED going to school. The school bus would pick us up right in the front of the house. We didn't have no good clothes to wear, just some old clothes that was given us from Carmen and Rhoda, clothes that they wore some time ago. They were older than us, but we were not that much younger than they were, and they said they had clothes to fit us. And Daddy was so happy that he didn't have to buy us school clothes.

I was going to Snowden Elementary School. My schoolteacher name was Miss Poole. And I had liked her, too. But the only thing I didn't like about her is she would call each pupil up to the front of the class, taking turns to massage her back. She would bring a comb to school and ask us to scratch her head. And this just made me start thinking about being home, doing the same things. But sometimes I liked doing it because that was like being teacher's pet. She called us each day, somebody had to either massage her back or comb her hair.

This girl name Francene Topp was a pretty black girl with pretty, pretty hair. I had kind of liked her, and two other girls name Marie and Ivy. But I didn't like the guy that I sat behind, Vernon Strawn. He was a dark, dark guy, real dark. He liked Francene Topp but he didn't like me, because she was real red and I was dark. And I got pissed off because he liked her and he didn't like me. But there were two other guys in my class, Bernard and Brian Anders, they were two twin brothers. They had liked me, but the other guy he didn't like me.

Ivy's mother would always fix her a good lunch, a good lunch all the time, and Francene Topp's mother would fix a good lunch. I never brought lunch to school. And I would always beg them for it, and Vernon didn't like me asking them for it. Every day I would ask them for something. So one day they played a trick on me. Vernon told Francene, "Ask Ruthie if she want your honey bun, and watch if she don't tell you yes."

I heard him told her that, so when she ask me did I want it, I knew I wanted it but I told her no. And they were so stunned when I said that.

So I said to myself, "I'll fix them. From now on, I'm going to steal their lunch."

So when they had to go to the bathroom or we go out to recess, I would steal their lunch, and I would steal their lunch money, I would sneak in their purse, I did, I just took their things. It got so bad with me doing that stuff until my teacher would go out the class for a while and if she'd tell me to sit up to her desk until she come back, I would go in her pocketbook and steal her money. I don't know why I would—I would just go in there and take her money. I even stole her wallet. I took it home, took all the money out, and I threw the wallet underneath the store, Joe Mink store. I threw it underneath there, and I took the money and spent it.

And we had a Christmas party. Everybody was supposed to bring something to school. I didn't have the money to buy anything, and Daddy said he wasn't going to buy anything at all. So I was crying and crying. I told Florence and them, I said, "Daddy know I got to take something to school, but he told me he ain't going to give me nothing to take."

There was a box of cereal that we bought, and that box of cereal had a little car in there. A red little car. I'll never forget, a little small red car. They told me that I would have to give whoever name I pull that. I remember I was crying and crying and crying, because it was so little.

I took it to school, but I never took it out. Everybody had to put their gift underneath the tree. And when we had recess, the teachers never locked the doors in the class. I was so afraid to let anyone see the little red car, I went into another class, open up the door, and I took so many presents. I put it all in my clothes. One present that I remember taking was a round locket with a nice design in it, and it was gold. It could have been not real gold, but it was a gold-looking locket. The box didn't have a name on it, so I put on there "From Ruthie," and I put it underneath the tree in our room.

When we had our party, it was Francene who picked the gift, and when she said it was from Ruthie, even the teacher wanted to know how did I get a nice gift like that. She didn't know some presents were missing in the other class. But that class didn't have their party yet.

So I figured the next day, recess, I would go and take more gifts. I went back in there, and I stole more gifts. And the third day, I started to go in and steal more, but I didn't know that they had two boys behind the closet to see who was this person stealing their gifts.

It was recess time. I went in that class, and I remember, as soon as I was about to touch that gift, the closet door opened. Two boys jumped out! I ran out of that class, I ran all the way around the building, I ran so fast. And they were running right behind me, and as I got all the way around that building, I came to the two double doors, I ran down that hallway, and I *roared* in the girls' bathroom.

Next thing I know, a teacher came in there and said, "Whoever's in there, come out here."

I was standing up on top of the toilet so they couldn't see my feet, and she said, "I know you're in here. Come on out of there." She came in there and she got me out. She took me to my teacher, Miss Poole, and then Miss Poole put two and two together. They told what they were missing, and she knew the locket. Then she remembered her wallet.

I break down and I cry, I told her yeah, I did those things. She ask me where was her wallet, and I told her where her wallet was. She wrote a letter to Daddy and they sent it in the mail. It wasn't given to me. She told him exactly what happened.

Daddy read it, and he beat me. He told me that he was going to take me to Mr. Joe Mink store and I better find that wallet. Sure enough, I went under that building and I found that wallet and I gave it back to her. She told me to never do that again and she would forgive me.

But that didn't stop me. I just continued to steal people's lunch and food and things. Daddy told me if I didn't keep my hands off of things that he would *see* that I keep my hands off of things.

And I started beating people up. Slapping them, beating them. Anything a kid would say to me in class, I would just slap them and beat them, and I got put out of school. First grade.

Daddy said if he got to take time off his job to take me back to school, he was going to beat my behind right in school. So he did have to take time off, because you got to have your parents come back to sign you in. He said, "If that principal tells me you did that, and you say you didn't do it, then I'm going to whip your behind. So you may as well tell me right now before we go in this building."

I said to myself, *I don't care. I'm going to lie to him anyway, because regardless if it's the truth he's going to beat me anyway.* So I stuck to my lie.

The principal told him that I did do those things, and Daddy slapped me right there in the office.

The principal said, "Mr. Fleetwood, no, don't do that. Whyn't you wait till you get home, and take care of that at home."

So when we walk out into the hall, Daddy said, "I'll finish you when I get home."

When I got home, he wasn't there. I knew when he came home that he was going to beat me. So when I heard the car pull up in the yard, I was getting all frisky and scared and Florence and them was getting scared because they know I was going to get a beating.

But when he came in the back door (because he always come through the back door), he did like he normally do. He came to the table. I ran in there and took his shoes off and his socks off.

Florence done put his food on the table. He et his food and put his glasses on and read his mail.

Then he said, "Gal, I ain't forget what I told you this morning. What I was going to do to you."

And I say, "Yes, sir."

"Go on out there to that oak tree and pull off a limb out there and put it down here till I get through reading."

I said, "Daddy, you want me to get a big one or a little one?"

"You just go out there and get one for me."

So I went out the back door, and I was looking at that tree—big huge, huge oak tree. I didn't know which stick to get, and I was taking up time, just taking up time, scared, scared. And I found one that was long and skinny, and I brought it in the house and I sat it on the table. The table was a little table, and the top of that table was green, with green flowers on it. And the chairs was brown wooden chairs but the center of the chair where you sat at was green. I got two of those chairs right now today that we had during that time.

And I remember when I sat the stick on the table, it fell in one of the chairs. He didn't say anything, he just keep eating his food. I went back in the room, waiting on him to call me to beat me.

I heard him got up from the table. I heard the

back door open. He went outside, he got another one, a bigger stick than the one I got.

And he said, "Gal?"

I said, "Sir?"

He said, "Come on in here."

Went in there. I was shaking.

He say, "Now take off all your clothes."

I said, "Daddy, can I please keep my drawers on?"

He said, "Take them all off."

I took off my clothes.

And he said, "Now get up on that brown table right there, stand up there."

I said, "Daddy, don't beat me hard, Daddy, don't beat me hard—Daddy, don't beat me hard!"

He started beating me and beating me and beating me. I was jumping up all over that table, I was screaming, I was screaming, I was screaming, screaming and screaming.

"Down the window, Daddy, please down the window so the neighbors don't hear."

He said, "The neighbors! I don't care about no neighbors! I'll *up* them windows. Open up them damn doors! *Open* up them doors. You don't want the neighbors to hear? I want the neighbors to hear."

And he beat me. He beat me. He beat me, he beat me, he beat me. He hit me so much that he happened to hit his own self, and when he did that, he went berserk. Then he took off his belt. He took off his belt then.

"I'm going to make water come out of your eyes," he said.

He didn't chop me with the leather end of the belt. He hit me with the buckle part. He had just chop me and chop me and chop me. I was screaming and yelling but I never did cry. Never did cry. Never did cry.

And after he beat me, he told me get on out his face and get my clothes. "You are a tough nigger," he said. I grabbed my clothes and I ran in my room and I was shaking and shaking.

Florence said, "Gal, I told you not to do that. You know Daddy going to beat you. You know you always lying, you always lying."

I said, "I can't help it. If I tell the truth he's going to beat me anyway."

After I put my clothes on, I caught myself going to bed. He called and told me to get out of that bed. He told me to come in there and squeeze this bump on his back. And I said to myself, this man—he already beat me until I were trembling and shaking, I had welts all over me, and he told me to squeeze this bump on his back!

I squeezed the bump on his back.

Then he called Naomi. He told Naomi that he wanted her to squeeze this bump on his face because it felt like it was a hair inside that bump. And he said, "Look over there and get that tweezer." Naomi squeeze it and it was bleeding, and she did pull out a hair.

He said, "I done tell Gal, if I got to take off

work for her one more time, that's going to be *her*."

I STARTED DOING them old bad things again. Same old thing, lying and stealing and doing all kind of stuff. I stole some tickets from a teacher that was for a play. I didn't take them home, I just throw them behind the heater in the class. They sent a letter to Daddy and said that they was going to call him, because they might've misplaced it, but they think that I stole it.

I knew they were going to call, so I went and got a knife and I cut the phone cord.

He was sitting there waiting on the call. He kept saying, "That phone ain't ring all day."

When he finally pick up the phone to use it, there was no dial tone. He pick the phone up and he look, and he say, "No wonder. The phone line pop."

Florence and them find out that I did it, but they thought that when we were cleaning I probably popped it, yanked it out. They didn't tell. The next day he got that fixed.

He told us that when we got back from school he wanted Naomi to clean up the bathroom and he wanted me to clean up the back room. So Naomi clean the bathroom up. I clean up the back room outside, and Florence cooked.

When he came home, he didn't go to the table. He went straight in the bathroom and see if Naomi had did the work that he told her to do. And Naomi did clean the bathroom real good.

He said, "Naomi, did you clean this bathroom today?"

Naomi said, "Yes, sir."

"*You* cleaned this bathroom today, right?"

"Yes, sir."

"Come here. What is this?"

Naomi was scared. "What is what?"

"What is this?"

I came down the hall because he was talking kind of mean at her.

He said, "Look at this stain you left inside this toilet."

I got closer to the door, and when I got there to looking in the door, she was by the toilet and he was behind her, and the next thing I know, he grabbed her head and he pushed it in the toilet and had it in the water.

Florence and them heard it, and they came down the hall. And Naomi was twisting, twisting her body trying to get out of that water, and somehow as she did it she happened to hit him.

He said, "Nigger, you going to hit me?"

"Daddy, I didn't mean to hit you."

The next thing I know, he boxed the shit out of her. He boxed her and boxed her, and she fell on her back. She was kicking and kicking and kicking, and we was all standing there, and he was beating her and beating her. Florence and Kitty asked him to stop. Naomi managed to get away and she ran outside through the back door.

I started getting scared, and I went back outside to check the back room to make sure that was clean, because she had already gotten a beating from the bathroom and she had *cleaned* it. He knew he had told me to clean the back room, but he called Naomi.

"Naomi, didn't I tell you to clean this back room?"

I said, "No, Daddy, you had told me to do it."

He saw a cord, an extension cord, on the step. He started beating me and beating Naomi with it. Florence came up and asked him to please stop, please stop. He stopped. He came in the house and sat to the table. Florence had his food ready. Then he right then call us in to come take off his shoes and his socks, and I told Naomi, I said, "I hate him. I hate that man. I hate him. I can't stand him."

He told us to sit to the table and start eating right then. And as we were eating, every time we put food in our mouth, he would look in our mouth. I was scared to open my mouth to eat.

After we got through, we clean up the table and move his shoes, and put it where we normally put it at for the next day's work. I don't know who made the bath water for him. He called Florence and told her that he was going out that night and wanted her to get some clothes for him. So she got the clothes out, and he left.

The phone rang—it was the lady he had gone to see, Miss Nightlaw, and she wanted to know did he already left yet. We told her that he had already gone.

I told Florence, I said, "I can't believe how he beat Naomi like that after Naomi clean up that bathroom."

"Gal, I don't know. I don't know what's wrong with Daddy. I don't know why he do that."

DADDY TOLD Florence and Kitty that he was going teach them how to drive, even though they weren't old enough. They need to drive because he was going to sit back and let them be his chauffeur.

It was a blue Chevrolet, at this point, he had a blue Chevrolet. He started Florence off driving at first. She needed glasses so he bought her a pair of blue cat-eye glasses, these glasses look just like cat's eyes. And they were *cat*, now, cat to the max. We called her Cat Woman. And he told Florence, he say, "You ready to drive?"

"Yes, sir."

He told all us to get in the car. But he didn't get in the car right then. When we saw him coming, he came with a switch off the tree in the car with him, and he told Florence, he say, "One wrong move and I'm going to whip you. Every time you make a wrong move in this car."

That was Florence first time driving, and it wasn't easy for her. She was backing up, she almost hit the house, and he just started beating her in the car, whipping her arm, whipping her leg. She said, "Daddy, if you keep hitting me, I won't be able to drive."

She backed out and we went towards Rifle Range Road. And she didn't stop at the stop sign, she just pulled on out. And he whipped her. He told Kitty the next day was going to be her day to drive and he was going to beat her if she didn't do right.

We end up going to Dairy Queen. We didn't get no ice cream or nothing like that, just drove through. But as we came back, Florence went off the road. And he started hitting her again. Florence was driving that car so fast right then, I really thought we was going to wreck, and as we pulled into the street, going down our side, he told her to stop the car and get out. When she did, he whipped her all around the car, and she got into the passenger side and he got into the driver side, and then he finished pulling up into the yard.

When he got out, he started whipping her as she ran. She stopped and turned round and faced him, and she said, "Daddy, are you going to kill me like you killed Mama?"

And when she said that, he boxed her face *up*—her glasses flew off—she tried to get away. She tried to run towards the back door, but we couldn't get in anyway because he had the key. And she tripped over the step. He opened up the door and he said, "You wait. You get in here and I'm going to kill you. I'm going to kill you."

Florence said, "That's right. Go ahead kill me. Kill me like you killed my mama."

That night we started crying. Crying and crying, crying and crying. And he beat her, and he beat her, with his big old rusty gator hands. He told Kitty, "You going to get the same thing, too, if you drive the way she drive."

I told Naomi, "I don't want to never learn to drive if we going to get beat just to drive."

He told Florence that he didn't want her to drive anymore. I think that hurt him, what she told him about Mama.

HE GOT some books. I don't know where the books came from—maybe the teacher brought them to the house—but they were my books. He said, "Gal, I want you to go in there. I'm going to be in there in a minute because I want you to read to me."

Tag and Spot, that was the name of the book. "See Dick run"—all that. I got down on my knees at that brown table, same table that he beat me on. And the book cover was green. He came and he sat on the blue couch. And he said, "Read."

And I remember saying, "The . . . ball . . ." and next thing I know—*Bam!*—he boxed my fingers.

He said, "It's not 'thuh,' it's 'thee.' "

As I'm reading again, that word came up again.

"Thuh . . ."

Bam! "*I said, not 'thuh.' 'Thee.'* "

He got up. He went outside, and he got a piece of switch off the oak tree.

"Every time you say that word 'thuh' and don't say 'thee' I'm going to whip your ass."

And I was so shaking and so nervous I was scared to say that word again. But it was in the printing. It came up again. And this time I said "thee" and he didn't hit me.

I kept saying the word "thee" every time I came to it.

He said, "Naomi, now it's your turn."

Naomi read right through the book, because she was smart anyway. She was honor roll; she was smart from the beginning.

He told Florence that he wanted us to read every day. Every day. Every day he wanted us to read, because I wasn't doing it in school.

That was when I started to stutter.

They teased me all the time. They told me that I was a stuttering jackass. A stuttering fool. I couldn't help it. I was so embarrassed when I went places. I didn't like to be around people when it happened. For quite a while, I couldn't say three words together. I knew the words but they won't come out. My first school speech I had was just to say "Happy Easter Day." That's all I had to say. I went up there and bowed, and I said, "Ha-ha-ha-happy Ea-ea-ea-easter D-d-d-d-d-day."

I was scared to open my mouth. It was so bad that I made it up that I couldn't see, so I could

get glasses. I told them I couldn't see, but I was
lying. I wanted the cat-eye glasses. Somehow, I
thought if I had those cat-eye glasses, I would
be able to talk right.

chapter four

a couple of miles from Hungry Neck, over in Remley's Point, there's a little church that has the face of Jesus on the roof. I think they made it with shingles in different colors. And it's still painted up there today, the face of Jesus. You can see it because the roof is a slanted roof, and the Jesus looks down on you. But believe it or not, the face looks black.

When we was little, we looked at it. We said, "We thought Jesus was a white man, but on here he's a black man!" And we really liked it, because he was black. And he is huge. When you're standing off, when you're walking away, look like he is just following you with his eyes, wherever you move. We always liked that picture. I don't know why they put it up there, but I liked it. Everybody liked it that saw it. I wished we had one.

In Hungry Neck, the roof on both of the churches is just plain, no pictures at all. The first church is Second Zion. Then, soon as you pass that, you see a old house, and then you see another tiny church, red brick. That used to be Mr. Wicker church, Sanctified people.

This white girl Diane used to lived behind the brick church, she and her brother. Diane liked us. Florence used to plait her hair. And they came over to our house to eat our oranges.

Daddy got the oranges, two or three big sacks inside of a blue car somebody gave him because it caught on fire and burnt up. And the oranges were burnt, some were even black. We got the sack, we had to peel it up from the floor of the car, and you could smell the burning. Even the oranges that didn't have a black scar, they tasted burnt. But we didn't care, we ate the oranges anyway. The first one I ate, it was still warm. But we just peel them wide open and ate them. Diane and her brother loved those burnt oranges.

We had another white family in the neighborhood, name Dew. Mr. Dew had a son name George, George Dew, who used to play with us all the time, and he used to ride our bus. We knew he was white, but to us he was black. His father owned all that land back there behind Beehive Road where they got those apartments at now, upstairs-and-downstairs apartments.

Mr. Dew had two airplanes, real airplanes, and a long dirt place where they would land and take off. That's how long it was. And sometimes he would get those things that people fly in the air, that say words on the back, and he would fly it through the sky. That was his business. One of the planes was blue-and-white, and one was red-and-white.

He was a nice man, and he used to take us for rides in the airplanes. Daddy never knew that we were back that side anyway. It was a street over. We would go out there and Mr. Dew would take us for a ride. But we never went off the ground! He would just drive us in circles on the ground. He would give us the hat that buckle around your chin, he would put one on top of our head, and the plane would be going around and around and around. We never got up in the air. But we would be hollering and screaming because it was shaking as it was going. It was shaking, we was bouncing and bouncing. Every weekend he would tell us "If you want a ride, come on out here. Mr. Dew will give you a ride." And every kid in the neighborhood would go there. We knew his son real well, and that's the reason he would ride us around.

There was a house back there, a old wooden house, you could barely see it, all the way back in the woods. It was the house of the Shivers family. And that house was old. The wood of the house was thick, it was straight boards up and down, and you could see holes in it. And the porch floor was all humpity-hump. Those people were very poor. I went to school with the daughter and the son, but one of the daughters was kind of retarded. Her name was Tulip, that's what her name was. But they never complained. And I think that was Mr. Dew land they were living on, I'm not certain. Because all of that was his, all of it.

Mr. Dew is dead now but his house is still there today, and his family is still there. They must have made a lot of money when they sold the land for those apartments, but when you see their house, you figure they have no money, that's the way they live. Now they're in the seafood business. They go crabbing and shrimping and fishing, and they sell it right there in the yard. And those old planes are still there, all green and rusty from being out there so long. The sons never took it up after he stopped. And they live right there just before you go around the curve to go to the old bridge.

We didn't watch much television when we were little. It was only one TV, and about the only time we watched it was when we were standing there, turning the station for Daddy or twisting the aerial, or now and then when he went out at night.

But in the afternoon, before he came home, we played hopscotch in the yard underneath the big old oak tree. Mrs. Vane son, Rafe Vane, would sometimes dig a trench from the tree and let us pour the water down, and we would see the water going down different trails. We would put a little boat in there and let that go around.

We used to play a game called Devil Devil Come and Get Me, and a game called Red Light Stop. And we played Double Dutch. We were good, we were very good at Double Dutch. And sometimes we'd get the clothesline and one of those big cardboard boxes, punch a little hole in it, and tie the line and pull each other down the dirt road. When we go around the curve the box would always keel over and I would scrape the tip of my nose.

And anytime it would start raining and the sun was out, we would say, "The devil fighting his wife, the devil fighting his wife."

But we didn't go swimming or fishing. We didn't know those things.

ON THE SIDE of the brick church used to be a wired fence, rusty one, too, and then another old house, belong to the man called Ice Jones. He had five or six horses back there. He was almost seven feet tall, slim, and he was dark dark black. His son grew up to be tall just like him, and we called him Ice Jones also. The son married a Filipino girl, and they were living in there too, for quite a while.

We used to throw little things at the horses to make them move, so we could watch how they move. We would stand close to the fence to make them swap their tail to hit our faces. I don't know why, I just loved those pretty horses.

And you know what? That man used to shine those horses skin! He did. He had a big old brush, and he used to clean them until their skin was silky and shiny. But I was scared to go through that pathway when it got dark because I thought them horses was going to get me. So I used to *zoom* down there. I was scared they was going to kick me, but they never bothered us.

Ice Jones had a field by the side of his house, and we would steal his sweet potatoes out of the field. He never fussed at us. We would bite that sweet potato raw and eat it, it was delicious. And he used to give us that stuff you peel it back—sugarcane—and boy did we eat that. It was sweet.

We used to wait on his porch to catch the bus. Old Ice Jones, I really liked him. He walked a cool walk, easy stepping like a Michael Jackson slide, but Ice is going forward with his. He always kept on suspenders because he stayed in the field or he stayed back there with his horses. But his wife was sick. You never would see her come outside. The few times that we did see her when we were on the porch, she used to wear a black curly wig.

ONE TIME it snowed. We didn't have any gloves, we put socks on our hands. And they were mitch-mack, we didn't care. Donny and Otis came outside to play with us, and we couldn't go to school for two weeks, that's how hard it snowed. The snow brightened up everything. All of Hungry Neck was bright and sparkly, except right then I noticed that our house didn't look as good as it used to. It looked a little dirty, in all that snow.

We licked our tongues in the snow, we made little balls and put it in the freezer. I wanted to see if the ice in the freezer taste the same as the snow so I licked my tongue in there, and when I licked it in there, it got stuck. And when I pulled it out, the freezer pulled off some of my tongue!

I was tasting all kind of things when I was little. Tasting and peeping, touching, listening. I was just curious.

MRS. VANE husband, Mr. Downey Vane, no matter what, when he get a watermelon, he would always cut the watermelon in half, and he would call nobody but Gal. "Gal, come on, get a piece of this watermelon." All the time. He had really liked me. He had one of his legs cut off from cancer in the leg. I would watch him when he stick his little nub leg in that thing. But when he take it off, that little knee would move. It looked strange to me, the way it could move like that.

Mr. Hack Ralston used to come out to Hungry Neck with a truck, sell hot dogs off of his truck. Another man, name Mr. Simpson, sell fruit, cabbage, any kind of fruit and vegetables that you want. He used to grow it hisself and sell it. He would go pull up in Mr. Buzz yard and sell it. He was a old man, had a green truck, and it look like a little house thing on top. And he always wore a hat, twist to the side. Mr. Simpson still living today. We would jump on the back of the truck and try to get some of his plums and grape, and the peanuts, the boiled peanuts is what we would really steal. When he would go in the gate and drink with Mr. Buzz there, he couldn't see us. We would peep from behind the truck and reach up, eat whatever we grab.

The milkman used to come through Hungry Neck and sit our milk right on the step in a wood crate. The milk came in bottles, not in cartons. We would open it up and drink the milk right there.

And what was really nice in Hungry Neck was the music we could hear. Rhoda Wicker used to play the piano. You could hear her voice singing from all the way down the street—she kept that screen door open when she sang. She played "The Young and the Restless," and I always loved it, because it was soft. It was so pretty. It sounded like a feeling, that music. I always liked to hear it. We would keep the windows up, just to hear it. She always sounded very happy.

And we would know always what time of day it was because this big ship out there would blow a horn, and we could hear that, too. Every hour. We would know what time it is. *Bommmmp*. And when it's twelve o'clock, it blows it longer. I don't know what kind of ship it was, but it was on the river out there. A big ship.

The ice-cream man had music, too. And it was black music! Al Green songs and the Jackson Five. We knew when he coming—if you don't hear Al Green, you hear the Jackson Five. But the ice-cream man was a white man. And no matter what, if you didn't have enough money, he's going to let you have that ice cream anyway. He always pull off on the side, where the grass was at. Sometimes he would pass us and we'd have to run down the street to get him, and we'd be counting up all our pennies, and he'll say "Well, what you want?" and I'll say "How much that cost? How much that cost, how much that cost?" pointing to different ice creams. I used to want the Push-ups and these one called the Nutty Buddy because I liked that sweet brown corn. He sold candy, bubble gum, and then cigarettes, and all that stuff on the truck. And when people in Hungry Neck started getting food stamps, he'd sell them ice cream out of food stamps.

Later we had another ice-cream truck coming in, in the afternoon. It was a guy coming through, but he would never stop. He played music, but he didn't even have no ice cream in there, he was selling drugs.

One more man came through the neighborhood selling food, but not only did he sell food, he came through there to find out what woman was single and what wasn't. He was a fresh man. But he didn't last long. I don't know who stopped him, but somebody did.

* * *

THE FAMILY I really liked was the Hermans. They had four daughters, and any time it's their birthday, their mother would throw them a party and always invite us. We never had a birthday party. But they did. They had a washtub they would full up with apples and water, and we would try to bite them. We played a game, Pin the Tail on the Donkey, and whether you win or lose, you go home with a prize. I was always jealous of them because they had the parties. The Sampsons did the same thing, and the Topps, and the Wickers. The Carveys did it. Everybody family had birthday parties, except our family. We even got invited to the Linkharts. They were the worst people. They were some dangerous people. They would chop your head off if you ever get on their wrong side, so I stayed away from them. But even them, even those bad people parents gave them parties. And we never had none.

Hungry Neck did have a playground, but at the time there wasn't much there. We didn't have those things they have now, the little animals that you can get on and ride and the merry-go-round and the slide. That was never there. Even the building wasn't there. Only thing we had was the cemented place and the two basketball poles with no net. We had to go all the way to Crabnet Beach if we wanted to go on a sliding board. Our baseball field was that area that they got all fenced off now, as you going around the curve. Now they built houses there. Me and Naomi played on the softball team, and we were good. When we won, we used to go to the Dairy Queen. Our coach name was Wing, and now he drives a city bus.

Every Halloween the playground would give a party. I would get me two bags of what they were giving out. The bigger kids would come out there just to watch us, and they would say "Look at Gal." People just had liked me. "Look at Gal. Gal ain't going home with one bag now, Gal going to have two bags." I would look in my bags real quick, then I would look at Naomi and say "Naomi, what did they give you?"

We never had a costume. We went out with our regular old clothes on. After the Halloween party, the playground lady told us, "Go home, do *not* go to anybody's house. *Go straight home.*" But we went and we knock on the people door anyway, our neighbors.

"Ain't you been to the party?"

"No, ma'am."

"That's why they have the party for y'all chirren, so y'all don't go to the houses."

But we thought, we going to just go to two more houses. We went to the Linkhart house. They got a path and pretty flowers on the two edge. And they got two pine trees as you walk up the step. The house was dark.

I said, "Naomi, ring the doorbell."

"I'm not ringing that doorbell, you ring the doorbell."

I rung the doorbell.

Mr. Linkhart, he had a big glass door, he push it open with his foot, and when we looked he had a big rifle. Pointing straight at us.

"If you don't get away from here—"

I left my candy. I dropped it. That man he pulled a gun on us! We ran and we ran, we told and we screamed to everybody, "The man got a gun!" The police came down there, said he didn't have no gun. But he pulled a rifle on us, we knew that.

Mrs. Sampson saw me crying and told Otis, "Otis, tell Gal come here." I was crying, and I told her I dropped my candy over to the Linkhart house. She told me don't worry about it, that she will give me some more. She give me those big old Hersheys, those big candies. Naomi and them had them little ones. I was satisfied with that. But I never got them two bag of candy back out of the Linkhart yard.

ONE NIGHT when we did watch television was the night when Martin Luther King died. I was sitting on the floor with my legs crossed, close to the TV, watching, because I had loved that speech that he made, "I Have a Dream." Always had loved that speech. And when they showed us the part where those people had the water hose and the dog, I said to myself, "Oh, God, how could somebody do that to anybody?" I saw the policeman, and I said, "Look at that fool."

All Daddy said was, "Don't you let me hear you say the word fool in this house again."

But I told Florence and them I am going to speak one day in front of a lot of people. They say, "Yeah Gal, yeah Gal." And after that I said I will never watch another show where black people get hurt. Even later, when I began to watch *Roots*, I didn't like it. When I saw that man got his feet chopped off, right then I hated it. I couldn't look at movies like that anymore. But when *Roots* came on TV again, I came into the room, and I saw the guy hanging. Right then I wanted to beat every white person that I knew. That's why I can't look at movies like that. These people haven't done nothing to me, but it's a thing that happens to me if I see it. That's why I prefer not to look at it. People said I should look at it because it's your history. And that is true. But I couldn't.

chapter five

daddy was a big man. He weighed about 210 pounds. He had a big nose and a wide face. His lips were dark—black from smoking cigarettes.

And one day, his teeth started bothering him. He didn't know which one it was, so he went to the clinic up by Dillon and had them all pulled out. They told him he didn't need them all out, but he said he didn't care, he *want* them all out. He got every last one of his teeth pulled out, and they gave him the false teeth. But he never wore them. Kept them in a glass in the bathroom. Only time he would put them on was when he'd go see a lady. Didn't even wear them on the job. He chewed with his gums. He'd eat meat, corn, he didn't need teeth. His gums were hard like teeth. But any time he'd get ready to go out and see a lady, got to have those false teeth.

And we were glad when he went out. That was another time of freedom. We knew he wasn't coming back until two hours before he had to be to work, so the house was ours. We could come out of our rooms, and sit to watch TV. We had fun, we played cards, invited Rhoda and Carmen over to play with us. We even got some liquor and played a game—if you had the most cards left you had to drink some. We would press our hair or listen to music or sew. We had a old antique sewing machine Florence taught us on. She started us with two white papers, and she would mark it, and tell us to sew on the line, to learn how.

Florence could really sew. She didn't need a pattern, she had her own designs. And she took the time to teach us and to fix our hair, Florence didn't have the tough hair like we had, she had really soft hair, and when she walked it would *bounce*. She was so pretty. When she pressed our hair, me and Naomi would put the straightening comb on the stove, and we would get the petroleum jelly. What Florence would do, she would part our hair and just out of spite she would put a lot of grease on, so when she'd get the hot comb to press it, to pull it and get it straight, the grease would hiss and melt down into our scalp and burn us.

I wanted bangs, so I put the curler on the stove. Florence smeared a lot of grease on my hair in front and rolled it up. When she unloosed the curler, the bangs dropped down, and she took her hand and mash the bangs to my forehead to make it burn.

I said, "Florence, don't do that!"

"Shut up your mouth."

She pulled my head back and sneezed in my face.

Kitty said, "Florence, why you always doing that to them?"

"They better keep doing what I say, unless they want them plaits sticking up all over their head."

I said, "The next time, let my plaits stay on my head, because you always burn me."

I was afraid she was turning evil then. I was afraid she would be just like another Daddy to me. And she start becoming *more* like Daddy. A little bit meaner every day. She spit on us. She began to dig in her nose and if we were coming down the hallway or by her, she would throw it on us. Then she'll start laughing. If she sneeze, she would get it and rub it on us. She would rub it on our legs, anywhere. She became so nasty, I didn't like to be around her. Knowing that Daddy beat us, still she became worse, along with him.

Then Daddy stopped beating her and Kitty for some reason. Then it was just me and Naomi. Florence seem like she got on Daddy good side. No matter what she said, it was fine with him.

When we were taking a bath, she would take her bath first and we would have to take our bath in the same water. I took my bath anyway, but I told Florence later, I said, "I don't want to

take my bath last no more. Everybody always
be before me."

She said, "You got to take it like I say take it
or you ain't going to take none at all."

I said, "No, I'm not either, I'm going to tell
Daddy."

"Yeah, and I'll tell Daddy that you be sneaking around with them little boys around here."

I said, "No, I don't be sneaking around here
with no little boys."

She say, "Yeah, you do. You be sneaking
around here with Otis Sampson and Donny
Wicker."

Which was true. But I didn't want her to tell
Daddy.

He would never like to see us laughing and
talking together. If he did, he would call one in
the room just to confuse us. He'd tell Florence
or tell Kitty "Gal didn't tell you? That she say
such and such about you?" And he lied. He
would try to divide us. He would say something that would make us mad at each other,
and they would get mad at me or I would get
mad at them.

Some things he told them about me, they
didn't really believe it, but in order to satisfy
Daddy they would act mean in front of him.
Then later they would say, "Gal, you know we
was doing that because Daddy was around."
And I believe that was what happened to us.
Because of him, we didn't treat each other
right.

* * *

DADDY STARTED stealing things off the Naval Base. He told me, "Gal, me and you got a job to do. You got to get up in the morning."

I said, "Yes, sir."

After we eat breakfast, me and him would get into his truck and he would go on the Naval Base, and park the truck, and walk toward these rusted dumpsters. He would open up the dumpsters and would tell me to sit and watch for people.

"If anybody come, blow the horn."

He would steal these heavy-looking metal stuff and throw it in the back of the truck, throw it in the back of the truck, throw it in the back of the truck. And when he got so many of them, enough that he wanted, then we would take it back home.

He would tell us to go outside, dump the trash in the hole, start a fire, and throw those big heavy things—looked like giant bullets—in the fire. After we do that it would be red, it would be so red. We had to get a big old hammer, put the metal on top of something else, and chop it because it was so hot and red you could crack it right then and it would just break right on up.

The person who wanted this from him said you had to burn it, then after you'd burn it, it would turn real, real red, and then when you crack it, it just opens. I mean, we would do that all day, after we came back from school. All day long. There was just so much of it. After we let it cool off, we would put it in the back of his truck. He would take it all the way up to North Charleston, to this man that had a bunch of junk cars in his yard. And Daddy would sell it to this man, and the man would pay him money.

Then he start wanting to be more greedier. We start going every weekend, every weekend, every weekend, and my neighbor Mrs. Vane, she said, "Gal, what you doing out there?" and we said, "Daddy got us burning up this stuff and cracking it for him."

He started taking wires, and we had to put it on the fire and let all the rubber burn off, and from there we had to get it and wind it up in a round circle, wind it up. It looked like copper when we got through. And burn these heavy big pieces like big bullets and then crack them. We was getting it every week, me and him, getting so much stuff. And I'm the person be sitting in the truck, being his lookout.

But with all the money he was getting, we see that he still wasn't buying us anything at all.

He came home and brought a huge old plastic bag. And he said, "Gal, Naomi, Kitty, Florence, I got something for y'all." Open up the bag, it's full of corn. Full of corn on the cob. I mean, *full* full. We had to take all that corn out and put them in bags, bag them up, and put them in the freezer outside in the back room.

So we ate corn and we ate corn and we ate corn. For breakfast, we ate corn. For lunch, we ate corn. For dinner, we had corn. It was seven days a week, for one whole month, we had nothing but corn. Corn. And Florence would always get the big corns and give us these little skimpy corns. After we eat ours, if she had any left on hers we would eat off of hers.

Later he brought home more bags—string beans that was pick out of the field, or some lima beans, and we had to shuck them and shell them and freeze them. There was okra, and we had to wash them and clean them.

Then Daddy finally brought some meat. But when he go buying meat, when he got it home, it was nothing but pig feet. Pig feet, pig feet, pig feet. Pig feet. Florence would boil it, and we eat it with gravy sometimes, or we eat it with sauerkraut, or we barbecue it, but it was always pig feet. Pig feet. I thought that was the only kind of meat that we was going to ever have.

Pig feet. Pig feet is what we et.

But as time went on he began to buy hamburger steak. We had some food then, we had food then. We was eating real good then.

But if I ever got sick or got hurt, I never saw a doctor. The only doctor I ever saw is back when I got my vaccination shot to go to school. And they gave me a little cube of sugar. Then when I had the pencil lead in my hand. That's the only two times I went to the doctor.

What puzzled me—I always wondered why

did they all have a card and I didn't. They all had a card—even Pam and the ones that didn't live here. A navy card. It's a card you can use on the base, or at the Naval Hospital. They went to the doctor all the time, but I never did because I didn't have the card. I wasn't his child—he never legally adopted me. Matter of fact, I didn't know how to say what I was to him. I wasn't his child, I wasn't his grandchild. Somebody told me he was my step-grandfather. But that didn't stop me from calling him Daddy. That's what I always called him, so to me that's what he was. To tell you the truth, I don't think I knew what a step-grandfather was, or even a grandfather. All I knew was Daddy.

When I was little, real little, and my grandmama was still alive, I used to search up in the last bedroom in my grandmama pocketbook. I wanted to see something with my name on it. I never did. Not even a social security card. Not a birth certificate. I just wanted something with my name on it. I would see Florence, Naomi, Kitty, everybody, but I could never find Ruthie. Never me. They said I used to steal out of her pocketbook—yes, I did, because when I couldn't find my name in there, I was mad.

AFTER A WHILE Rhoda and Carmen Wicker became a little bit more friendlier towards us, and I was good friends with their brother Donny, me and Naomi were, and we'd go to Otis Sampson house, the second house from us, into their backyard all the time because they had a plastic pool, and their daddy and mama built them a tree house in a tree and with that long ladder. And we didn't have none so we used to always go over there.

One time, one of the guys knew me and Naomi was up in the tree house. He came and pulled the ladder off, and there was no way down. Not unless we jump onto one of the trees and try to slide down but if we did we would get all scratch up. So we stayed up there, hollering and screaming, hollering and screaming. Otis Sampson mama or daddy never came out of the house.

We was up there for quite a while, and we knew Daddy was home. We just *knew* he was home, and that really got us scared. Because we wanted to beat him home. Finally Otis father came out there, and he up the ladder back up.

We came *sailing* down there. We ran behind Mrs. Vane house, through her hedges, and when we look, we saw the tip of Daddy car.

So we knew he was already in there, and we knew he was going to be mad. And soon as we got in that door—

"Gal and Naomi! Where y'all been at?"

We told him we been at Otis house, playing in the tree house.

He said, "I'm going to whip y'all behind, because y'all know better than to go out. I told y'all. Y'all don't go to nobody house around here. I want y'all home when I come home. Get on in here and take my shoes off."

I took his shoes off. I said, "Daddy, you want me to do anything else for you?"

He said, "No. Because I'm going to whip your ass when I'm finished." So me and Naomi knew we was going to get a beating.

But just then, Mr. Larue came over. That was one of Daddy's buddies up the street. Before Daddy could have a chance to even remember, I guess, to beat us, they started talking and they started drinking. I was so happy. And every time Daddy called me I was right there, because I knew he was calling me to get him some more ice, and I wanted him to drink and drink and drink and drink. That way I knew he wasn't going to beat me.

He never finished moving his plate off the table where he had eaten at. Him and Mr. Larue was sitting there laughing and talking and drinking. Finally Mr. Larue left, and I just knew that he was going to beat us.

And I heard a noise, *rrrrererrerr*, and I said, "I wonder what that is." When I went in there, he had passed out. His head was in his plate and he was sleeping. His head was stuck in his plate, sleeping. He was drunk. Right then I was very happy.

I tried to move the plate from underneath his head because I was supposed to be washing the dishes. It was a white plate with gray trimming round it, and I got those plates here right now, today. And as I was pulling the plate, he opened up his eyes and he looked at me.

I stood still, still.

And the next I know, *plop*, his head went right back down. So I let it stay there.

When I went back in our room, I smelled something. It was polish, Florence and Kitty was putting polish on their fingernails.

So I said, "Oh boy, I sure wouldn't mind having me some polish."

They said, "Girl, you better not put no polish on your hand, you know Daddy going to whip you."

I said, "I'm going to get me some polish."

The fingernail polish was green. It was green fingernail polish. I put it on my fingers, and I let it dry, but some of it was getting messed up because all of it didn't dry.

Florence said, "Girl, Daddy see that polish on your hand, he going to whip you good."

"Y'all got some on there. Y'all going to get a beating too if I get a beating."

The next morning I made the coffee, and I put the coffee in his room. I was trying to hold the saucer with the cup on in a way that he wouldn't see the polish on my hand. But I knew that he would see it because it was green. His light was off in the room, but I had to turn it on when I set the cup down. So I had my hands underneath the saucer.

And he didn't see it. He got up and he went into the bathroom. I knew I had to take his food in, and I said, "Florence, please take his food in there," and she said, "Nunh-unh, I'm going to let you take his food in."

So I took the food in there, and when I sat the plate down, he said, "Gal, what you got on your hand?"

I said, "Polish."

He said, "Polish?"

"Yes, sir."

He ain't say nothing. He ate his food and put on his shoes and socks and got his clothes on, and he went on to work.

I told Kitty and them, "See? Daddy ain't do nothing to me."

Daddy came home that afternoon, he wanted to eat in his room, he didn't want to come to the table. We took him his food, but he had wanted *me* to bring the food in there. So I took the food in the room, and he told me to stand right there, don't even move, until he finished eating.

I stood there. I didn't really know what he wanted.

Then he said, "Kitty, Florence, y'all come here. Who put this polish on Gal hand?"

"Gal put the polish on her hand herself."

He said, "That's all I want to know."

He pushed his table to the side and he got up, and I was standing there, right in the front of the dresser. And he went into the kitchen. I heard him fumbling in the drawer, where the silverware was at.

When he came back, he had a butter knife in his hand. And he tell me to get his plate and take it in the kitchen and come back. By the time I come back he had already pulled the table back to by his bed.

He said, "Stick your hand out here."

I stuck my hand out there. He grabbed my hand and he got the knife and he scraped and he scraped and he scraped and he scraped, until he was cutting the skin, taking that polish off. And I told him that I was hurting, and I was bleeding, and I was screaming and I was yelling, and I was saying "Please stop." And he got that butter knife and he scraped and he scraped, every last one of my fingers. Every last one.

"If I ever catch any damn polish on your hand again, I will kill you, nigger. You hear me?"

"Yes, sir."

I went into the bathroom and I turned the water on. My hands was shaking and bleeding all over the sink. And I thought, "Florence and Kitty going to get the same thing, because they got polish on their hand." But he didn't touch them.

After I had dried my hands off, I went back in the room and I looked up on the dresser, and I saw that bottle of green polish, and I went and I threw it in the trash.

That night my hands were burning and stinging and still bloody from how he scraped them so bad. Florence and them got frightened, and they took theirs off their hand. And I really started to hate him then. I really started to hate him and hate him and hate him. I hated him.

He told me that the next morning I'm going to get my black ass up and I'm going to fix his coffee and I'm going to do it by myself.

And I started thinking when I was lying in the bed. I said, "I'm going to kill this man." I said, "I'm going to kill him." I said, "I'm going to kill this man."

I couldn't sleep that night, because I was trying to think, how could I kill him? Just *kill* him. And I took the flashlight, and I went outside by the fence in the back.

This tree, it had some berries, and they used to call them poison berries. It was blue berries, the berries were blue, but when you squeeze it, it look purple. They had always told us, don't eat them because they're poison berries.

And I started thinking. *These are poison berries. And he hurt me so bad.* And I said, *I'm going to kill him.* So I took the shirt I had on, and I opened it up. And I picked so much of these berries, and I put them in my shirt. And I ran back to the house. And I hid them inside a bag underneath my mattress.

The next morning, he called me and said, "Gal, get up and fix my food."

I got up. I put the coffee on. He told me to

wake him up when the coffee done. I was scared to go get the berries, because I didn't know if Naomi was watching me. But I snuck and I got them anyway. And I made his coffee, and I got them berries and I squeezed them and I squeezed them and I squeezed them, every last one. I squeezed every last berry that I put my hand on. I said, "This is how he's going to pay for it. I'm going to kill him today." I said, "I'm going to kill this man today."

When I took the coffee in his room, my hand was shaking. I put it on the table, and I said, "Daddy, I got your coffee."

He got up, and he started drinking the coffee. I went back in the kitchen to cook his food. And I could hear him, when he had drunk some and put it back on the saucer. He had drunk that cup, and he called to me to fix him another cup.

But I didn't hear him no more. I kept walking back and forth past his bedroom to see if he was dead.

And as I was coming back down the hall, he almost ran me over, running to the bathroom. He went in the bathroom, stayed in there for a while, came back out. I said to myself, *He ain't dead yet.*

I flew back outside, and I got some more berries. And I squeezed some more and I squeezed some more in there. My hands were purple. And the second cup of coffee, I put more in there. He went back to the bathroom again. He said, "Gal, what the hell you put in my coffee? This stuff making me go to the bathroom all morning. I got the runs. I'm going to be late. What you put in here?"

And I said, "Nothing."

I thought he had me. I got scared. I thought he knew I was up to something—but all that berry did was get his stomach to run off. Like I said, I wanted to kill this man. I had the intentions to kill him. I thought I was *going* to kill him. But all it did was make him shit.

After I put his shoes on, and he got dressed and went on to work, I was mad because I didn't kill him. And I started thinking, *There got to be something else. There got to be something else around here that I could kill him with.*

I TOLD Kitty what I did.

"Gal, you're kidding. You didn't do that."

"Yeah, I did," I said. "I tried to kill him. I'm tired of him beating me, Kitty. I'm tired of him beating on me."

"Well, I ain't going to tell nobody."

I said, "Don't tell Florence, because she'll tell, she'll tell him. But to tell you the truth, Kitty, I don't think nothing can kill Daddy. I think he will outlive us all and never die."

Back behind us, Miss Coralie had chickens. One day I saw the chickens eating those poison berries. I stood there, and I watched the chickens, waiting for them to drop dead. And they didn't. They just kept on eating.

DADDY WAS EVIL, and I was evil, too, as a child—but I was evil because I was being treated evil. And I was the black sheep of the family. Sometimes I would hear them tell me "You ain't my sister. You ain't no kin to me. All of us are light-skinned, and you are black." Even other people would say "Gal, you can't be kin to them. Why are you dark and all them are light?" But it was true. They are all light, and I am black. Their hair was prettier than mine. My hair was all kinked up. *But*—they all were fat. And I wasn't.

Kitty was the only one I told that secret to—about trying to kill Daddy with the berries. Nobody else knew, and still don't know today. I know that she must have cared and was looking out for me, because she never told that secret. She laughed about it with me later, but I knew I could trust her. That was important.

I never understood why that man beat me so much. More than he did the others. Maybe he was mad at somebody else, and that person wasn't there, and he took it out on me. For a time I thought that I looked like my real mama so much that it brings back memories to Daddy, so he beat me. And then I thought, "No, that can't be it. My grandmother's name was Ruth, my name is Ruthie ... maybe the *name* got to him." He always called me Gal, didn't like me to be called Ruthie. When he took me somewhere, he never told nobody my name was Ruthie. He always said Gal.

chapter six

when he had came home that day, he didn't come right in the house. I heard him talking to somebody outside. It was the next-door neighbor, Mrs. Vane. She asked him could I start coming over there, ironing some T-shirts for her husband, some sheets and pillowcases, and do a little vacuuming around the house. And he told her yeah. So I started cleaning for her.

She had me to come over there three days a week, cleaning, cleaning. I cleaned her big old house and she end up giving me two dollars. But she kind of liked me, started liking me so much until I was over there the majority of the time, and I felt good doing that, because I didn't have to be around Daddy that much.

Mrs. Vane would always plant pretty plants. I liked to be in her yard, it was a *garden*. And our yard was a old mess. I used to go over to her place, bruises on me, and just sit out there with all her flowers until I could calm down. I guess at the time she wasn't paying it any attention.

But she did ask me, "Gal, what's that y'all be doing there, out there in that backyard?"

"That's some stuff Daddy be taking off the base, and we got to burn it."

"Why y'all be cracking it like that?"

I said, "I don't know."

And she said, "You know, that stuff against the law. Fleetwood better be careful and remember everything you do in the dark comes to the light, or else they going to have to send all of y'all in a home or something."

So I start thinking. I said, *Send us in a home . . .* I thought, *That way we would be away from him.*

Mrs. Vane told me that her son Rafe was coming home and he got two little kids, and if I didn't mind, when they stayed there, ask Daddy could I stay up till twelve o'clock. And he say yeah. So I stay and I baby-sit the kids, and when I came home Daddy wasn't there. Florence and them was up drinking.

And I start drinking.

They drinking this liquor he used to always buy, come in a bumpy bottle, that's what he called it—Bumpy Bottle—because the bottle is kind of rocky.

Florence said, "You remember that game we used to play, and if you get caught with the extra cards, you have to drink? Well, Rhoda and Carmen asked about it, and we going to start playing that again when Daddy go to work."

Started doing that, and I was still going to Mrs. Vane house back and forth, cleaning up.

And we would steal the liquor from Daddy because he would go on the base and get it cheap, or go to the Coast Guard and get it by the case. He would get it by the case, and give it to his lady friends, Miss Nightlaw, Mrs. Quince, Mrs. Finney. And he would come home with cartons of cigarettes, I mean every kind of cigarette. We started smoking. Drinking and smoking.

Daddy got busy selling the cigarettes and beer, besides all that metal and wire that we stole off the base. And he was gone for a couple of days and we didn't see him. We didn't know what was going on. Come to find out that they had arrested him coming down James Island and put him in jail for driving drunk. Kept him for two days.

When he did come home, he told us what happened, and he said, "Here, Gal. Put this on the top of the chifforobe." (I still got that chifforobe home, a antique chifforobe.) He said, "Put this on the top of the chifforobe." It was a big giant plastic bag full of seeds. Full of seeds.

"Tomorrow, I want you and Naomi to go out there in the yard and clear this area out for me. Dig all y'all can dig. Pull every grass you see— pull it up."

That morning we got up, we ate breakfast, cleaned up, then went outside And we dig. It was, oh man, so long that we dug. He told me to go inside and get that bag of seeds that he gave me. And we know we was planting seeds but we didn't know what we was planting. I remembered those seeds we planted in Mississippi, that came up all pretty vegetables. So we planted it.

Time went by, we could see something there. It was growing, growing, growing, and we could see him watering it.

Mrs. Vane would look out there, and she'd say, "Gal, what's that your daddy got growing in the backyard?"

"I don't know. He got a garden out there."

She knew exactly what it was. But I didn't know what it was.

He got a lot of plastic bags, and he brought home more seeds. And I remember him telling me, he said, "You know what? These seeds I got can make me a lot of money."

So he went outside and brought in so much leaves, just so many leaves. So many leaves he brought in. And he was bagging them up and bagging them up. Florence told us she knew what it was, and she said, "When Daddy go out again, we going outside and we going to get some."

So sure enough, Daddy did left. We went outside in the backyard and we just take them leaves off and she said, "The guys say you put it in some aluminum foil and put it in the oven and let it dry out."

Put it in the oven, and let it dried out. And she said, "Now we got to roll it."

We tore open some cigarettes and try to roll it in the cigarette paper, but it wouldn't roll. So we went and we got a couple of Florence's Tampax, open up the paper, and we roll that. We rolled it up and we smoked it.

Florence was falling all over the floor. She said it was like she couldn't feel nothing on the bottom of her feet, like she was on a cloud, she was falling all over the floor by the hallway, and Kitty was just hollering and screaming, and Naomi was laughing and laughing. I was laughing and laughing and laughing. And I remember Florence saying, she said, "Once this stops, I don't ever ever want no more," and Kitty said, "I don't either, I know I don't want no more." And I said, "I don't either."

But, next day, because I felt what I felt, and I knew what it was then, I started going in the backyard, I start taking it every day. I was about nine. That's a shame.

And I started smoking cigarettes. He would call me or Naomi to come light his cigarette on the stove for him, and at first I would just sit on the stove to light it, but I started taking puffs. Pall Mall. That's the first I smoked. There was no filter at the end. I started stealing his cigarettes. I started taking Florence tampons and just rolling up reefer, just rolling up and rolling up.

I got so smart at it, I took the tobacco out of my cigarette and put some marijuana in, and then I put the tobacco back in. I'd get up, and after Daddy went to work, I'd go early in the morning and smoke marijuana.

One day I was standing in the kitchen to the sink, and I had to hold on. It was like I couldn't even move. It was like I was just *stuck* there. I didn't move for a long time. By and by I started walking to the stove, and when I got there, I started rocking on it. I don't know why, but I remember I was doing that. And Kitty caught me—rocking on the stove.

"Girl, what's wrong with you?"

I said, "Nothing. Nothing."

And I still had some of that green leaf. I decided that I was going to let my friends, Marie and Barbara, try some of that.

Daddy had a old car in the backyard. I would go behind the car and take those Pall Mall cigarette, and that leaf, and we'd go behind there and we would smoke it all day long. We would smoke it so regularly that before we would get up to come from behind the car, the two girls and I would be on top of each other, rocking.

Then I start thinking to myself, I know a girl who I could get to rock with me. Francene Topp. I started calling Francene over to the house. But she didn't like to smoke. She didn't like to smoke at all.

We had this brown blanket, it's a blanket that say USN. Daddy stole it off the navy base. I took it outside and folded it, and I lied out in the backyard. Francene was coming, and I stuck my head out, I said, "Come on under here, Francene, see what's going underneath here." And when she got in underneath there, I just started rocking all over Francene. For some reason.

But then later, as I kept smoking that stuff, I started getting migraine headaches, so bad I had to hold onto something just to hold myself up. So I stopped smoking it. I left it alone.

Daddy was getting worse and worse with money. He was having money but he wasn't *having* it—because he was giving it to his lady friend. And he must have known that something was missing up there in his closet. He came and he told Naomi that he know somebody was smoking and somebody was drinking in this house. Naomi said, "There ain't none of us doing it." He said, "Well, I'm going to find out who's doing it."

So he said, "Come get my shoes on, Gal."

I put his shoes on.

After he left, I thought he was going to be gone all night, so I said, "Hey, I'm going to get up and I'm going to drink." I got up, I started drinking some of that Bumpy Bottle. And it was cold during that time, too; it was getting kind of cold. I turned the heater switch on in the hallway. I wait until I hear it click, so I could be warm in the bathroom. And as I'm sitting in the bathroom with the door open, I'm just smoking and I'm just drinking, and smoking and drinking.

I didn't know that the smoke would gather in one ball, to where the heat was at. If you got it heated up, the smoke stays in one ball. But it *travels,* you can see it going down the hallway. All I know is I heard a door slam. And that hallway was foggier than fog. It was *foggy.*

And that was him.

I dashed out that bathroom so fast, and I dive in my bed, and he came through that back door.

"Who been smoking in here? Gal? Naomi?"

Nobody answer.

I mean, I was scared.

He came in there. He turned the light on. He said, "Somebody been in this house smoking. Now I know somebody been in this house smoking, because all this smoke in the hallway."

I said, "Daddy, it's not me. Not me."

Florence said, "Yeah, Gal been smoking, Daddy. Gal been smoking."

"Gal, come here."

Went in his room. He took out five cigarettes. Told me open my mouth.

I opened my mouth. And he try to stuck it down my neck. "You want to smoke? You want to smoke?" and he's pushing it down my neck, pushing it down my mouth.

I said, "No, I don't want to smoke, Daddy! I don't want to smoke!"

But he didn't beat me. And I went and I spit all that tobacco out of my mouth.

He told Florence that I was smoking. But he didn't too much bother me about it. I don't know why. I guess he knew he had a trap then. "Well ... Gal smoke ... Naomi smoke ... I don't know how they get the cigarettes, but—if I don't have none, they'll have some for me."

He would come in the room while I was sleeping, or pretending I was sleeping, and he would get my cigarettes, take one out, and smoke it.

He put cases and cases and cases of beer and boxes and boxes and boxes of liquor in the closet and so many cartons of cigarettes. He would take it to a lady on Yonges Island—she was a bootlegger—and sold all the things. And she would pay him money for that stuff which he got it cheap, and then he would take the money and give it to a lady name Bernice Quince.

And she'd come over to the house and demand for Daddy to do things for her and didn't want him to do anything, anything, for us at all. So come to find out she had a daughter, and the daughter was my age, too. So he said, "Y'all, I'm going to bring Bernice daughter over her, and I'm going to let her spend the night." And he said, "I'm going to be gone for a couple of days." He went outside, and he got some of that marijuana and put it in a bag.

The girl came over and spent the night. The next morning, we had fix some grits, and when we got to the table, she said, "I'm not going to eat this garbage."

I looked at Florence and Florence looked at me, Kitty looked at Naomi, we all looked at each other. I was mad, and I said, "Garbage?

You *going* to eat this. We got to eat slop, you got to eat slop, too," I said, "because my daddy is taking all our money and giving it to your mama."

She said no he isn't.

I said yeah he is, and I slapped the grits up in her face.

She started hollering and screaming, and hollering and screaming. Next thing you know, Daddy pulled up in the yard.

She ran outside, and she told Daddy, "I'm going to tell Mama."

Daddy almost broke his neck to stop her from calling her mother, because if she had tell her mother something bad had happened to her, Bernice would treat Daddy like a dog. She was twenty years younger than he was.

So Daddy stopped the girl. He said, "Come on, come on, let's go get some ice cream." He took her to buy ice cream. And when they came back, she had bangle bracelets. Real bangle bracelets, all on her arm. And he never had got us nothing. Not even a Christmas present. At Christmas, Mrs. Wicker gave us a box of some hand-me-down clothes from Rhoda and Carmen, and Daddy said, "Now I don't have to buy y'all nothing for Christmas." All we ever had for Christmas was one time, we did have one silver Christmas tree, and on top a round light, with four different colors, that goes around.

Naomi got mad about that girl's bangle bracelets. And Daddy knew it.

He said, "Well, Naomi, it's going to be your time to clean the bathroom again." I start thinking about the same thing that he done to her before, knocking her down the toilet.

He said he got to take the girl back home, so he took her back home. Daddy came back. Naomi cleaned the bathroom up again, just like he asked.

Some stain he found again. I guess the daughter had told her mother what happened, and he took it out on us. He started beating Naomi, beating Naomi. Right then the toilet back broke right in half. He got his belt and started beating Naomi and beating Naomi some more, all over the body. The only part he missed was the bottom of her feet. I started getting so frightened, I started getting so scared. And Kitty was shaking and Florence was shaking.

I ran and looked out the window, I wanted to see who neighbor house light was on. Only person house light was on was Mr. and Mrs. Wicker. I tried to dial their number and he saw me on the telephone.

"Who that you calling in there?"

I hung up.

Naomi said, "Gal, Gal, please, please, call Mr. Wicker—call Mr. Wicker!"

I try to call, but I was scared Daddy was going to beat me. Naomi breaked away from Daddy, ran out the front door with hardly any clothes on because he had already ragged half of it off her, ran across the street, told Mr. and

Mrs. Wicker what was happening—that Daddy was beating her for no reason.

Then Mr. Wicker—they were Christian people—came over and tried to talk to Daddy, and Daddy cursed him out and told him to go mind his business. Mr. Wicker said that he was going to call the police on Daddy if Daddy didn't stop beating Naomi.

Naomi said, "Yeah, Mr. Wicker, call the police. Call the police, because when the police come, I'm going to tell the policeman the stuff Daddy got growing in the backyard."

Then I said to myself, "Thank you Lord, thank you Lord, I am so happy. I'm so happy. Call the police, call the police." That way, when the police came to take him to put him in jail because of the stuff that he got in the backyard, that way we don't have to be beaten by him no more.

Daddy had gas in a can outside, that he would usually use in the lawn mower. After he heard what Naomi said, he ran out the back door, he got the can, he poured gas on every plant, every single plant that there was. But he didn't have time to burn it. The policeman was knocking on the door.

A voice said, "This is the Mount Pleasant Police."

When he came in, Daddy was sitting to the table with a cigarette in his hand and drinking liquor, and looking like nothing ever happened.

The police say that they had a call from a neighbor saying Daddy was beating a young girl. Daddy said, "I didn't put my hands on her. I didn't do nothing to her." Then he started cursing.

"*I* am the king here. This is *my* house. If y'all don't get out of my house—"

That man said, "Look here, Mr. Fleetwood. Let me tell you something. Right now, I can take you on in to jail if I want to, and then these kids would have to leave the house."

Naomi said, "Yeah, he beat me, he beat me because he said I didn't clean the bathroom up good."

I jumped up and I said, "Naomi, tell him what Daddy got in the backyard. Tell him, Naomi."

And the man said, "What you got in the backyard?"

And we said, "He got some marijuana in the backyard."

Then they called in another car. Next thing we know there was four policemen car in the yard. One said, "Show me where it's at."

They all had flashlights, and we went out there with the flashlights. We looked—and it was like it was never there. Nothing. It was all gone. It had shriveled all instantly when he poured the gas on. Then I started getting really scared, because I figured when the police left he was going to beat me for saying what I said.

The policeman told us there was nothing back there, and there was nothing they could charge him with, and there was nothing that they could do about it. He said, "Mr. Fleetwood, if you put your hand on any one of these girls again, I'm going to come and I'm going to lock you up."

So Daddy didn't touch us that night.

HE WAS STILL going out and seeing Mrs. Quince, and then he finally took us to the lady house. She lived on Saddletree Road, and she lives on Saddletree Road today. I thought we was going in a mansion. I couldn't believe it. She had the telephone that he bought her that you hold one part to your ear and you talk in the other one. Then in her bedroom she had a American red-white-and-blue telephone. She had a *big* color television. Her daughter had a big color television. The room was so pretty. She had everything you could think of. And we had nothing.

We were just so shocked at what he was doing for her, and he wasn't doing anything for us. Then I started hating her. I hated that lady. I hated her guts.

So when we got home that day she called the house and I was very rude to her, very rude. She told Daddy that I was rude. And I told Kitty and them that I didn't care if she told Daddy, because I hated her.

He told me that he owe me one. He said, "I owe you one."

And I thought, "Shoot, he ain't owe me nothing. He ain't owe me nothing." I said, "Kitty, y'all, I'm leaving." I said, "I'm leaving, I'm leaving, I'm running away."

Naomi said, "Gal, you know if you're running away, Daddy going to find you. He going to really hurt you."

"I'm running away. I don't care what nobody says."

I said, "Naomi, you want to go? If you want to go, you better come on, we going to leave."

I packed some clothes and I put it in a brown bag. But I hid it behind the back room. And I went to school though. We were still in school. When I came home I went around the back, I got the bag of clothes.

I remember I had on a flower dress, gray and burgundy flowers in it. I ran down the street, and I turned on Nebo Street. I went to the man house that had liked my mama a while back. Marlon. And I asked him could I stay with him and his wife, and he told me yeah. And I told him what happened.

The same afternoon, Kitty came down there, and she said, "Gal, we got to talk." And she was driving then, too, she was driving. We drove down to where the boat landing is. She said, "Gal, Daddy said tell you that he going to beat you anyway when you do come back, but if you don't come back now he's going to call Social

Services and let them pick you up and put you in a home."

I said, "I don't care, let them put me in a home. I'd rather be in a home, Kitty."

She grabbed me, and we were holding each other, and we were crying. And she said, "Gal, I don't want you to go in a home."

Three days later, I went back. But he didn't beat me. The whipping was gradually slowing up a little bit.

I WAS IN the front yard. I remember I was jumping rope. Daddy had his window up and I heard the phone ring. I couldn't hear what he was saying, but I heard him talking. Then I heard him say "Gal," and I said "Sir," and I ran all the way around the back and came in the back door.

When I came in his room, he said, "I had a call. Your mama dead." He said, "She got burnt up in a fire. Somebody killed her."

And I remember just standing there looking at him. And I remember I twist my feet, so I was standing on the side of my shoes. And then I remember walking out of the room. I went back in the front yard and sat on the step. And I was just thinking. I said, *I didn't really know who she was.*

She played the drums. She liked Mary Janes candy.

Her name was Leitha Homer.

Daddy said, "You and me and Kitty, we're leaving out of here and going to Philadelphia, because we got to arrange a funeral."

And I said, "Okay."

chapter seven

i told everyone in school that I had to go because my mother died, and I was going to Philadelphia. Me and Kitty and Daddy did left out, and we went to Philadelphia. That was the first time I have seen traffic lights on the side of the road instead of in the middle. First time I seen them, when I went to Philadelphia. We ran some lights before we noticed where they were.

But when we got there, the funeral was already over with. We were late. So, I asked them could I please just go see my mama grave. They told me yeah.

The casket was still just sitting in there. But there was nothing for me to see, because she was burned completely. There was nothing but a picture, in the casket. Kitty and Daddy was standing farther off from me. And I walked up to the hole, and I remember kneeling down, and as I was kneeling down, I remember the sand that was dropping down in there, and I said,

"Mama, I love you. I love you." And I got back up.

They told me that we were going back into town where all the people were at, sobbing and crying. I remember walking up the steps, six steps. There were people on the porch, people that my mama knew. I didn't know anybody. I remember that I opened the screen door, and when I walked in, the house was so crowded and so full of people. I was just walking in slowly, and people were taking my hand, and saying, "Oh, look at little Leitha. Look at little Leitha. Oh, this one look just like Leitha."

It didn't bother me. I was just walking through the house. Me and Kitty got something to eat in the kitchen. Daddy said we had to hurry up, because he wanted to stop in Baltimore and see his sister Ida.

A lady grabbed me and hold my hand real tight, and I asked her, "Could you tell me—could you show me the building that my mama got burned up in?" And I said, "What happened to her?"

She said, "Your mother was involved with this man. And she must have cheated on him. So he tied her up to a bed and poured kerosene all over her and started a fire."

"Why did he do that?"

She said, "I don't know. When they found her body, it was all burned up. The feet and the hand part was still tied to the bed."

And I said, "What man would do that to her?" I said, "Did they find him?"

"No, because nobody don't know who killed her."

She took me there. And I stood there in front of that apartment building. You could see the burns on the outside, around the windows. I just stood there and I just stood there. And I just looked, and I just looked.

And then I remember saying, "Mama, why did you come here? Why did you leave me?"

The lady grabbed my hand, and we walked back down that sidewalk, and Daddy said it was time for us to go because he wanted to see Ida, his sister.

Ida owned her own restaurant, and she had her house on the top of the restaurant. When we got in there we ate breakfast that morning and then we stayed. We spent the night there in Baltimore, and then we came back home to Charleston.

When I went to school the next day I wore a red shorts with a white blouse to match that Mrs. Vane had bought me new. I felt different, I felt strange. And I don't know why, but I walked out of my classroom, and out the double doors, and onto the basketball court. I was standing in the middle of the basketball court, and I was just looking around, and I started crying. I started to cry for my mother. It just suddenly hit me that she was dead and never coming back. I remember telling myself that I loved her, knowing I hardly ever saw her, but I loved her still, because she gave birth to me. And I said, "Mama, why did you leave me? Why did you leave me?"

Someone went and told the teacher that I was crying on the basketball court. They couldn't calm me down. I was yelling bad things, I was saying "I hate you Lord, I hate you, you motherfuck."

They called my house and there was nobody there. And Mr. Wicker, they got in touch with him and told him to come pick me up by the school because I was sick. He said it would be about an hour before he could come—he was driving a bus for retarded people, and he would come on his lunch break. Before he got there, I remember standing up and just looking off into the sky. And I fainted. I fainted, and next thing I know, I was home.

Before that day, I really had no one to love. Love was a poison word in our family, not even Kitty ever said it. But now I had my mother. I imagined her. I pretended. I pretended that she was talking to me and I was talking back to her, but I was putting in the words for her. Even though I couldn't see her face, even in my imagination, I was saying, "Mama, I love you. Why did you leave me?" And I would answer back for her that she loved me, and she wished that she could have tooken care of me, but she couldn't because she didn't have the money, and she wanted me to stay with my grandmother. I said, "Why didn't you take me to Philadelphia with you?" and she said she couldn't because she was in a gang. I said, "But you know you left me in a place where I was beaten so badly, and Daddy didn't love me." And then I answered back, "I didn't know, Gal. I didn't know who your real father was, and I couldn't tell you who he was." I asked, "Why did you name me Ruthie?" And I answered back, "Because I love my mother."

I didn't really know her, but she became real to me by my imagination.

Daddy start telling me later, "You're just like your mama. Every bit of her. You're a liar, you a cheat, a thief. You're just like her. And I don't know who in the hell your daddy is."

I was so mad, I said, "Well, I'm going to be just like her then. I'm going to be just like her." I remember saying that. "I'm going to be just like she is."

I went back to school and I took it out on any and everybody that I saw. I remember this white girl named Cindy Buck. I slapped her—I mean *slapped* her—and I saw my handprint in her face. I was just mad. Because my mother was dead, and it really was bothering me.

And I continued. I beat her up, and made her bring me money to school, and—I don't know—I just went crazy. I beat up Francene Topp, I slapped my friend Marie, anyone who crossed my path. I thought it was good to be mean. Being a big macho girl, being a tough nigger. Having the kids in school scared of me. It was a thrill thing to me. I wanted something that they had that I didn't have.

I would say my prayers at night. I would say, "Mama, why did you leave me?" I couldn't get that off my mind. I just couldn't help myself, couldn't help it.

I would ask Daddy almost every day, "Did they find the man that killed her?"

And he said, "No."

DADDY TOLD us to continue to burn those things in the backyard, and I just, oh, couldn't do it. But I had to. I didn't have no choice because he would beat me if I didn't. I didn't tell him that I was scared of the fire because of my mama. I didn't like fire, I didn't like it at all.

But I was watching it, the way the flames came up. One day I took the plastic curtain down from the bathroom window. I wanted to see how a curtain melt, how something would burn and how it would feel. I held it up on a stick over my foot, and lighted it, and let the curtain drip on me. It burnt and dripped and stuck on me, and I screamed. I had to peel it off my skin. And it just came to me—oh, God, can you imagine my mama then, screaming and hollering and being burned alive?

Daddy came out there wanting to know what was wrong with me. I was trying to tell him that I didn't want to burn that metal anymore. But he just beat me. I couldn't tell him, because it didn't matter if I did.

He said, "You and Naomi, y'all load that stuff in the truck." He said, "Matter of fact, this going to be y'all last time doing that. Y'all going to find y'allself a real job," he said, "and I mean a real job, too."

So somehow he got in touch with somebody, and next thing we know, he told us that we would start working at the shrimp dock. It was two and a half miles away from the house, right there on the creek. The first one, Hobcaw Shrimp Company.

My mother was still on my mind. Just constantly.

Daddy said, "Y'all can walk to work. I'll show you the way to walk. You'll walk through the Lakes."

That's what we called it, the Lakes, because it used to be lakes there. Now it was white people's houses, with trees and lawns. First we would cross the highway, and then we were walking through the Lakes. But really we would have to run, because there were people there that would have their dogs loose, that would chase us. The people would sit in their yards, and they would see these dogs attacking us and didn't call them back. They didn't want us to walk through there, even though we were just walking to work. One time I was alone, and I was riding a bike. I made sure that I was at full speed, and I had my legs up, so if a dog try to snap at my legs, they would be up in the air.

And then, soon as we got over the bridge, the shrimp dock was right there.

Kitty and Florence wasn't even working, they didn't have a job. It was me and Naomi he made start working. All summer long we would go and head shrimp up to about eight o'clock at night, nine o'clock, and then weigh the shrimps. Even after school started, we kept working, afternoons and nights. The man today there knows me. He liked me and Naomi, the man that worked on one of the boats. He'd always give us free fish and free crab, and we would bring it home, and we had to put it in the bags. On the way home, people would stop for us, but when we got into the car they would down all the windows, because that's how stink we would be, coming from the dock. And Daddy would take all our money.

We worked there for quite a while. I was talking to this guy, his name was Elmo Rush, but they used to call him Hammer Head. They called him Hammer Head because he had a hard head. He was bowlegged, a nice brown-skin guy. Daddy was going to come pick us up one day, but Naomi and me had finished early. So I went underneath the bridge with Elmo, and me and him was talking and kissing. That was all it was. I wasn't interested in more than that. We was just talking and kissing.

I didn't realize that Daddy had already pull

up just that quick. Naomi was out there standing up and I was nowhere to be found. And when I came back around, I didn't see Naomi, and the boat man said, "Girl, Fleetwood done came and pick up Naomi, and you in trouble."

I asked him to take me home, and I remember that when we pull in the driveway, I open the door before the car stop and jump out and run to the house, and when I reach to open up the house door, it opened by itself.

I didn't know that he was behind the door.

I was walking in real slow, nervous and scared, and *bam*, something hit me from behind, and then hit me on the top of my face, then I remember I fall down to the floor, and hit my arm on the coffee table.

"Where you been at, you whore? Where you been at?"

"Daddy, I just was underneath the bridge."

"You ain't been underneath no bridge," and he started beating me, and beating me some more. I backed up from the living room into the dining room, and I almost hit the dining table. I managed to get around the table, and I fell in the blue chair that was against the window. I had some pink rollers in my hair, and one of my rollers came loose. I remember him boxing my face from left to right, left to right. When I tried to get up, he knocked me back.

I heard a *crack*, a *clingalingaling*. I didn't realize he had knocked my head *through* the window. There was glass in my head—I reached for it—and I pulled the glass, and I looked at it, and I said, "Daddy, my head is bleeding!"

"I'll make it bleed some more!" And he boxed my face. The blood came pouring all down my shirt. Florence and them was screaming, and he finally stopped. I felt the left side of my head burning, and the blood dripping down.

On the floor I saw four pink rollers—and my hair still rolled up on them.

I didn't even know he had yanked the rollers out. I picked them up, and I stuck them in my drawers, because I wanted Kitty to see. See what he had done.

He got mad because the glass was broke. He wouldn't take me to the doctor.

When I went to school, I pulled that side of my hair over towards my face, towards my eyes, so nobody could see the bald spot in my head. I start wearing flowers in my hair, on a comb. Later, when I pulled the hair back you could still see the bald spot, so I wore one of those bands to put around your head. That way I knew nobody could tell. It was still stinging, but eventually the hair started growing back and back.

But Daddy never changed. He was still the mean old monster that I knew he was.

And it came to me one day—Daddy was a slave driver. That's really what he was. He wanted us to honor him like he was a king and bow down to him.

* * *

WE THEN BEGAN going to this place down the street at the community center. We got a club together, and the first band that we ever got down there to come and play was the Grand Ams. Daddy let me and Naomi go out to the center with Kitty and Florence because he wanted us to keep our eye on them, make sure they didn't mess with any mens. But we didn't care, we wouldn't tell him anything anyway.

Florence met a guy named Darrell and Kitty met a guy named Jerome. Come to find out that both of them were two cousins, and they were on the football team. They started dating and stuff, and Naomi met a guy in the same neighborhood, his name was Johnny Pine. Since Daddy was going out constantly all the time and never home with us, they decided to let the guys come over.

That night Florence was with Darrell, Kitty was with Jerome, Naomi was with Johnny. And I was in there watching out to see if Daddy pull up. But I went in the yard and got some of that marijuana and started smoking it again and actually passed out.

When I woke up all I heard was footsteps running. I couldn't see anybody, but I heard the window up—because it was a wooden window, hard to pull up, and it made a noise. They knocked the screen out of the window. When I got in the room, Jerome and Darrell and Johnny had left their pants and their drawers all over the floor, they even left their wallet, everything.

They ran out of the window naked because they were afraid that Daddy would catch them in the house. The minute Daddy was putting the key in the door, all of them jump out of the window.

They ran, past Mrs. Vane house and on the dirt road called Truluck Street. They never came back that night, and I don't know how they got where they went to with no clothes on.

EVERYBODY FIGURED it was time for us to see guys. We always sneaked about it because Daddy wouldn't let none of us see anybody. We had another party down the street at the Sampson house.

Daddy said, "Naomi and Gal, I want y'all back here at twelve o'clock, no later than twelve o'clock. Not even a *minute* after twelve o'clock."

And we said, "Yes, sir."

I told Naomi, I said, "We'll fix that. We'll put the clock back an hour. That way we can stay till one o'clock, and he'll think it's twelve o'clock."

Went out, and we stayed out until one. But when we walked in the door, it was dark and he was sitting there. But you could see him when you open up the door, because the kitchen light shined on him. And we saw him sitting to the table.

"Gal and Naomi, what time is it?"

"Daddy, it ain't no more than 'bout a few minutes after twelve."

"You're a damn liar, too. Somebody here

switched that clock. Now which one of y'all switched that clock?"

We said we didn't switch it.

He said, "Well, I going to tell you one thing. I'm going to whip every butt in here till I find out which one of y'all switch that clock."

Florence and Kitty didn't had to worry, because they didn't had to be home anyway until one o'clock. So he said, "Get in there and take them clothes off. Whoever first, come on."

I was trying to push Naomi, to let her be the first to get the beating, and she said no she ain't. She's not going to go. So I said, "Forget it, I'm just going to go ahead on and get it, and get it over with."

I knew I had to get up on the brown table, stand up on it, and get beat. Just beat beat beat. I stood there and stood there.

He said, "I'm going to make you cry this time, nigger. I'm going to make you cry." And I stood there and I stood there, and I wouldn't cry. He beat me and he beat me and he beat me until he got very tired, very tired. But that didn't stop him from beating Naomi. He beat her too.

But somehow, when he hit her with the belt, that part that you stick in the hole got stuck on her back, and she grabbed it and somehow she managed to snatch it out of his hand. Florence and Kitty came in and said, "Daddy, what are you doing?"

He told them that somebody switch the clock back.

"I did that," Kitty said.

He looked at her. I think he knew she was lying, but he didn't say anything. He stop beating Naomi.

WHENEVER I got beat, Kitty would always come to ask me was I all right. She was afraid for me. Florence was never afraid for me, but Kitty—I could see it, even if she didn't tell me. I could see her looking, and I could tell she felt sorry for me, and she wished she could do something to help. But she couldn't. She was afraid.

Kitty used to wear this short blue satin dress with a panty made underneath it. They used to call this dress, a long time ago, called it a Sizzler. And these white shoes with the heels so thick, looked like big clogs. Florence never dress like that, but Kitty love to have her body out. Naomi like all of her body out. But I was that person that was kind of shy, didn't like that kind of stuff.

We used to go out partying. They all had boyfriends, but me, I was scared of guys. I don't know. Just scared of guys. It took me a while to even talk to a guy.

When Daddy would leave, Jerome and Darrell and Johnny would come over, and Florence and them would pick the bedrooms that they wanted in the house.

They introduced me to a guy named Erwin Gervais, but they called him Hawk—because his nose was shaped like a bird beak. He came over with them. You could hear the bed squeaking, and kicking in the wall, and Erwin said, "Ruthie, why don't we do what they're doing?"

I said, "No, I don't want to do what they're doing, 'cause I'm scared." And all we did was kissing. I dated him for a long period of time, never gave sex to the guy, but then come to find out that he was dating one of my friends, too. But it didn't bother me. She was the one who's giving him some, and not me.

Daddy decided later to let Florence and Kitty take company. But before they would have company over, they would have to tell him, two or three days before time. And when the guys did come over, Daddy would sit to the table, at the dining-room table, while they were in the living room, and he was just sitting there, watching them. Just watching them. And I told Naomi there was no way I was never having nobody to come here at all.

But somehow, I ran into this guy name Lorenzo Lang. He was married to a friend of Florence's. I would be outside every day, and I would see this guy walk past all the time, and I knew he was an older man. But I just had liked him, for some reason. He was a sweet man. He would always speak to me. It was coming towards my birthday, and he said, "You know what, I don't mind taking you out."

I said, "Well, I can't tell Daddy or none of them, because if Daddy found out, he going to hurt me."

He said, "Don't worry, nobody's going to know."

So, the phone rung for me that day. And he said, "I'm going to take you out to eat on your birthday."

I knew nobody else was going to take me anywhere on my birthday. I said okay. I was going to lie and tell Daddy I'm going to do something for Mrs. Vane, because he will never call her house.

So, the car pulled up that night. And it turned the lights off. Right beside the street where Mr. Buzz house was at. I told Daddy I was going to go on to Mrs. Vane house. He didn't care, because he was going out anyway. So, Daddy left out of the house before I did, and the car pulled up in our little driveway.

I knew that was Lorenzo. And I opened up the door real quick.

But it was his wife and her mother.

She slapped me in my face. "You little slut, you little whore! Lorenzo don't have nothing to offer you. Lorenzo got a child and a wife. And if I ever catch your little black ass back in my red Pinto again, I'm going to *kick* your ass."

Her mama said, "Where is Fleetwood? Fleetwood home?"

"No, ma'am, he ain't home."

And the mother standing right there let her

slap me in my face again, but I couldn't do anything. I was scared. And she said, "And if I ever catch you in the street, I'm going to run you over."

After they left out of the house, I was so scared and so nervous and I was wondering what happened to Lorenzo, because I know I just talked to him. But I never saw him that night. The next following day I went to talk to Rhoda, and I was telling her what happened. Coming back from her house, I stopped to that stop sign by the Sampson house, because I always looked to see if any cars coming. Soon as I got out on the street, I had to end up jumping in the ditch because his wife saw me. She almost ran me over. So I guess she really meant what she said.

ONE THING about Daddy. You had to tell him when your period come on. If you didn't tell him, he would call you.

"Gal? You ain't tell me nothing this month."

"Daddy, it ain't on yet."

And the minute your period go off, you better tell him it gone off too. All of us. Every last one of us. He wanted to know when it was on, you better come a-running, and you better tell him when it's off.

He was doing a lot of drinking. He become more drunker and drunker, until he was passed out every day and there was really nothing that he could do. He was still working and stealing, but he would get up in the morning and put liquor in his coffee to have a good day. He would go to work drunk, he come home drunk. I guess his work was pretty good and that's why they didn't bother him.

Matter of fact, he got awards for his work, awards and plaques—and every one had a picture taken as he gets the award and shakes the man's hand. He had seven of them. "For Excellent Work." He cooked on the ship for twenty years, then he put twenty years in at the Naval Weapons Station. But they never knew the life at home. He lived a double life. Work was work, and home was beating ass.

But he started getting drunker and drunker and drunker and drunker. We would sneak out while he was sleeping and get back before he wake up. We would even take the phone off the hook so he wouldn't hear nothing.

One night he was so drunk he called me and said, "Get this tag off my foot." I said, "Daddy, ain't no tag on your foot." He said, "Get this tag off my damn foot!" so I pretended and said I got it.

Daddy dated a lady in Hungry Neck, too. He used her in case he couldn't get to one of the others. He would send me to Joe Mink for a half pint to give her, and then send me back for another bottle for him. He would get her drunk and have sex with her in the dining room, in one of the chairs. One night they went outside in the backyard in the old junk car he had out there. He didn't care, he just did it anywhere, and all of us knew. We was up and awake and saw it. After they were finished he'd send her walking back home half drunk, and he would fall to sleep or head out for one of his other lady friends.

And no one else in Hungry Neck knew what was happening in our house. We never told no one nothing. We just went on like everything was always fine.

WE WERE STILL good friends with Carmen and Rhoda. Rhoda was still playing the piano and singing songs. They were both pretty girls. They had these big teeth in their mouth—those teeth was *big*, and they were white and pretty, those big old teeth. And I always said, "Boy, I wish I had me some big teeth like that."

Some other children moved into the neighborhood, in that old green house with white windows, and when I saw them, their teeth was sticking out of their head. More big teeth. I used to call them the Hoonka-Boonka children. Their butts poked up high and they were bowlegged, too. The boy, every time he talked his teeth was sticking out his mouth, and I used to go home and say, "Oh Lord, please give me some teeth like that boy." I just wanted to see how it would feel, to have that teeth. When I would see him I would say, "Hey, Hoonka-Boonka boy."

And he would always get mad at me. He said, "That's all right, I ain't going to tell you that these people going to open up this little store back here."

I say, "What little store?"

He say, "The house right there is going to be a store." So I went home and I told Naomi and them that we're going to have another store besides Joe Mink's. The family last name was Garling. The mother name was Ora, she had a son named Donny and one named Nat. There was already another boy by the name of Donny, so in order to get their names right I would call Ora's son Ora-Donny, but the other boy I would just call him Donny.

They had this small store over there, so we had two stores to go to. The daddy's name was Flip, we called him Mr. Flip. And most of the time he would be drunk, so when we would see him drunk we would ease our hand behind the glass and sneak back there and steal candy out of the store. There was always somebody to catch us, but we always run past them.

When I gave Mr. Flip the money, I put it on the counter.

"Don't put the money on the counter! When you go to the white man store, you put 'em in the white man hand. When you come in my store, put my money in my hand like you do the white man!" And that's true. People when they pay a black person they throw it on the counter. But they want you to put the change in their hand. So what he said had meant something to me, when he told me that.

I used to get shamed sometimes to go there. I would say, "Mr. Flip, Daddy want to know—"

"You ain't coming in here to claim nothing today! Your daddy owe me now! Your daddy still owe me. Tell your daddy when he pay me, then he can get something else."

Then when that didn't work out there, Daddy would send me back to Joe Mink store, to credit from there.

Daddy used to get food stamps from somebody. He would get $150 worth of food stamps for $75. Cash money. And that's when he bought a lot of grocery, when he could use the food stamps. Somebody who was desperate for money would sell them to him. We would get a phone call, a man named Lamott would say, "Tell Fleetwood if he wants some stamps, come on across the bridge because the guy here now." Daddy couldn't use the stamps on the base, so we went to a store on Johns Island. That store is still there today. Daddy could buy anything he want with food stamps in that store. Washing powder, Clorox, beer, cigarettes, things you not supposed to get with food stamps.

Marie and Ivy started to want to go down to the boat landing, so they could get into them dirty blankets and do them nasty things with their boyfriends. Somehow they found an area off of Rifle Range, a dirt road you go down. Right now today that place is boarded up, a silver gate was put in there. But they used to go down this dirt road, I don't know how far down in there, and go on top of the car and have sex on top of the car. And I'm sitting inside the car.

I wanted to know what it was all about. I listened. But I didn't do it.

ONE DAY Daddy told us that he was going back to Mississippi and bring up one of the other sisters. Out of the blue, he wanted another one to come to Charleston. We were figuring that he wanted to get them one by one, slowly.

So we went down there to Mississippi. Aunt Beezy said, "Oh, Clovis, please don't take that baby," because she had had Sylvie since she was a infant, three days old. It was a hard thing to take her away. But not for him. He put her in the backseat. He left Pam and Evelyn. Sylvie was crying the whole way in the car, the whole way, she didn't want to leave Aunt Beezy, she didn't want to leave. But I said, "Don't worry, everything will be all right, everything will be all right."

Got back to Charleston, Sylvie was still crying, she was so skinny, and every one of her teeth in her mouth was rotten. I mean every teeth in her mouth was rotten. There was not one white teeth in her mouth. Every teeth was rotten. They always used to call her Rotten Mouth. She was a person that wouldn't talk to nobody, wouldn't say nothing, I guess she was lonely because she left Pam and Evelyn down there. As time progressed on she got used to us and we all just went along like sisters, like normally.

Daddy never really hit Sylvie until one time she lied about the ceramic turkey. Florence used to make ceramics. She used to go on the naval base—there was a ceramic shop out there that you could go and make ceramic things, and do it in the big oven. She made this turkey. The turkey was brown, and the gobble thing on the nose was red where it slashed across the face. We had it sitting outside on the freezer in the back room.

Sylvie used to go out there with a blanket and say, "Turkey, are you cold? Are you cold, baby? I have a blanket for you." Somehow one night she managed to knock it off there, and it smashed.

Daddy wanted to know who break that turkey.

Sylvie knew that we used to get beaten, and when he asked her, she actually kind of collapsed—and he knew it was her.

She was little, but he beat her anyway.

When I saw that, I told Kitty and them that I was thinking about leaving home, and Kitty said, "Ruthie, you better not be leaving home, you know Daddy find you he going to really kill you."

Florence say, "Well, I ain't worried about it because the day that I graduate I'm leaving the next day. I want to get out of Charleston."

Our aunt in New York, Esther, called, and she

said she was coming down because we were going to have a family reunion. Somehow Florence got to talk to Esther aside, where nobody knew, and Esther wanted Florence to come that following summer just to come to New York to see how it was. So she went to New York for the summer. She met a man named Preston Rudd. And when she came back she had a box full of material he bought her, I mean any kind of material that you wanted, satin and velvet, gabardine, silk, leather.

She said, "I know one thing, when I graduate from school I'm leaving. I made money up there, sewing clothes for people in Aunt Esther's building. And that's where I want to live. New York." Preston Rudd kept calling her long distance, and right after Florence graduated from high school, she left the next day. Just like she said. Right to New York.

Then that left me, Naomi, Kitty, and Sylvie.

chapter eight

kitty started talking to a guy right in the neighborhood, we never even knew he lived there, name was Tupper. Tupper Gates. And she wound up gotten pregnant from the guy. But she didn't tell us.

She was planning to go to State College in Orangeburg. Daddy already paid for her to go. Already bought her a little refrigerator, a fan, whatever that she needed for school.

I told Kitty, I said, "Kitty, I'm going to run away before you go."

Kitty said, "Girl, you better not."

"Yes, I'm going to leave."

I told Naomi, I said, "Naomi, if you want to go with me, you better try and save your money up. I'm saving my money up, and all I need to do now is find me a newspaper so I can find out where I'm going to live at."

I was working at Shoney's at the time, so I had money to go. I began putting my clothes in brown paper bags.

Sylvie started crying. She said, "Gal, Naomi,

if y'all leave me, Daddy's going to really beat me. Please don't leave."

I said, "Sylvie, don't worry. I promise, once I get settled, I promise I'm coming back to get you. I promise." She kept begging me don't leave, don't leave.

I kept looking through the newspaper, I called so many different places but I couldn't find a place that I could really afford to pay for. I told Kitty, and she said, "Well, Gal, I tell you what. There's a place that you go in North Charleston that have a book and tell you about apartments or trailers and you got to pay them a fee." I remember going to this place, and this place exists today. We went there, but I couldn't find anything. Then somehow I looked through the part where they have trailers for rent, and I finally found a trailer with two bedrooms, one bath, a living room, and a kitchen. In Rosewood, way up in North Charleston. That trailer was $110 a month, but it was on the lot with another home and another trailer.

When I went there, I explained to the man what was happening and why did I want to leave and go. I told him that I am still in school but I just wanted to get away from home. He told me he was a retired policeman, and I didn't have anything to worry about because nobody was going to come here and harm me or hurt me.

The house was a green house. The trailer in the front was a newer model trailer, and that trailer was green also. But the trailer behind them was a white trailer with blue trimming. And that's the trailer that they had for rent. That was going to be my trailer.

I paid for the first month rent, and they didn't even ask me for any deposit. I told them that I don't know when I'm going to get my lights turn on, when I do move in, because I didn't have any money. They actually got a extension cord, maybe two or three, and connected the trailer to their house so I could use their electricity.

When I got there the week afterwards to start moving in, I didn't have plates or fork or knife or spoon. They came and they gave me all of those things. And I told them that the only problem I'm having is I got to go back and forth to school, which was about ten miles, all the way across the river. But the man said that was up to me, there was nothing that he can do about that.

Kitty said, "Gal, I don't think you should stay here. This is a bad area, and you know, a girl like you, living out here by yourself—"

"Kitty, I don't care, I want to get away from Daddy and I am never ever returning."

I asked Naomi, I said, "Naomi, if you're going, you better get your clothes and we're leaving."

Sylvie started crying and crying and crying. Kitty said, "Well, Sylvie, now you know I'm going to school pretty soon, and I won't be here."

But all the time when she was telling us that, she was already pregnant with this child that none of us knew about. Then as weeks went on, I noticed her stomach was getting big. Kitty said, "Gal and Naomi, y'all, I got something to tell y'all." She said, "I'm pregnant."

I said, "Girl, Daddy going to kill you! What you going to do?"

"I don't know," she said, "but I'm going to school. I am *going* to school."

Daddy asked why she hadn't been telling him about her period, and she had to say she was pregnant.

He said, "Goddammit! You're going to get a abortion and you going to get a abortion tomorrow."

"Oh, no, I ain't. I ain't going to get no abortion. I'm not going to kill no child."

"You mean to tell me you already let me spend all this money on you for school and you gone end up pregnant? Who that damn nigger is? Who is that damn nigger?"

"I'm not going to tell you."

"Gal and Naomi, get in here! Y'all know Kitty been pregnant all this time and y'all didn't tell me anything?"

We said, "No, sir."

"Sylvie?"

Sylvie came in there.

"You know Kitty was pregnant?"

Sylvie was shooken up, knowing that we was

going to run away and leave her behind. She said, "No, Daddy, I didn't know."

"Well, somebody in here lying."

Kitty said, "I know one thing. Ain't nobody going to hit me in this house."

Daddy said, "No, I ain't going to be beating nobody. But I bet you one thing. You are going to carry your fat behind in the morning and you going to get a abortion."

That's when I said, "Naomi, we have got to go." I said, "Naomi, we have *got* to leave out of here."

Kitty said, "Y'all ain't going to leave before me." She called this girl name Audrey Biddle. Audrey came that night, picked Kitty up, Kitty left, end up at the school in Orangeburg. Me and Naomi, we packed our bags and we called a guy that lived on Truluck Street, name Brian Hampton but we called him Rooster because he's big and fat. Rooster drove a baby blue Mercury, and he would take you anywhere as long as you had money to pay him.

And I said, "Rooster, this is Gal." I said, "Whatever I tell you, please, please do me a favor. Don't ever ever tell Daddy."

And right then he said, "What you doing? You going to run away?"

I said, "Yeah." I said, "Rooster, please come right now. Daddy left out of here and I need to be gone before he gets back."

"You got the green?"

"I got it." I knew I was going to have to pay him probably four or five dollars.

He said, "I'll be there in five minutes."

I grabbed whatever I could grab. Sylvie was in tears and pulling us and pulling us. She didn't want us to leave.

When we saw that Mercury pull into the yard I told Sylvie we had to go. She pulled us and she pulled us and she cried and she cried. She said, "Gal, please y'all don't go."

"Sylvie, I promise you," I said, "I'll call you tomorrow."

We left, going across the bridge. Rooster took us to Rosewood. We got there to the trailer. I paid them money. When I put the key in the door to open it up, I turned the light switch on but there wasn't any light. They had disconnected the extension cord because I wasn't in there yet.

We had a lighter. I told Naomi, "Let me light a cigarette first." I lit a cigarette and then we was walking down the hallway trying to find our way.

"Naomi, I'll let you have the last bedroom, that's the big one, and I'll take the middle bedroom"—even though she wasn't working, she didn't have no job. She said okay. That last bedroom had a air-conditioner in there.

"Naomi, I don't think we should sleep in these rooms tonight. Look at the couch. The couch pulls out like a bed—we'll sleep on there."

There was some sheets in the last bedroom. We put the white sheets on the couch. Then we lie down on top of that. Then we put another sheet on top of us.

All of a sudden, we heard a *sst, sst*. And felt things on top of us. It was so dark, but the sheet was white, and when we looked, it was full of cockroach. I mean *full* of cockroach, the flying and biting kind. And you could hear them. They were dropping from the ceiling and crawling all over the sheet. We jumped up out of that couch so fast, and we ran back in that last bedroom.

"Naomi, man, I can't stay here."

"Look at all these cockroach."

But we didn't have no other place to go. I couldn't touch those sheets. We slept back there on the naked mattress.

The next day I didn't go to school, she didn't go to school. The people in the front house found out that we were there. They came and brought some food, and we et the food that they gave us. They told us we could keep the lights as long as we need it.

Come to find out Naomi had already told the guy who she was talking to—Cass—that she and I moved. I don't know how he found the place, but he came there, and he tried to take over the place, like he owned my place! I didn't say nothing to him. Naomi didn't want to go to school, wanted to stay there and not do nothing.

The guy started taking Naomi to and from school, but he would never give me a ride.

Every morning I had to get up at five o'clock, catch the city bus downtown, and from there get a ride across the bridge to go to school—then back across the bridge again, take the bus to the north area, and hop a ride to work, then hop a ride home. But I did it. I was determined to finish school. I wanted to prove to Daddy that I would make it. He was so sure I was going to drop out.

By the time I get home, Naomi and Cass have already eaten, went in the bed, and made love. Dishes piled up everywhere, the trailer in a mess. She wouldn't do nothing. So I got fed up with it. I told her she's going to have to leave. Cass took her on out. I don't know where they moved to but she never went back home.

I had a social security check for a hundred dollars. They had been sending checks ever since my mother died. I didn't even know she worked. But they sent me a check every month, and they said I would get it as long as I was in school. A hundred dollars a month. But all those years I never saw the money. It had on there "Pay to the order of Ruthie Homer/Clovis Fleetwood," and he took all the checks, for seven years. But I fixed him. When I decided to run away, I called social security, and they told me to come down there and fill out a form. I gave them my new address. And that next month he was waiting on the check. Kitty told me that Daddy was so mad he got up on top of the table, and he said he was sick and tired— stomping the table with his foot—tired of Gal, Gal took his money. And Kitty said the table collapsed, and he fell on the floor.

I used that first check to get a phone in the trailer and I called Kitty. They had sent her back home from school when they found out she was pregnant. I gave her my number, and I said, "Kitty, please don't ever give Daddy the phone number." I told Sylvie I would come get her, but she was happy now that Kitty was with her.

And I was happy to be out of Hungry Neck. Things was more busier in North Charleston. There was a lot more places that I could go to without trying to get a ride. There were bus stops everywhere I wanted to go. If I was walking, there's a cab—if I have money I can stop for a cab. And I liked meeting a lot of people, not seeing the same faces constantly. I ran into all kinds of different people. But living in Hungry Neck, it was always the same people, same faces—and they were always watching. In Hungry Neck I had to walk maybe a mile just to get to a bus stop, but in North Charleston all I had to do was walk twenty feet and I was right there to the bus stop. There were new people in North Charleston, and they left me alone. They didn't try to be nosy because they didn't know who I were. All they know is they saw me. I could come and go as I please. I didn't have to answer to nobody at all. I could cook when I wanted to. I didn't have to clean up. I didn't have to pick the corn off anybody toe. It was like being free.

North Charleston was tighter. Houses was jam-packed, apartments here, there. It was more dangerous, but I wasn't afraid. Hell, *home* was dangerous. I was willing to take on anybody that came my way. I always would pray to myself. One time I was walking for a job, all the way from Mall Drive up to that Wendy's, way up there just before you get to the Northwoods Mall. I walked. Miles. But just before I got to Gaslight Square, a lady was walking, and she was dressed church-wise, and she hand me this little book. I just grabbed it, and I took it. I was pouring down sweat. I said, "Oh, Lord, please let me get this job." I didn't even know where I was going. I just told God to direct me to the right place. I passed so many places that I could have stopped to, but I didn't. I ended up at Wendy's, and they hired me that day. That same day. And I thought it was meant for me to run into this lady.

THE PHONE rung one day, and I said, "Hello?"

"Gal, this you?"

I said, "Who is this?" I didn't even recognize his voice.

"You mean to tell me you was so hot in your pants that you needed a man so bad you had to run away from home?"

I said, "How—how did you get my number?" Stuttering. I said, "D-don't call here no more." I slammed the phone down.

The phone ring again.

I didn't want to pick it up. I knew it was him. I let it ring two or three times and then I pick it up. I said, "What do you want?"

"Just like I told you. You was so hot in your pants, you needed a man so bad you had to leave home."

I don't know all the curse words I said to him, but I know I told him that I hated him and that he would never ever put his hands on me again. I slammed the phone down.

The phone rang again. It kept ringing and ringing and ringing and ringing, until I just went away. Later I unplugged it so it wouldn't ring no more.

The next day while I was at work, Kitty stopped by my job. She said, "Gal, please forgive me, I didn't mean to give Daddy the phone number. But, you know, he sounded concerned about you."

I said, "Kitty, he lying to you so he can find out where I live at so he can come and get me."

I warned the people next door, to tell them what was happening. They said, they see any cars that don't belong on their property, they would handle it.

Marie found out that I ran away from home and I had my own place, so she figured that was a place for her to hang out, too. It didn't bother me because I didn't have any friends where I was at. She started coming over every day, every day, every day, and all we did was drink, smoke, drink, smoke. Smoke marijuana, smoke cigarettes. When I'm not working, we would walk down the street. As you get towards Rivers Avenue there was a green laundrymat out there. We would go out there and take a bottle of Bull, sit out there in the front, and laugh and talk about people while they were coming in and out of the laundrymat, and just smoking dope right in front of them, even the old people, we didn't care. We didn't care at all.

We did that every single day when I got off work and when I wasn't working. Then we decided that we needed to start going and partying. End up one Friday night going to this club off Rivers Avenue, went in there and start dancing and drinking some Mad Dog Twenty-Twenty. I saw Carmen Wicker in there, too. She said, "Girl, Ruthie, your daddy ask about you, you know."

I said, "What y'all tell him about me? Don't tell him where I live at."

"Girl, we ain't going to tell Fleetwood where you live at."

I said, "Because y'all know how he go."

"We ain't going to tell him where you at. Don't worry about it, but we just want you to know that he ask about you."

"Well, if he ever ask y'all about me again, just tell him y'all don't see me no more."

While I was saying that to her, this guy was watching me, just watching me and watching me. He came up to me and he say, "Hey, can you dance?"

I said, "No, I don't want to dance."

He said, "You think you pretty? You ain't pretty, you ugly. Ain't nobody want to dance with you anyway."

I looked up at him. "I don't know why you saying that to me. I don't want to dance with you."

"Yes, and you think you fucking pretty. You ain't fucking pretty, bitch, you fucking ugly."

I was the type of person that just say anything to a person, and I didn't care. I started to talk back to him, but Marie said, "Girl, Ruthie, you better close your mouth, girl, that guy there he drunk, girl, he might try to hurt you."

I said, "Yeah? Let him put his hands on me."

But the guy didn't bother me no more. There was a faggot that they knew, that came to our table and he said, "Hey, don't sweat it. You ain't got nothing to worry about."

Another guy kept watching me. He was a nice-looking guy. Any man that used to ask me for my phone number, I always give them the wrong phone number. So Marie said, "Ruthie, you see that boy keep watching you?" I said, "Yeah, he better not ask me to dance, because I ain't going to dance with him. You know what,

I think we better leave early, I got to go to work in the morning."

She said, "Yeah, we'll leave early."

When we was leaving out of the club, some-body tapped me on my shoulder. "Hey, you know, I been trying to get your attention all night long but you wasn't paying me no atten-tion. What's your name?"

And I always give them the wrong name. But somehow, "Ruthie" came out. I don't know how it came out but it came out. I said, "Ruthie."

Marie looked at me, because she know I never give anybody my real name.

Then he said, "Well, if you don't mind, can I have your phone number?" He had a pen in one hand, and had his other hand open up to write the phone number on. And I always give them the wrong phone number. Somehow, the right phone number came out.

Anyway, the guy name was Peach. Peach Millican. And when he called me, I was sur-prised that he called me because I figure I had gave him the wrong number. So then I said, "Well, I'll go ahead and talk to the guy." Started talking to him and everything, and he was driv-ing a blue-and-white Impala. He asked me how I was getting back and forth. I told him I was going to school and working, but I didn't have any transportation. He gave me his car to use every single day.

But come to find out Peach had a girl friend, which I didn't know about, and they was about to get married, but he didn't tell me anything. I called his house one day. His mother answered the phone. She called me a slut, a whore, saying that Peach has a girl friend and I'm interfering into their life. So I told her that it wasn't me, it was him. I told her that she could have her son, that I didn't want her son.

All the time, this guy was whoring around. I didn't know it. Then he came over, and me and him and Marie drank all night long. I was so drunk I didn't really know what was going on, until Marie had to put me in the cold shower. About four or five in the morning, I end up going to bed with the guy. Still drunk. I remember lying on my back, and he was lying on top of me, and he said, "I got to get up and go to the bathroom."

When he went to the bathroom, I felt something crawling on me. When I looked down, it was a crab on me. It was a crab, crawling; it was a little baby crab. I didn't pay it no attention. I grabbed that little crab and I look and I squeeze it in my hand, and I felt more on me, but I didn't know what that meant. I just thought it was some bugs. I killed seven or eight of them. I didn't even tell him when he came back from the bathroom.

The next day I told Marie. She said, "Ruthie, girl, you know that means Peach had sex with that other girl, and he came and had sex with you, and he is not clean. Somebody ain't clean. Girl, you mean to tell me you let that boy give you the crab?"

I said, "Lord, Marie, what can I do?"

From then on I said I wasn't going to mess with Peach anymore. When he called, I told him what was happening. He told me that I wanted him more than he wanted me, so I'm the one who gave *him* the crab.

I said, "I didn't give you no crab."

So I am going down to the hospital downtown, Medical University, and I was shamed to go in there and tell those people. They had to stick me with this long needle, for the infection that that guy gave me.

I told him that I didn't want to see him anymore. So me and Marie, we just started hanging out again together.

I cut my family off completely. I stopped calling them up, Kitty and them to Daddy house, I wouldn't call them, I wouldn't go over there or nothing.

But next I know, Naomi and Cass got married. They had the little wedding up there at the little church in Awendaw, and they had their reception at Snowden School. After that, Naomi changed. She wasn't the same person that we knew. Her attitude changed, her language—her talking—changed. It was like she was born in the city somewhere, or in some other state.

Kitty was close to having her baby, and I wanted to go back at the house and stay with her. I was scared, but I hoped Daddy wasn't going to touch me because I was a little older then. Daddy was going out and going out and leaving Kitty home, and even though Kitty was adult, supposed to be in college, she needed somebody.

One night she was hollering and screaming, hollering and screaming, "Gal, Gal, Gal, please come rub my stomach, Gal."

I started rubbing her stomach on the tip of the side. She told me, do it a little farther down. I had to keep moving my hand. She said, "Harder, Gal, harder, Gal," and she was shaking and shaking and shaking and shaking in the bed. "Harder, Gal, harder," she say, "Mmmm," and her legs were shaking, and her feet were shaking real bad. I kept rubbing and rubbing.

I said, "Kitty, Daddy ain't here. Ain't nobody here. You want me to call Tupper and them, tell his mama?"

Kitty say, "Oh, Gal, yeah, yeah, please call."

When I called, their sister was home, but she said, "Tupper ain't here, and we ain't got no car. Y'all daddy ain't home?"

I said, "Ain't nobody here," I said, "Kitty about to have this baby."

And I couldn't call a ambulance. Because if you're living in Hungry Neck and you call a ambulance, if you don't have a hundred dollars, they will not pick you up. At least that's what I was always told. And we didn't have the money. Kitty started hollering and screaming again. I rubbed her and I rubbed her and I

rubbed her. That must have went on for at least
about two or three hours. Then it was late in the
morning. I called Tupper and them house again.
Finally somebody finally pick up the phone.
Then they came rushing over there, took Kitty
to the hospital. She had to get a C-section.

Then who came home but Daddy.

He wanted to kill somebody because Kitty
went without him taking her. Tupper and them
had to take her because he wasn't there, but he
went storming to the hospital, storming.

The next day he brought home a bassinet, a
white bassinet, blankets, Pampers, milk, some of
everything. But he wanted her to have killed
this baby.

Kitty name the baby Jewel. She let Jewel sleep
inside the living room. Mrs. Vane came over,
said, "Oh, look at this baby. This baby is so
pretty." Everybody came over to see the baby,
see the baby. Tupper wanted to see the baby so
bad, but Daddy said, "You let me catch that nigger in this house, I'll put some lead up his behind so deep, he won't know if he coming or
going."

I said, "Kitty, it's a shame Daddy ain't going
to let Tupper come see the baby."

After Jewel was about three weeks old, I was
going to the mailbox, and there was Tupper, just
standing to the mailbox. Behind his back he had
a bag of Pampers. He said, "Gal, give this to
Kitty." As he gave it to me, a car was coming
down the street.

A white Chevrolet.

I had the bag in my hand. Tupper started walking away. Daddy didn't even put the car in park real good. He jump out of the car, snatch the bag out of my hand, and throw it back at the boy. He told him that he don't want him to buy Kitty nothing. Nothing for that baby, nothing whatsoever.

I guess Tupper said in his mind, the hell with it, I ain't going to come see her no more.

Daddy started going on the naval base and buying everything cheap for Kitty. Kitty start feeling better later, and she started back smoking.

Audrey Biddle came over. "Gal, you know what? If y'all don't get your life together, y'all going to hell."

I said, "Why you say I'm going to hell?"

She said, "Because if you ain't got Jesus in you, you going to hell."

I said, "Well, I tell you one thing. When this world come to a end, and if the Lord got all the Christian people to go up above like angels, I'm going to grab onto the bottom of your feet, Audrey, and I'm going to hold on, and I'm going to heaven with you."

She said, "No, I'm going to kick you right back on down, let you go to hell."

Kitty started listening to all that stuff. She didn't want to smoke anymore. She didn't want to do anything anymore. She had gotten so Christiany, it was Jesus this and Jesus that. She started giving me her clothes, her pants, her short dress, her everything. She started wearing these long dress—not to the knees, I mean almost to the ankles. Then she started wearing these blouse to cover up everything, all her neck, and these little round thing on top of her head, look like little doilies to me that people put drinks on. They start wearing their hair this old-fashioned way, all pulled back like some old lady, and bunch up on top. Kitty asked me would I keep her baby for her when she go to church—and I said yeah, because the baby never would go to sleep for her anyway. So I start keeping the child, keeping the child for Kitty every day.

They go to church one o'clock in the afternoon. *Hope* they will come home two o'clock the next morning. That's how much church be going. The tambourine be beating, the spirit be going at it, as they say. You can tell when they coming home. You hear them clapping, clapping. I said, "Why don't they stop it. They make me sick." I told Sylvie, I said, "I hate Audrey. She came and took my drinking partner away. Kitty don't smoke no more, Kitty ain't drink no more." I said, "I hate Audrey."

Every time I turn around—"Gal, when you going to give yourself to the Lord?"

I said, "Audrey, you think I am going to hell?"

She said, "Gal, even if you five years old and

you know right from wrong, you going to burn forever in hell anyway."

I said to myself, "Why would God kill, or burn, a person at five years old?" I said, "I don't care, I'm not going to turn saved, I'm going to turn saved when I get ready to." They started asking me all the time to go to church, go to church. I would tell them I got a toothache, just to not go to church and keep out of church.

I went one time, and I saw they force you to go up there to the front. They try to make you. I said, "I don't want to do it because what if I say yeah, I'm going to get saved and take Jesus as my savior, then I turn around and I go smoke tomorrow and I go drinking? That means I'm lying."

They said, "Well, just ask Jesus to come into your life." They wanted me to see this movie, a movie that would turn your life around. I told them I didn't want to go see it. They tell me all the time, "Gal, you need to turn your life around."

I guess about six months later, Kitty started acting a little different. She kind of pulled away from Audrey. I said, "Kitty, what is it? You miss Florence?"

"I don't miss Florence. You know what, Gal? I miss smoking. I miss drinking."

I said, "Kitty—please, Kitty, please—Kitty, start smoking again!"

"No, I ain't going to do it."

So I went and got a cigarette. Kitty said, "Oh

no." Then she said, "Yeah, Gal, let me have one."

Gave her a cigarette. Kitty said, "Ah, you just don't know how long I waited. Gal, don't tell Audrey."

"I ain't going to tell Audrey."

It was like Audrey was taking control of our house. She wasn't doing what she was doing in her own mother house. She was coming in all the time, didn't want to look at TV, wanted to play gospel music constantly, and clapping and shouting and saying all kinds of stuff. Audrey noticed that Kitty was rejecting her, didn't want to hear the gospel, didn't want to hear anything.

Kitty really started drinking and smoking then. Boy, I was so happy. I was just too happy. Kitty started wearing those short-up clothes again, those tight dress, these plaid pants with the big elephant legs and her big Afro on her head. We loved Afros, that was the style. As long as the Afro was round, that's all we worried about—long as it was round.

Somehow, Audrey frightened Kitty. Told Kitty that the Lord told her if she didn't come back into the church and turn her life around—I'll never forget this—that the Lord is going to come and take her baby from her and kill her child.

Kitty got scared. Kitty got so scared that she went back into the church again. I said, "Ain't no Lord can tell Audrey to tell you that he's going to kill Jewel."

But in a way I had believe her, too. Every night and every day I told Kitty I cannot let Jewel sleep with her anymore. I kept Jewel constantly. I would get up all times of night. When I would come home from school, I would get Jewel and take Jewel to the store. I was afraid to leave Jewel with Kitty. It was just a thing. Jewel got so adapted to me till she started to call me Mama. She knew Kitty was her real mama, but just called me Mama too.

As time went on, I noticed Jewel was still living. And Kitty was still living. And Audrey was still living, and I was still living. I said, "She lied!" I said, "Kitty, come on, please, Kitty, do it one more time."

Kitty said, "No, Gal, I'm scared. Audrey say Jewel is going to die."

But then she decided she going to try it one more time. She going to smoke and drink again. This time, Audrey brought a man name Brother Henderson, and a lady, Sister Marie. She brought them to the house. Those people had Kitty out of her wits. Kitty put on a long dress so long I thought I couldn't even see her shoes. And she had on a jacket to go with it, and the jacket was so tight up to her neck, I said, "Kitty, why you got to wear those long clothes, look like some old lady?"

"Gal, it's a sin for you to wear pants. If you read the Bible, it says something about 'man's garment.' "

"Kitty, you mean to tell me if I get saved, I can't wear pants?"

"No, you cannot wear pants."

"I can't wear earrings?"

"No, you can't wear earrings. You can't wear lipstick, you can't wear makeup, and certain ways you got to fix your hair."

"I never heard that. I'm not going there. Nobody can pay me to go there."

The church was called the Circle of Love, and it's still right down there, the Circle of Love. Kitty started going every day, constantly. If you would put a piece of bubble gum in your mouth, she say, "Did you thank the Lord for that? Did you say your grace for that?" And I started getting into this habit, that even if I take a drink of water, I would say, "God is great, God is good." I would drop something on the floor, and I was getting ready to eat it, she would say, "Kiss it and tell the Lord Jesus wash it off for you." I started to believe all this stuff, all this was just going into my mind.

And I believe I started getting frightened of life itself.

I said, "Lord, if I die today, I'm going to hell. God, I like to smoke cigarettes and I like to drink. I'm going to quit one day." But these things just keep ringing in my mind. I'm going to hell no matter what I do. I was saying, "Lord, don't take Jewel away." Because I had love Jewel. And I had gotten so close to her, but I thought that he was going to kill Jewel, because of what Audrey said.

When Jewel started to walk, Kitty was still going to the Circle of Love. Then all of a sudden Audrey had this other church for Kitty to go to. Up there near the school, in a area called Wambaw. They started going to this church in Wambaw, and Kitty ended up meeting a guy in church. A country man.

I could notice the different change in her. Her face even got lighter; you know you can see a lightness in a person's face when they are happy. And she said, "Gal, you know, I meet this guy up there, his name is Luther. He is a real nice man. He going to come over here one day."

So Luther start coming over there maybe about a month after Kitty start going to that church. I was kind of glad that she was dating him, because he was a safe person—always talking about church and the Bible—and I figured that when he came to the house, he was going to change Daddy. And Luther did start reading the Bible to Daddy—but I looked in the room, and there's Daddy sitting with his Bumpy Bottle in his hand, drinking it and smoking cigarettes while Luther read him the Bible. I knew right then, there was no way it would work.

Luther was a dark guy. Looked dusty, dingy-looking. With a little small Afro, little beady ears—his ears wasn't no bigger than a nickel. He had a green Toyota, a dark green Toyota. At the time I had a dog name Tippy. Red fox dog. Rooster Hampton gave it to me because he didn't want the dog no more. My dog was with me everywhere I went. He'd go with me to the store and sit by the door until I came out. The dog used to bark every time Luther come in the yard.

When Luther came there about the third time, I was in the kitchen washing dishes, and I heard something pop loose. I felt hot water coming on my feet. The pipe had come loose underneath the sink, and I shut the water off real quick. Luther said he know how to fix it. He went under the sink, twisting pipes.

"It's fixed, I got it. Gal, turn the water on."

Jewel reached her head in there looking to see what he was doing, and I turned the water on— the hot water.

He didn't have it on tight. That water start shooting up all over the place, Jewel fell on the floor, and the hot water burned her back. We finally go the water shut off, and Jewel was kicking and screaming. Kitty picked her up and put some ice on her back real quick. "Gal, bring her in the bathroom, bring her in the bathroom!" We ran and we put Jewel in the tub and put the cool water on top of her back. Kitty had some bandage, and she put Vaseline on the burn and bandage Jewel's back up.

Luther he was so sorry, because he had just met Kitty recently, that's only his third time at the house. After we tend to Jewel, Luther went back and re-fix what he did wrong, and it worked that time. But he felt so bad, he said he was going to leave. Kitty went outside with him. He grabbed Kitty hand and he was going around and around with Kitty in a circle, trying to get her dizzy, and the next thing I know Kitty was hopping on one toe, hopping and hopping and hopping. He was twisting her around so much until one of his steel-toe shoe kick her big toenail off her foot. Kick it completely off. Kitty came in the house hollering and screaming.

I said, "Dammit, Luther, you done burn the baby, now you kick Kitty toenail off, what else are you going to do today?" I was mad, and I think really I was worried that Luther was going to take Kitty away from me—I was going to lose her again.

He say, "Oh, Gal, I feel so bad, I just feel so bad, I got to go." Kitty's toenail was completely off. The big toenail.

Went in the house, poured alcohol on it. She tie a piece of sheet on there, she tied it so it wouldn't come loose. Luther told her that he was so sorry. And he don't know whether or not he was going to ever come back to the house again.

Daddy kind of had liked that guy—because he was a church-going guy, Daddy know Kitty couldn't get in too much trouble. So, Luther waited for about a week, then he came over to the house. When he came, I was mad with him because he had caused so much confusion in the house. And I was afraid that Kitty was liking him too much. I was afraid they was thinking about getting married.

So I let my dog out because I wanted my dog to bite him.

Tippy went outside. And all he did was go underneath Luther's car to sleep.

"Y'all want to go to Hampton Park?" Luther said.

So I told Kitty, okay, we're going to Hampton Park. Luther said he'd go in the country to get a few things, up in Wambaw, and he'll be back that afternoon.

My dog must have didn't heard Luther crank up the car. He ran my dog over, underneath the car. Luther had no choice but to go back farther, because the dog had got hisself hung up, and was just barking and barking, and I was out there hollering and screaming, seeing my dog hurt like that. Luther got a brown plastic bag out of our house and on his way back to Wambaw he threw the dog out in the woods.

I told Kitty, "I don't think you should marry that guy. Don't marry him. Please don't."

But church kept going on, and they kept going to church, and Kitty fell in love with Luther—and she did get married to him. He had his own trailer, so it was better for her.

Then Kitty was gone out of the house. And Jewel was gone.

So I went on and left, too. Not back to the trailer, but into another area, in North Charleston off of Palmetto Avenue. The Sunset Apartments.

chapter nine

t h a t   w a s   a rough neighborhood, right there by the first gate of the naval base. All the sailors would usually come at night to go to that little club right there—it's closed now, but it was right there by the 7-Eleven.

When I moved to there, I moved with no lights—I didn't care—I walked around with candles, for months and months, until a black guy name Maurice, that we called Rabbit (and he is black, he is blacker than tar), he stole a meter off somebody else box and put it in my box, and I had lights for a long time, illegally.

Until one time when the man was coming to check the meter, Rabbit forgot to take the box out. I told them that it wasn't me, that somebody else did it, and the management didn't make me move off the property. He just told me that after that they would put locks on these boxes so you won't be able to steal anything.

I still didn't have a car. And I had to get back and forth to school. That was my main goal. I had to have transportation. I even said to myself, I wonder if I can meet that guy back again, the one with the blue car. Peach.

I did see him again, and he explained to me that he was seeing another girl but he love me and he can't do without me. And I fell for that. I went right back to bed with that guy. And the same day I went to bed with him, I got pregnant.

I was mad at myself. I didn't even like the guy. And on top of that, I was getting ready to graduate pretty soon.

BUT DURING THAT time Daddy got sick. He had sugar. And that's the first time he started having to take insulin. He would go to the doctor and get it, but as time went by they started giving him those needles and telling him that he had to do them himself.

I knew anyway that he wasn't going to come to my graduation, because he believed that I wasn't going to graduate from school. But I sent the invitation to him, knowing that I was probably about a couple of months pregnant. Nobody else knew.

At the graduation, it was so many people— the Municipal Auditorium, in 1979, June third. But I looked, and I kept looking, and one time I stood up to see if I see Kitty and them, but I really couldn't tell whether or not they were there. When they call my name, Ruthie Homer, my principal gave me a look—he knew something was wrong with me, in my life, I believe, it was just a look that he gave me.

And then I heard "Hey, Gal!" and then that's when I knew that they were there. Sylvie came, Kitty came, and the lady that I used to work for, cleaning up her house next door, Mrs. Vane, she came. Then I saw Mrs. Vane stood up, and she waved at me. And after I got my diploma and came down the opposite side, I saw when Mrs. Vane left. All she did was stood there to hear my name call, and she left.

After the graduation was over, I asked Kitty why didn't Daddy come.

"Daddy is sick, Gal. In the hospital. That's why Daddy can't come."

I said, "It's meant for him not to come. I'm glad he didn't come. But I just want him to know. You make sure when you go back to the hospital—tell him I did what he thought that I would never do."

She told him just what I said.

PEACH'S MOTHER notice that something was wrong with me. I had met her finally. But the third time I saw her she said, "Ruthie, you sure getting kind of big around the waist there."

I said, "No, ain't nothing wrong with me." But I knew I was pregnant.

And Mrs. Millican started cooking food for me all the time, all the time. Gradually she saw I start eating more and more and my plate start getting higher and higher. She realized that I was pregnant then. Then my stomach really started to show, really started to show.

Without me knowing, Peach gone by Daddy house, talked to him. And believe it or not, Daddy loved Peach. He loved that man, I don't know why—maybe Peach got a little of Daddy in him, and he sense that. But he had love that guy.

Peach ask me to marry him, and I told him that I was not going to marry him. Then I start thinking, I said, "I better marry him, because people going to start talking now." Because they say it's going to look bad if a girl pregnant and ain't got no husband. We was taught that when we was little—it's going to look bad if you having a child and you ain't got no husband. And I said, "Well, I'm going to go ahead on and marry that guy. That's what I'm going to do. I don't care."

His mother wanted to plan the whole wedding and everything, and that got on my nerves a little bit. I didn't know that she was on the other end of the phone when I was talking to his sister, and I told his sister that I don't give a damn what his mama said, I don't want her doing anything for me. And sure enough, Mrs. Millican was on the other end of the phone.

She called back and said she didn't know I felt like that towards her. I told her, well, hell, I did. I was mad at everybody. I was already six months pregnant. My stomach was way on out there. And the wedding was two months off.

Kitty said, "Gal, I got a dress for you, you can use my wedding dress that I had."

I was scared to try Kitty gown on because I figured my stomach was too big. And when I tried that dress on, looked like I had a big mountain inside of me. I was shamed to be walking down the aisle, knowing everybody was going to talk about me. Daddy told me that he is not doing anything for me, he is not coming to no wedding, so I can go get married without him because I was nothing but a whore and that's all I was. He said all I wanted to do was graduate and be a whore.

I told Kitty, "I don't care, he don't even have to come. He ain't been at my graduation."

But I couldn't believe it—that man went and got him a white tux, walked me down the aisle, and when the preacher say "Who give this young lady away?" he said "I do," and he sat down. But he was drunk. He was *drunk* drunk. The church was packed but I felt bad because Daddy was drunk, and I was so big, pregnant, I looked like a big Humpty-Dumpty. And I could hear the people talking as I'm walking down the aisle.

Peach had on a white tux, too. The wedding was right there at Shiloh Baptist Church. We had the reception at the little hall. When I got out of the car and into the building, people were standing in lines to shake my hand, kiss me. And they had brought so many gifts.

But after that night, the next morning when I

woke up, I didn't see no gifts. I didn't see anything. His mother took everything. She took the leftover food! She took everything to her house, she opened up my gifts to see what she wanted and see who bought this and who bought a cheap gift.

She told me that she don't think it was good for me to stay home by myself, so pregnant, while her son was working. So I said I would spend a few nights with her. I knew I was going to have that baby soon. Peach was working for this company called Wirt Construction, off of Montague Avenue.

A week later, sure enough—he came home, and my water break, and he was rushing me to the hospital so fast in the car, I was bouncing, and the least little bump I was hollering and screaming, hollering and screaming. And I knew we didn't have no insurance.

The doctor said, "I don't think you know anything about birth control pills, do you?"

"Yes, sir, I do."

"No, I don't think you do. How in the hell you going to have a baby and you don't even have insurance and you can't even take care of this baby?"

When I had to open up my legs for him to check, to dilate, he pushed my knees like I was nothing, like he hated to do it. I remember I said to myself, "Oh Lord, I don't have no money or anything at all to help me."

Kitty had given me a bottle of oil. She said,

"Take this and put it on the Bible on certain scriptures, and pray over it. Wherever you are and you don't want any kind of evilness around you, just rub it on the door, or spray it. Anybody that touches the door, the power of God will protect you." This is what was told to me.

I remember, that man came in there and he just did me rough again, just *rough*. The way he poke his hands in me, it wasn't the right way. I knew it wasn't the right way. And he left out of there, and I start crying and crying and crying because I couldn't believe he was treating me like that.

So I managed to get out of that bed, and I got that bottle of oil, and I pour some in my hand and I didn't care, I just threw it, anywhere in the room. I rubbed some on both of my knees, where he opened my legs. I managed to get to the doorway, and I sprinkle it, and some scooted out in the hallway. And just as I got back in the bed, the nurse came. She said that I had dilated good enough and it was that time.

When the man came back in that room, I said, "Oh Lord." My hands were greasy, but I remember I was rubbing them together—and I said some little scripture, I don't remember what, but something.

The doctor said, "Hi! How are you doing?"

And I raise my right hand to God, he was not the same man. He *was* the same man, but he had changed. He didn't even look like the same man. "How are you feeling?" he said.

I said, "I don't know," mumbling—because I was afraid to talk.

When he touched my leg it was gentle! It was easy. He said, "Baby, it's time for you to go."

And I remember when I got into that delivery room, he gently put my leg into those two saddles, I mean real gentle. I remember his words, he said, "Push, baby. Go ahead. Push, Ruthie, that's right. Easy. Very easy, Ruthie."

And I remember I was giggling to myself until I had to laugh, and the baby said *boop*, and popped out, and he almost dropped the baby. He grabbed the baby, and he said, "You got yourself a beautiful little girl."

And that man was so sweet and so nice. He never mentioned anything. All he asked me after I had that baby, he said, "Ruthie, if you want me to, you know, sometimes people don't have money for having a child, and it cost—but if you want me to I'll tie your tubes for you right now so that way you don't have to worry about that in the future."

I told him I had to think about it. He told me to let him know, while he was fixing the instrument.

But then I changed my mind and told him no because someday I might want some more kids. I told him no, but he told me that was okay.

That man didn't ask me for one penny. I don't know how the bill got paid. I couldn't believe that. He had started off treating me like I was a dog, but I guess it was mainly because he wasn't going to get paid.

Since I didn't have any insurance, a girl who was paying got my room, and they push me in the hallway. I had to be in the hallway. That's how crowded it was. Slept in the hallway. I had my legs cocked up any kind of way, or laying down any kind of way. People walking past me constantly, constantly, but I et right there in the hallway, which you know it really didn't bother me.

And when they came to pick me up out of the hospital, they brought me a pink blanket, something that looked like a T-shirt, and I remember Mrs. Millican had some kind of old hat to be put on my head. I told her I was not putting no hat on, and she told me if I didn't, I could catch pneumonia.

So I told Peach when we left out, off of that ramp, after I got in the car, I told him that we were going straight to our house—I'm not going to his mama house. That boy drove me straight to his mama house. She took the baby, Mary, and she say, "Oh this baby look just like Peach, hee-hee"—that's how she act—"Sure look just like Peach."

I said, "She look like a little wet rat to me."

She said, "But I know this my grandbaby."

I guess that was the main thing she was looking for, to see if this was her grandchild.

Anyway, I stayed there about a week and then I started getting frustrated, because she doesn't smoke. She doesn't do anything. She's one of them church-going ladies. We decided we going to move from where we were, into this area next to the fairgrounds. A mixed area. Nice homes, white and black. Found this house on Senorita Street. A nice fenced-in-yard home, with a big giant pear tree in the back. It had three bedrooms in there and everything.

After we settled down in there Peach started driving for Rudy's Cab Company, driving a blue-and-red cab car.

I noticed that there was a black lady always to this white man house, the white man living right in front of me. I used to peep out my window just to look. Then there was some white people live next door to me, heavyset lady, she had a tall husband, and they were sweet, nice people but they were nosy. And I had a old white couple living on the other side of me— they came to greet me into the area, they brought okra, they brought beans, they brought fish, because they had a big boat in their yard. They came over saying that they welcome me and that they saw when I came in, I was carrying a baby, and everybody love babies. They wanted to hold Mary. I was surprised because nobody had ever done that. They gave me clothes and all that kind of stuff.

I started noticing the white man right in front of us. Older man. And I saw the black lady over there. I see her, and I say, "Oh, she fucking him." That's how I said it. But when she would be there, he wouldn't be there—and she'd be gone by the time he come home. But I kept watching that for some reason, just kept watching it. Then I finally got a good look at the man. And all the time I didn't know the man was watching me, too.

I would take the baby out on the step. And sit down and feed the baby, and this man would come out there, and he'd hail me and I'd wave him back. He always keep on a red hat. And he always wear plaid shirts. And if it's not blue jeans, it's corduroy pants with boots. That's the way he always dress. He drove a truck that was beige and red.

The baby was starting to get a little bigger, so I said to myself, when I put her down to go to sleep, I'm going to sneak out and go to the store. I had to walk about two blocks out of the neighborhood and go to the store. It was a Magic Market. I used to walk there, get me some beer and cigarette and come back. Then one time when I get back in the house I can't find the baby, the baby stuck behind the pillow, she already roll herself behind the pillow. That scared me.

Peach mother must be was calling to check on me—and when she call maybe I had already left and went to the store, and by the time I come back she already hung up. She start telling Peach that she would call there every day for me and I'm never home.

She say she even send her sons Paul and

Levon up there to check on me, said they heard the baby crying one day and I wasn't home. They saw me coming from the store. So I guess that's got Peach curious about where do I go, where do I be. He start asking me where do I be going at because his mama say she called and I'm never there.

I said, "I be going to the store."

"You be leaving the baby in the house by itself?"

"No, I don't be leaving her," which I was lying.

So I started taking the baby with me. But it was so hot I had to put a diaper over her face because the sun would be beaming on her—I didn't have one of those strollers that have those hood on them. I said to myself, "I don't have to answer to them. The hell with them. I don't have to answer to them for nothing."

Peach start keeping the cab car. They let him keep it home. I went outside one day and just sat in the cab by myself to smoke a cigarette.

For some reason I pulled the ashtray back. It was full of cigarette tips and the tips were red. *Lipstick.* And little pieces of paper. *Phone numbers.* Lipstick, phone numbers.

The cab was park right in the backyard by the screen door. The door was open but the screen door was closed. I looked up at the screen door, and I saw he wasn't coming, so I took one of the numbers out of the ashtray and I put it in my pocket.

I said I'm not going to never tell him. I'm going to call this number. Called the number. Sure enough, girl answered the phone. I said, "Hey, I'm Peach's sister. Peach told me to tell you that he was going to meet you—"

I didn't know what I was going to say. Somehow she must have knew I was up to something. She hung up the phone.

The next day I told Peach, I said, "How come you always have all these cigarettes in your ashtray up here?"

"Because I be driving people, taking people different places."

"But they ain't supposed to sit in the front, they supposed to be sitting in the back when you pick them up."

"It ain't nothing. It ain't nothing."

So a few days gone by. I notice he have something on his neck. I know I didn't put it there. Because I hardly ever had sex with him anyway.

I said, "Oh, no." I said, "Oh, hell."

Then he decided he wanted to have sex with me, but he wanted to have a rough sex. Rough sex. He held me down with his two elbows. I said it was hurting me, but he took the telephone cord and he wrapped it around both of my arms to the bed, and he wrapped my feet to the bed.

When I got the first tie on my leg, all of a sudden she just came to me. Right then. I don't even know if I saw Peach. I knew what was happening wasn't the same, but I just suddenly saw my mother. And I thought, *Now I know how she felt. I see now. Nobody there to help her.* I could feel how she felt. I could see her, and feel the kerosene pouring. *Nothing she could do.*

He pulled my clothes off of me. He jumped on me and sticked it in me. I remember, he still had on his T-shirt, and I was turning my head from left to right and my arms was pulling and hurting.

And when he was licking my chest, I really felt like something low. To have somebody just licking. And it reminded me, the way he looked at me, it was a look the way Daddy used to look. A look to *look* at you.

When he got through, he wiped himself off, and slowly, slowly, he decided to take me loose. When he got ready.

So I figured that's the way sex was going to be with him all the time. And I said to myself, *No.*

He never did like that to me again.

I would drink, when I knew I was going to have sex. I had to be like that. I had to be high, to do it. I tried to be prepared, I would keep a bottle hidden somewhere. And he never knew I was blind as a bat drunk. But at times he caught me off guard. He was the type of person that wouldn't tell you I love you or anything, before he wanted it. He would just do it.

So, in a way, I didn't really know how to have sex with people. That's why I was kind of scared to have sex. I didn't want to have sex with nobody.

chapter ten

i walked to the store, had the baby with me. I ran into Marie, I hadn't seen her since the wedding. I was so glad to see her. She said, "Girl, what you been doing? I ain't know you live around here." I said, "Yeah. I usually walk up here to get some cigarettes." When she found out where I lived, she started coming there. She started getting me to go out with her, this place and that place. But everywhere I went that baby was with me, just with me.

We decided one day we going to go on the naval base. Went to the bowling alley, and I was carrying the baby, too, while I was bowling. Holding her in one arm and rolling that ball down with the other. Then I realize I knew a girl in there, name Barbara, from Hungry Neck. And she said, "Ruthie, what you doing walking with that baby on your hip like that? You better go and put that baby down over there. All that racket and stuff be over here." I said, "Yeah."

I said, "Damn, Marie, we can't find nobody to keep Mary for me. I shouldn't be bringing her in here." So we called Marie's sister, and she said she'll keep the child. We took Mary up there, off the Hike, that's where the sister was living at now. Let her take Mary, and went back to the bowling alley, some tight-up pants on like normal, like we would wear.

And this white guy was watching me. I knew he was white, but his skin was real dark, and he was just watching and watching and watching. I kept going on the phone to call and make sure the baby was all right. The next time I went to the phone, the guy was by the phone.

He wasn't talking to nobody. When I hung up, he said, "I don't know who that guy is that stood you up. But if it was me, I wouldn't have stood you up like that. You been out here a long time, then you left and you came back."

I just looked at him. I said, "I ain't calling no man."

He said, "Well, you mean to tell me you don't have no boyfriend?"

I said, "No. But I am married."

"You are?"

"Yeah."

He said, "Well, is it all right that we talk?"

I said, "Yeah, fine."

So he asked me did I drink. I told him that I drink. He start buying me some beer, just laughing and talking, laughing and talking. And he said, "Do you come here often?"

I told him no.

He said, well, if I ever want to talk with him,

he say he is on the U.S.S. *Clayburgh*. His name is Jeffrey Lagaret Brewster. And just give him a call. He said it's going to take a while for him to come out to the quarterdeck but he would be there.

I said, "Nah, I ain't going call him." But I kept that phone number. I did keep that phone number.

Called there. I don't know why I called, but I called there. Me and him started talking, we started talking. And he was just a person for me to just talk to, and he was so nice. I would meet him at the bowling alley. Then all of a sudden we started kissing a little bit. I was thinking, *Boy, if Peach catch me, he going to kill me.*

I never thought I would be attracted to a white guy. It was just something that happened. All of a sudden I was not attracted to any black guys at all. It was like they were attractive but they didn't attract me. All of a sudden I turned and became attracted to only white guys. I don't know exactly why I did, but I guess I was afraid a black guy might hurt me. I knew there was a lot of good black men out there. But they were hiding.

The man across the street, one day I saw him going to his mailbox, so I went to my mailbox.

I said, "Hey, neighbor, how you doing? I always see you out here, but you know we never really spoke."

He said, "Yeah," he said, "Well, anyway, my name is Furman."

I said, "My name is Ruthie." I said, "Your name is Furman what?"

"Rand."

"Oh." I don't know why, but I ask him where he work at.

He worked at Gold Star Shipping, way down there on East Bay Street. He say, "You know, I seen your husband all the time. And you are too much of a pretty girl to have your husband having all those women in his car like that."

I said, "You seen them?"

He said, "Yeah, I seen them."

So I start thinking, I say, "Oh this man probably just want me or something."

I said, "Well, who is that black lady you be having over there with you all the time?"

He said, "Oh, she cleans for me. After my wife left and my daughter is gone, I don't have time to do too much work. All she does is wash clothes, a little bit of cleaning, that's about all."

He said, "Whyn't you come over one day?"

So I told him okay.

I waited for Peach to go to work. The baby was sleeping. I went to Furman's house. He's got a beautiful home. Sitting down in the den, and he got this big old animal that's stuffed, a deer or something. And he got some old antique rifles, right by his fireplace. And he had a cat. And I've never seen a table like that inside of a person's house—look like a picnic table, with two side seats, but it was shiny. I told him, I said, "My, this is a nice house." I said, "How many rooms you got?" just walking farther on in there. And he show me the bedrooms, and he had two bathrooms. I started getting kind of frightened. I said, *Oh, this man might try to get me.* So I said, "Well, Mr. Rand—"

He said, "No, don't call me that. Just call me Furman." He said, "If you ever need anybody to talk to, you can come on over here."

Then I rushed back across the street. I was afraid Peach was going to come home and find me not there. When Jeff called, I told him that Peach is going to work that night and for him to come on over.

He said, "You going to have on something sexy for me?"

Jeff and me weren't having sex, we just played. Just having fun. So I said, "Well, okay. Yeah, I will."

When it got dark, Jeff got a cab from the naval base, up to my area. I heard when the car door shut, and I saw the cab when it backed up. I told him when he come, come to the front door, because when Peach comes, he goes in at the back, and Jeff could run on out the front door. So Jeff was standing in the door. And he always wore black. Got to be black. And his hair is black too. I had on a white little negligee, those kind with the little skinny straps, and I was standing to the door, to the side.

He asked me what I had on. I said, "Well, come on in and I'll show you."

The baby was in the bed sleeping. And as

soon as I had closed the door and I was getting ready to kiss him, a light came into the yard. Heard the car went around the back.

Jeff said, "What—what is this?"

I said, "Oh—Jeff—that's Peach!" I said, "You got to go, you got to go!"

That boy ran out that house, jump over the fence, ran down the street. Next I know Peach was in the house. The cab company must have told him.

He looked underneath the couch. He went back in the room, he looked everywhere, he searched every room. He knew something was going on. I was frozen. It was because I had on what I had on.

And I told him that I had that on for him. Knowing that I was lying.

Peach left. Right after all that searching, he left. He had a feeling I was giving it up to somebody else, which he was himself anyway.

The phone rung. It was Jeff, and I told him that Peach left. He said it ain't no way, he is not coming back there, he said he ain't coming back there again. He said now he got to wait on another cab to take him back to the base. So I told him the best thing for us to do is meet on the base.

He didn't want to meet at the bowling alley. He wanted me to start coming on the U.S.S. *Clayburgh* ship. So I start seeing him on the ship. And my baby, I was taking Mary with me. I told him I wanted to bring her, and he said he didn't mind. And it was kind of nice, because after a while, everywhere we went on the boat, everybody knew me. All the guys knew me. We even went out in public, to restaurants. We didn't care, we just went. I said, "Too bad—if Peach find out, he just going to have to find out."

Being on the ship was like being important. That's what it meant to me. I felt important because Jeff asked me to go—on the base, and on the ship, with all those guys—and he didn't care who saw us, what color we were. And I felt important because they were in uniforms. And because I could get to eat on the ship. And look at movies, walk through the ship, meet his friends, his captain—it was exciting. I really liked it.

There was so much to do on the base. You could go bowling. You could go eat a Colossoburger, you could go to the club. Jeff always wanted me to come on the base. I used to dress nice all the time, and I liked that. To be black, too, and to look nice around those people, black and white . . . I liked that.

Jeff did tell me that he had a son, from a black girl. Showed me a picture, and showed me pictures of all the black girls that he had dated. He said he never dated a white girl in his life. I didn't believe him. He was from Presley, Indiana. He called his brother and told him that he met a girl down here, and his brother said, "What color is she?" and he said, "Well, you should know me by now." His mother wanted to see a picture of me, so he sent her one.

He liked Mary. He would always ask me, when I was coming, "Are you bringing Mary with you?" So I would take her on the ship.

Standing on that deck, you could see all the water and the other ships. And guys dressed in their black sailor crackerjacks with the white hat, and guys looking at other guys' girl friends, and everybody nice and friendly. Very nice and friendly.

A couple of nights I took Mary to Marie's sister so I could be alone with Jeff. But Jeff wasn't the type of person that was out for sex. I used to kiss him and rock up on him, but not with my clothes down. I had my clothes up and everything. He was just a nice person. But then one night he asked me, did I ever suck dick before. That kind of surprised me.

I told him no, I never suck nobody dick before in my life. So I did his. It was so little and teeny, real little, and I thought, "This can't do much." I decided I'm going to have sex with him. We went to one of his friend house. It didn't bother me at all because while we were doing it, I didn't feel nothing. Nothing. I mean, nothing. I didn't even know sex was ever like that, you could feel nothing at all. And I didn't mind.

He told me that he had to go back out to sea for six months. I asked him, I said, "Jeff, while you gone, you going to send me some pictures and letters?"

He said yeah, but he said, "You remember, you got to put them in a place where your husband can't find them."

I had a big old blue pocketbook, it was a tall pocketbook. And in the back there was a lining. I decide to barely rip the pocketbook lining just enough to fit the envelope and the pictures in there. That was my secret place that my husband would never find. I got so much letters. And I taped so much tapes, even in the tub, and I tell Jeff all kind of things, and I had so much letters and so much pictures that I was getting from him, weeks and weeks and weeks.

All this time I didn't know that Peach knew exactly what was happening. All this time he knew. He was playing a game with me, like he didn't know. But I was realizing that when I would put a letter in there, I notice it wasn't as thick as it was. But I didn't pay that no attention. Until I got a phone call one night.

I was high as a kite. I was smoking up, smoking and smoking. I answered the phone.

"I didn't know that you didn't love my son."

I said, "Who is this?"

"This is Mrs. Millican. I guess what Peach said about you is right. I didn't know that you didn't love my son. You mean to tell me that out of all these men in the world, you carry yourself down so low to a white man, Ruthie? A white man?"

"What are you talking about?"

"Come by my house and I'll show you."

Me and Jeff had took some pictures together on the ship, we took billions of pictures, and he sent me some. She had pictures of me and him, kissing, she had pictures of my tit in his mouth because we took pictures like that, just playing, holding the camera up, and then the letters. The letters.

I dropped the phone. I just dropped it. I knew right then, that was it. Then I had to face Peach. I really panicked. I didn't know what to do. I said, "Dammit, what am I going to say now?"

When he came in, he stood with his legs apart and his hands in his pockets, his elbows sticking out like a Western cowboy, and did his mouth with his lip going under his teeth, and his eyes stretched up at me.

I knew it was war.

"Ruthie. So tell me, how long have you been seeing this white fucker?"

I said, "I don't want to talk about it."

He said, "No, how long have you been seeing him?"

I said, "I don't know, I really just met him."

"Ain't no damn way. I got letters with the date he was writing you. Ain't no way."

I started backing up from him because I knew that he was going to hit me. I backed up into the room and against the high bed. He knocked me back and slapped my face, and the next I know he was boxing me on the top of my head, and I was holding my head, both hands on top of my head, and squeezing my face tight so I wouldn't feel it. But he was hitting me all over my head, so I was moving, and then he start hitting me in one spot right on top, and it started bleeding, bleeding, bleeding. I knew the blood was dripping down, and dripping down on me, and when he realized that he saw blood, he said, "Oh, my God, Ruthie, what have I done? I am so sorry, forgive me, baby, forgive me." And I started crying, and he started crying.

I went in the back to clean myself up, and when I came back, he started to ask me why did I do it, what was it that caused me to do it, was he not doing the right thing? And I told him that I didn't know. I told him that I really didn't know. He told me that I was lying, and it looked like he wanted to strike me again, but then he didn't. He left out of the house.

I called his mama and I told his mama what he did. She told me that I deserved that.

"My son went out of his way to buy you a washing machine and a dryer, new carpet to go on the floor, new beds, even leave his car home for you—but you want a white man dick. Nobody is going to disgrace my family like that."

So I hung the phone up on her. I thought, "I got to get out of here, because now the family is against me. What can I do?"

What I did, the next day I called her on the phone. I said, "Mrs. Millican, I need you to do me a favor."

"What is that?"

I said, "I'm leaving Peach. I don't care if you tell him. I'm going to be leaving Peach soon. But I just need you to take care of Mary for me until I find a place to stay, and I'll get her back."

She said, "Okay, Ruthie, that's up to you. But don't have that baby in the street like that because you know you can't be running from place to place."

"Just answer this question. Will you just do me that favor?"

She said okay, that she would.

I didn't tell her exactly the day I was leaving, but I told her I would be leaving soon. I called the cab company. I just grabbed what I wanted to get, I didn't care about nothing else, the furniture and all that. Cab picked me up. I told the cab please not to tell Peach where they took me at, because I knew he was going to come and look for me. Sure enough, he called the cab company, and I heard the lady talking on the little mike, on the radio thing, and she told the driver to tell me that Peach just called, but don't worry, she would never tell.

I told the cabdriver to let me drop some things off at Mary grandmama house, that means dropping her off too. So when the cab took me there, I said, "Mrs. Millican, I'll be back to get Mary within a week or two. I just need to go find me a place first of all. I'll be back to pick her up."

She said, "Okay, Ruthie."

Mary was barely walking. I saw her after Mrs. Millican closed the screen door, she was walking down the hallway to the kitchen.

I told the cabdriver I need to find a place to live and he told me about some small apartments in the Sunset, the ones that just got a living room in it, you can pull the couch out as a bed—so I decided I would go back there. The manager, he remembered me. I explained to him what was going on. He went ahead on and gave me the place.

I found a job at Western Sizzlin, the one way up on Rivers Avenue. Got a job there, and I started working. And I had money now to get my girl.

I called Mrs. Millican to tell her that I was coming to get Mary.

She said, "If you bring your unfit ass to my house to get my child, I am going to call the police, and I will tell the policeman and the *public* that you are a whore fucking a white man, and you destroyed my son's life."

I almost broke my own hand hanging up that pay phone. I went over there to her house. Her son Paul pushed me and pushed me, and they wouldn't let me on the property. And my little girl was crying, my little girl was screaming, up there behind the screen door.

I said, "I'm getting Mary."

I ran past that boy so fast, and when I got up to that step I felt something hit me in my chest. Mrs. Millican was a big woman. She had put her foot out, and she kicked me in my chest, and I went tumbling back over the stairs.

She said, "You damn drunk!"

And I was drunk, too. I was drunk, I was upset, and I was drunk.

She said, "Mary, see how your mama go? Come on, baby, you don't need to see nothing like that."

And from that day, she never let me come to see that child.

I said, Well, I'll wait another week and I'll call her when I'm not drinking. But that drove me just to drink, I was drinking worse and worse.

I called her with a sober head one day. She said, "Now you sound like the Ruthie that I used to know. Look here. Don't you ever call my house and threaten me about no child, because, see, far as I'm concerned, you are nothing but a whore, and on top of that you never loved my son, from the giddyup. You only married him because you was pregnant."

I said, "Dammit, I told you—"

"Don't you be yelling your voice at me."

I told her that I was sorry, because I thought, "Damn, if I keep on, she not going to let me see the child." So she said, "Well, let me sleep on it, and you call me back tomorrow and I'll tell you."

That time I was really upset.

Then the black guy that lived by me, the one named Maurice—Rabbit—he knew I was upset. Right there by the pay phone there were stumps. (Those stumps are right there today, right there sitting there.) I went and I sat on a stump, and I remember I was moaning back and forth. I didn't even have no cigarette, I was just mad. Rabbit came out there and he walked around me.

He said, "Hey, hey neighbor, what's wrong?"

I was hitting my head.

He said, "I can tell you're bad off." The pay phone was connected to their building, and he probably heard me slam that phone. He said, "I got something to take care of your needs."

He came back outside and he had a joint bigger than I don't know what. Policemen always stay up in that area, because it is so bad, but at that time I didn't care who saw me. Old people saw me, I didn't care. I cursed them—I was just mad.

Then I think I must be got so much marijuana in me, and I was drinking Bull, too, I don't know how I got home but I was throwing up all over the place. And the next day, it was like I was dying of thirst, I hadn't had no water for I don't know how long. I said, "The hell with it, I'm going to catch the bus." I caught the Harmon bus, because you have to catch the Harmon bus to get to where Mrs. Millican live. Got on the bus, got up by Melrose Plaza, the Piggly Wiggly. Had to cross over Harmon Avenue and past the Taco Bell, then cross to old Berkeley Street and from there over the railroad track and through a little pathway. And there was three houses there before I got to her house. One green one, one pink one, and one yellow one. Her house, the last house, was blue. I knew Mary was in there.

They must have seen me coming. They came to that door, and I tell you, I wanted to rag that lady head off. They still denied me seeing that child. Wouldn't let me see that child, wouldn't let me see that child. They kicked me out of their yard and sent me back across the tracks.

DADDY HEARD about what was going on. He started riding with this other man, they started car pooling. Daddy would meet him at the Blue Heron Hotel on Palmetto Avenue, right across from the Sunset Apartments. And there was a big restaurant there too. He would go inside there in the mornings and wait. He found out I lived right across the street.

He came there.

"How could you be so dumb and let them people take your child from you? How could you be so dumb? I thought I taught you better than that."

I said, "She tricked me. She actually tricked me. And I trusted her and I believed that lady."

Daddy was still talking that nasty talk and that mean talk, but he started changing a little bit towards me. I would call the house and tell him I needed money, and he would say, "Well, be at the hotel seven o'clock in the morning and I'll give it to you." I called him and he gave me money, to do little things that I needed, then when he would have to wait for his ride to pick him up in the afternoon, sometimes he would come to my place, knowing that I drink and smoke. "Gal, what you got, what you got strong to drink?"

Give him a little drink, he drink.

One day I went to try to see my daughter again, they wouldn't let me see her, not even for a minute. So I called the hotel and ask them was Clovis Fleetwood still there. They said, "Yeah, he still here."

I asked Daddy, I said, "Daddy, you got anything on you strong to drink? Because these people making me upset again."

He said, "What the hell I'm going to give you my liquor for—so you can go fuck on it?"

That's his exact words.

"N-no," I said, "I'm upset because they won't let me see Mary."

He said, "I ain't no fool. You want me to give you my liquor so you can get drunk and you can go fuck somebody."

So I thought maybe he was right, that I was really the type of person that do do that. I started thinking, yes, he is right.

I had become that type of person. I was a young girl living in the world by getting what I could from men. I didn't care how I hurt them. I didn't care. I used them. I dated them and used them, I took their money. I dated Jeff, but I dated other men too. I would tell them, hey, I want this much money. It was like a game to me, I enjoyed it, and I always had money. Always had money. I said to myself, "I am always going to be in control of all men from now on." It was like I had to be the boss. Nobody else was going to boss me.

And I probably hurt some people. I didn't care.

I was out to hurt and destroy and get what I can from men.

I didn't care how old they were. I didn't care if they were seventy years old. I wanted what they had. I figured what they had was mine. I didn't care what color they were, either. They *owed* me. They didn't really owe me anything, but I felt that all men owed me something, and was going to pay. I was making them pay for my granddaddy. That was what I was doing.

And I made the old mens pay more money.

I was turned off on black men because they would hurt me. I wanted to know how a white man would treat a black woman. Jeff, he was totally different. He never hit me. So I figured a white man was all that I ever wanted. That's what I tried to do to this older man, Furman Rand. He was a wealthy man, and I figured he wanted a young girl. So I did sexual favors for him. Not intercourse, not like that, the other thing. And he would pay me two hundred, three hundred dollars. I had it made. I told him, hey, thirty minutes, I want this much money. I got bills to pay. Furman Rand was a kind man to me, and I knew he was a lonely man, but I didn't care. Even when I didn't do it for him, I would call him on his job, and say I need this much money. And I got it, because he wanted to help me. So I said to myself, "That's my one ticket. I'm going to use this against men for the rest of my life." And I did it for a long time, even though I was still involved with Jeff. I would give Jeff drinks and drunk him, I would give him marijuana and make him be fucked up—sneak out for two hours, meet men and make money, come back—and Jeff never knew. And never questioned me. We got along.

It was like I *had* to get that money, and I *had* to do this. It was something I had to do. And when I got the money, I felt real good. I said to myself, "Now they will always pay."

I would be gone sometimes three and four hours, and come back, and Jeff was still sleeping. I could have been with three different guys. I would go way off, I would go in cars not knowing whether I would get in a wreck—but I would do it. Just do it. And I would have all this money and Jeff would never ask me where I got it from.

It wasn't the money that I wanted though. It was something else. I never looked for money in a man. Never. When Jeff left to go out to sea he never sent me any money, and I didn't want it. He couldn't afford it anyway because he was sending money back to the girl that had the baby from him. But when he was here, he would give me anything that I asked him for. He always write and send little gifts.

Jeff didn't eat like black people. He liked pizza and salad. And sandwiches. When I would cook rice and collard greens, he would say "Oh no." When some guys were coming over, he said, "Ruthie, would you mind getting some pizza, some soda and some beer, and some liquor—and make sure you make a big bowl of salad."

I said, "They don't eat black-eyed peas and collard greens?"

"Don't cook that food for those guys."

But the thing about it, when the guys came over that night, they were all black! They were all black guys. I think they really came over to watch my floor-model, that I was renting from Mister TeeVee. And to smoke. They wanted a place to hang out. Once they come from out to sea, they didn't want to sit on the ship. Some of them would go home, but some wouldn't.

So sometimes I would cook Charleston food for them. I remember when we invited some of them over, I cooked red rice. I knew there is a lot of black guys that won't eat red rice from a woman. And this is a true thing. A woman can use her period—put it in the rice—and that man eat it, and he will do anything she ask him. She will control his mind. So these guys came over, and nobody was eating that rice. Just sitting at the table.

I et some. Jeff et some. And I said, "Mitchell,

y'all don't eat red rice?" I said, "It's delicious,"
just having some fun with them.

"Noo-noo-noo," he said.

I said, "Oh, come on. Now why would I do
that." But you can ask any black guy, they'll tell
you. If you cook them red rice, they are not going to eat it. They'll tell you in a heartbeat, don't
give me no red rice. They'll eat white rice,
brown rice. Red rice? "No, ma'am, unh-unh."
Not unless they really know you and really trust
you.

Girls do that, to entrap a man. But not me. I
didn't need a man like that. I was in control
without any of that.

I FOUND OUT that white men could scare me,
though, and hurt me too. A friend of mine,
Carolyn, asked me to go eat up on Montague
Road. We went in to eat, there was a policeman
in there, a lot of white people, some blacks. As
we were eating, she said, "Ruthie, you see those
white guys over there?"

I turned around and looked.

She said, "They're looking at us, from the
time we came in."

I figured they wanted to flirt, you know. Talk,
whatever. When they got up they had on jeans
and T-shirts. I noticed they were really staring at
us. I figured they were looking at two pretty
black girls, that's what came to my mind.

We got up, went out the door.

They were sitting in their truck.

Carolyn had a old Maverick, blue one. We heard the truck crank up. Then the lights came on. The truck pulled up next to her car, and as she was fumbling in her purse for the key to unlock the doors, I was just looking at her. I knew they were there, but I didn't look at them.

They downed the windows.

"Hey, you niggers. Hey. Niggers."

My heart started pounding. She and I felt the same. It was like, *Don't say nothing. Open the door fast as you can, get in, lock it.* I guess she panic a little bit. She couldn't get the key in. I'm thinking, *O-pen-the-door-UP!*

"Did you hear us? Hey, you niggers."

Finally got in the car. Locked the door.

"Gal, did you hear that?"

I said, "Carolyn, don't take me home now, don't go to your house. Don't turn off on no dirt road, because if you do, we are gone." Sat in the car awhile. I knew they wasn't going to do anything right there, because there was a policeman in the restaurant. Finally the truck pulled out. Me and Carolyn rode around thirty minutes before she dropped me off. I said, "Carolyn, the minute you get home, please, call me." We never saw them again, but that scared me. It was the first time something like that happened to me, *directed* to me like that. They didn't touch us, they just spoke the words, but I never had a contact like that so close. So scary.

I thought, what kind of life am I having? All

I had was Jeff, and I knew he wasn't really the right person for me.

Sex wasn't a big thing in Jeff life. We had sex, and he would say "Was it good?" and I would lie and say yes, which though it wasn't, because I never felt anything. I never knew when he was finished. I couldn't tell. It was good that he wasn't hurting me, but it wasn't *good* good.

And he was into a lot of drugs. I never saw him do cocaine, but pills. My apartment was his partying place, and one night he gave me a little tiny pill. It was purple. He called it a microdot. He said I could take half of it or take it all. I said, "This little teeny thing?"

I swallowed it. And within five minutes, I saw a little man walking up on the ceiling. All the guys were in there, and they were all laughing at me. We were sitting on the couch, and I couldn't stop laughing. I kept seeing the little man.

"Jeff, get the little man off the ceiling."

"Ruthie, there ain't no little man."

"He's right there!" I knew I saw a little man pacing up and down across the ceiling.

I was paralyzed. I wanted to move but I couldn't move. I was still.

I wondered were they going to pull a train on me, but they weren't. It didn't happen. The next day I remembered what happened, but I was in a trance. I was mad at him for that, because he let people see how I acted with that drug. I told him I never ever wanted it again.

He wanted me to try all kinds of drugs. I told him no. He said, "I just wanted you to sniff something." It was in a little brown bottle, it was a liquid. He said it was a fast high. I sniffed it, and in a second I couldn't move. It was a thirty-second high. To be with him, I guess, I did it.

I got addicted to marijuana. Even on my jobs, I used to smoke dope in the bathroom, cigarette in one hand and joint in the other one. I even used to get high with my bosses, in the freezer at Burger King. Because you could never smell it in there. We would say we were counting inventory. Get high in the freezer, and then come back out and make those hamburgers. High as a kite. Most of my bosses were like that. I could spot the people who did drugs. You know who you can go to.

Jeff liked to drink, too. It was New Year's Eve, and Jeff said he was going on the base to meet his friends. I told him I wanted him to stay with me, but he say he will be back an hour before New Year's come in. And I was crying on that bed, a couch that pull out like a bed, and I sat there and watch the balloons, on TV, in New York Square, wondering where was Jeff—where was Jeff? About 2:30, he put the key in the door. I had the latch on and I wouldn't let him. I asked him where he was.

He said, "The craziest thing happened to me, Ruthie. This big fat woman kissed me at exactly twelve o'clock—"

And I started crying. I was very upset. I told him that I wanted him to leave and I didn't want him to ever come back. He said he wasn't going anywhere right then, he would leave in the morning.

I said, since he did that to me, I would fix him. When he went to sleep, I stole all his money out of his bag. He must be knew I was going to steal it. He stuff it in his duffle bag, way to the bottom. And I found his wallet. I stole all his money. He didn't find out until he went back to the ship. He tried to break my door down. I told him I was going to call the police if he didn't leave. He told me he wanted his money back. Then I told him I was sorry, I was going to give his money back, come on and move back in. He moved back in, and three weeks later he went to Singapore. He told me to be at the pay phone at a certain hour. But when he called me he told me that he didn't care for me anymore, he didn't want nothing to do with me anymore, because he fell in love with a girl in Singapore.

I dropped that pay phone and left it just hanging there.

I said to myself, I can't deal with any more mens.

I wasn't being with females, then, either. Marie was out of my life. I had invited her to my house one night. I went in the back, and when I came out, I caught her hand in my purse. My best friend. She was stealing something from me. That threw me. But I didn't say anything to her. I said to myself, "I am going to do what I can do, what I have to do, there will be no more females in my life, I don't care about having friends. I don't care about nobody."

I got so I didn't even like to go outside. I was a hidden person.

chapter eleven

i was living in the Sunset Apartments, and I was renting a television from Mister TeeVee. The white guy, name was Kevin, was the area manager, and if you didn't go in and pay your payments on your set or furniture, whatever you were renting, he would come and knock on your door or leave a little note.

One particular afternoon, I had on a blue pair of shorts and a white T-shirt, and black sandals. I had on lipstick, makeup, and my Afro was round, the roundest Afro. I saw the green van pull up, and it had "Mister TeeVee" on it. I said, I know he ain't coming to get money from me, because I'd already paid him. I closed my living-room curtain real quick, so he wouldn't know that I'm home. He knocked and knocked on the door. I wouldn't answer.

The old man across the street, his name is Eddie, old man Eddie, nice old man—he told Kevin, "Ruthie in there. I just seen her come from the store. She in there. Just keep on knocking."

I thought, "Damn, Eddie gave me away." I said, "Who is it?"

"It's Kevin."

"I don't owe you no money."

"No, I need you to introduce you to somebody, because I won't be running this route anymore."

"Okay, just a second."

I took the chain off the door, and I open up the door.

There was this brown-skinned black guy standing there. Looking dead in my eye. Long, curly hair. Skinnier than a pencil. And I saw the biggest smile on this man's face.

I put my hands on my hips, and I said, "Well, who is it going to be?"

"This guy's name is Ray Bolton. He's up here to visit his aunt on Wadmalaw Island, and he's going to stay a few months to make some money before he goes back home to Florida. I just wanted you to be aware that he's the new guy, going to be your area manager."

"Okay. Okay."

And this guy never took his eye off of me.

I said to myself, "Look at this young boy here looking at me like this."

The next day I was going to the gas station, Phillips 66 right there on Palmetto Avenue. I had on the same clothes I had on the day before, but this time I had a scarf on my head. It was blue with white flowers in it. And I saw this

Mister TeeVee van coming through, and slam on brakes.

He said, "Hey, excuse me—but can you tell me where 2246 Palmetto Avenue is?"

"Well, it ain't down here. Gotta be down that side down there."

He said, "Do, ah, you remember me?"

"Yeah, I remember you."

He said, "I'm new to this place, and I'm trying to find out the houses."

"Well, go straight on down. It's either that green, two-story building, or the houses across the street."

He backed up, he turned to make a U-turn. As he got to the stop sign, I was still standing there watching him. He put his reverse light on, he backed up.

He said, "Excuse me, can I ask you a question?"

"What?"

"Is it all right that I come and see you?"

"You don't even know me."

"But I don't really know anybody. I'd like to get to know some people."

"Well, I guess so. Hey, do you smoke dope?"

He said yeah.

I said, "Well, you can come see me if you bring me a bag of dope."

"Okay. I'll do that."

About 3:30 in the afternoon, this car pulled up right by my window. I didn't know that was him. I peep out the window and saw this guy, and I close the curtain. I said, "Why this guy is sitting out here?" Later on that night, he knocked on the door. I let him in. He brought the dope, and he said, "Here you go."

I said, "Now, what are we going to have to drink with this?"

"You want some beer or something?"

I told him yes.

When he went to get the beer, I went in that bag and I stole a bunch of dope out, and I put it in a napkin and balled it up and stuck it in my pocket. I fixed the bag up so he wouldn't know. But he didn't even look. We sat and drank, we smoked and talked.

The third day, he came and asked me did I want to eat lunch with him. He said he had brought lunch with him. He brought two end breads, with cheese and baloney. He had a orange. He had a soda.

"I don't eat end bread," I said. "I don't like that kind of food."

"That's all I have." And he had it wrapped up in a old bread bag, too.

He said, "You know, if you not busy, I really don't know my way downtown. If you can go with me and show me some places, I would really appreciate it."

I said okay.

We was riding down to the project, and I said, "Now, you remember that this area is very dangerous." I look back in the van and I saw a long black case and I knew it was a rifle, but I didn't say anything. I thought, this guy is just a punk. When we stopped, he reach down, and he grab his little book with the names and how much they owe, and he walked up the little sidewalk and up the steps, and he knocked on the door.

Nobody didn't answer. We knew somebody was there, because there was two cars. He kept knocking. I was still sitting on the passenger side. I noticed I saw the curtain peep, and I saw somebody peeping, and he saw the person peeping too. The lady asked him what he wanted, and he said he came to collect the payment or come to pull her set if she didn't pay the money.

A man opened up the door, and he said, "Can I help you?"

Ray said, "Yeah, I told the lady that was looking out the window that I came to either pick up the money or pick up the set."

The guy said, "You're not bringing your ass in here, you're not going to pick up no set out of here."

Ray backed up.

All of a sudden four or five people started coming out the door. Ray was still on the porch. He looked back at me and I started getting scared. One of the guys pushed him.

Ray was scared.

He ran to the van and opened up the door and he reached in there, and he grabbed that black case.

The girl said, "He got a gun! He got a gun!"

Everybody ran back in the house. Ray acted like he was going to take the gun out. The guy opened back up the door and got the television and threw the television out, broked it up. Ray ran back in the van and got on his radio and said, "I'm going to need some help down here, I'm going to need some help real bad."

Kevin, same guy who introduced me to Ray, came zooming on down there, and first thing you know policemen was up and down all over the place.

After we left I said, "Damn, I don't want to ride with you no more, not on a job like this, and you carrying a damn gun!"

The case was sitting in the middle between me and him. When we stopped at a corner, he said, "Ruthie, let me show you what this is." He unzipped it and he opened it up.

Pool sticks!

"That's all it is," he said. "Somebody left it in the van. I don't own no guns, I don't like guns. Don't even know how to shoot a gun."

I said, "We could have gotten killed! The people didn't know! The way you handled that case, they thought it was a rifle. I'm ready to go home, Ray."

But he had one more stop to make, to collect for some rental furniture. We drove up to this area called the Hike. Knocked on the door. There were a bunch of guys standing around. I told Ray, I said, "Look here—"

He said, "Ruthie, we already been in one incident. I'm being careful. There's a couch that she have, and two end table, and a love seat. If she don't have the money, we are going to have to pull it." He said, "Are you willing to do it?" So I told him yeah.

The house was a old wooden blue house. The girl in there she must have didn't care or didn't give a damn. She said, "Come on in and take your shit. It ain't worth a damn anyway." Went in there and I felt bad. What we took out of her living room, there was nothing left. And I really felt bad taking that stuff from her. She had two kids.

The kids were on the couch that we had to get. And I knew that she didn't have any money, just by looking at the kids and her. She grabbed one and pulled the other one and sat them on the floor. The kids were just looking up at us. They didn't know no better. After we took the last piece of furniture out of there, I turned back around and looked at the kids. And I remembered the time when I didn't have any furniture.

We got in the van.

Ray said, "You don't like doing this, do you."

I said no. I said, "Did you see them kids in there?"

He said, "Well, Ruthie, they don't have the money. This is my job. My job is to take it. I don't like it either, but—"

"They probably done pay on it for a year, you know. And all the company going to do is clean and sell it and get more money for it. The way I felt when I was in there, when I saw them two kids, I didn't even want to touch it, Ray. There was nothing else in there! I don't think this is the kind of business you should be in. You can find something else. It's not worth it."

He looked at me. He said, "You're right." Then he took me on home.

THE FIFTH DAY, he came again. And this guy, he told me he loves me, and he wants to marry me!

I said, "Get out of here. You don't love me. You don't even know me!"

"Look, I'm not lying. I do. I love you, Ruthie, and I want to marry you."

He said it was love at first sight. But me, no. I wasn't interested in him. I was just interested in what I could get from him. But I tried not to hurt Ray, because he was so sweet. He was a very very sweet guy. You could tell he was sad about something. I didn't know what it was then, but he was sad because his father had died.

But that's how I met him. I met him through Mister TeeVee. And the fifth day from when we met, he wanted to marry me. He said he loved me the first time he saw me.

And this man didn't even ask me for sex until two months later. I was glad, but I was wondering. I thought something was wrong with him. No guy had ever dated me for two months and didn't ask me for nothing. And that's why I really really respected him, because he wasn't after my body. He sure wasn't after my money, because I didn't have no money. And I wanted to kiss him, but it was two weeks before he even asked me can he get a kiss! And we finally kissed, but it was a quick little kiss. I thought, "Well, he give me a kiss, now I wonder when he's going to ask me for sex." I figured that was going to be the next thing. But it wasn't. It was like he was waiting for me or waiting for the right time, and we did it for the first time February 28. We mark it down in my book, and we said we would always celebrate that day, the twenty-eighth of February.

I MET HIM in 1980. And he never quit asking me to marry him.

I had to get a divorce from Peach. Ray was pushing me to get it, he was determined that I was going to get this divorce. I told him I was going to get it, but he wanted to be there, to see and hear everything that went on, so he would know for sure. He said he was never married in his life before and he didn't have any kids.

I lived with him three years, and the fourth year I said yes, I would marry him.

His family planned everything for the wedding in Florida. They paid for everything, the reception hall and the food, the dresses, everything. Mrs. Bolton made me a dress, and her sister made the veil. The wedding was going to be at her house—she even bought a brand-new red carpet for the stairway, where I was going to walk down. A friend of theirs was going to bake the cake, so it would be cheaper. The Boltons didn't have money, but they were willing to do all this for me.

Ray went down there, and I was supposed to meet him on the following Saturday, the day of the wedding. I said I would be there—but I didn't show up. I backed out. They had already had me in the newspaper, and pictures of him and me in the newspaper, and the date and the time and where the wedding was going to be at. His family had already gotten dressed for the church!

But I skipped out. I said to myself, "If I marry this man, he might beat me up later." And I couldn't do it. Couldn't get on that bus. They had to give all the presents back, and they lost their deposit on the hall, and all the money they spent on the food. I felt bad about that, but I was just too scared to go.

Ray came right back to Charleston. He wanted to know why I changed my mind and didn't marry him.

I told him that I really did get frightened about it. We was at the table. It was getting kind of late in the afternoon, and we had two candles to the table. I was sitting right across from him, and I lit a cigarette.

"Ruthie," he said, "stop right there."

"What?"

"Don't move."

"What are you talking about?"

"Ruthie, you're not going to believe this, but I had this dream before. I never saw the person's face, but this is the dream I had. I was sitting to the table with a girl, there were two candles here, and the whole room was the same way this is now."

"Aw, Ray, get out of here."

But he said he was really telling the truth, and it was meant for us to be together.

I said to myself, "Yeah I think so. This is real. This is the guy for me." So I said I would go to Florida. Ray went on back, and I took the bus a few days later. I thought, "Well, either I'm going to make it with him, or I won't." But I made sure that I had money, just in case anything happened, I could catch the first bus out of there and come back home.

I got to Florida early in the morning, about 6:30. I called his mother house and told them that I'm here at the bus station, to come pick me up. I didn't know they had a long way to come. Ray told me he was from Orlando, but he really wasn't. He was born in Orlando, but they lived way out in Tolley, little country town.

I was there at the bus station, sitting, waiting, to 3:30 in the afternoon. Still sitting and waiting, wondering when they were going to come.

By that time I had fire in me to kill anybody. I had waited there all day, not knowing anyone or even where I was, afraid that I was going to get hassled by some man. And then when his sister and him finally got there, I was crying and cursing, I told them I hated them, hated his family, because I had to wait in the bus station. His sister Cassandra was driving a Beretta, a red Beretta, and I was sitting in the backseat with Ray, and she was just looking at me in that mirror, and she didn't say a word.

When I got out of that car and got into that house, his mother and the rest of his sisters and his two brothers—it was like they knew me all along. When I walked in the door, they hugged me and they kissed me.

But I couldn't do it. When they grabbed me, I just stood there. They were smiling, and they were so happy that I was down there. And then the sister that came to pick me up, Cassandra, that's when she finally hugged me and kissed me, and she said she didn't do it to me at first because I was so upset.

Mrs. Bolton showed me the room that we would stay in. It was the prettiest room I have ever seen. I have never had anybody that gave me a room so nice. She had pretty carpet on the floor, and the bed was a king-size bed with a blue spread and ruffles to the bottom. I have never seen one like that. And she had big giant straw fans on the wall. She said that was her master bedroom that she had for herself, but since her husband died she never slept in it. Nobody did. We were the first to sleep in that room.

There were two other doors in there. The first door, I opened up and I couldn't believe it. The bathroom was so big! And it had a walk-down-in tub, a blue one. Then, the other door that I open up, I have never seen a closet that long before in my whole life.

The room had three different windows to it, and sheer white curtains. They were all stained-glass windows that she stained with a kit you can buy out of the store. Something that she lights, and it burns and it melts, and she can make it in any kind of design that she wants. Our windows were stained like a checkerboard—red, yellow, and black. She made a table for us out of little ceramic tiles, made it herself.

All kinds of things in the house she made herself. She had the two prettiest red big macrame hangings, with a glass in the center of each one, and two china dolls. It was big and long, hanging in the living room right in the middle.

I thought they were rich when I walked in the house, because she had so many pretty things. But come to find out they had no money. She had made all those things. She did it herself.

And the table was set—so formal, I didn't even know how to act at the table. I didn't know what to do. We had steak, we had barbecue, we had chicken, we had the works. And I said, "These people don't even know me."

I didn't eat a lot. I et a little bit of food. His mother and me, we talked and we talked, and we took a walk, and we went to her sister house, and we went to her sister-in-law house, she introduced me to them, and they hugged me and they kissed me. And all the family came over, and they were so happy to see me.

It was like I was in a different world.

That night I said to Ray, "This going to ever stop? Why do everybody keep grabbing me and kissing me? I'm not used to that."

"Well, Ruthie, you know, my family always been like that."

"My family ain't ever been like that. Why they always got to touch you and stuff?"

Living in a house with people, I had to be up early in the morning. It was fixed in my mind. It was trained. When I got in the kitchen, I saw Ray's brother Zack had already got out all the food. He was outside, but the food was on the counter. I made the coffee and started cooking.

His mother got up, and when she found me in the kitchen, she said, "Ruthie, you don't have to do that."

"I'm used to doing this. I need to do this."

Zack came in, and he started cooking. I told him not to cook, but he said no, he was going to cook for me. I let him cook. He brought the food to me upstairs, and I didn't feel right about that at all. I came back downstairs, and I told them that I was going to cook breakfast, lunch, and dinner for everybody. I did. I couldn't help myself.

And they loved Ruthie's cooking. His mother

told her daughters, "See there? Y'all need to be like Ruthie."

"Yeah, but Ruthie a country girl. That why Ruthie like that."

I said, "No, I been raised like that. I just can't help it."

I cooked, cooked, cooked. And I started cleaning. They said, "Ruthie, do you need something from the store? Do you want to go someplace?" And they would give me things. I wasn't used to people giving me things. I wasn't used to none of that. I had even called off the wedding, but these people still took me in, they still wanted me there. They gave me that nice pretty room. They always want to make me happy. Me—happy.

They bought me clothes. They gave me a ring and a necklace. They'd buy me funny cards, little jokey cards. Candy, a black-and-gold pen set, some shoes, any little things that they would see. And sometimes funny little things, tiny little funny things.

Like a toy mouthpiece. A *lip*! You wind it up, and it opens and shuts. It had no teeth, just a lip. That was the funniest thing I got. Zack gave it to me because he said I talked a lot.

They knew I always wanted long hair, and they gave me a weave—it's hair that you can connect, like people that have extensions in their hair. It was auburn, and it was curly. Mrs. Bolton put it in my hair, and I had long hair *all* the way down. You couldn't tell me nothing. I was swinging it, slinging it.

Cassandra and her sisters bought me a big picture. You could tell somebody hand-painted this picture, and you can plug it in the wall and it lights up in certain little holes. It was a picture of a house and a water fountain, and the water lit up like it was coming down. Yellow, gold, green. I wanted to see how somebody made a picture like that so I actually pulled the back off to find out how they did it. Come to find out they used Christmas lights, and aluminum foil behind the picture to make that shininess for the water. I had never gotten a picture like that.

His mother would make things for me. We would sit down and we would laugh and talk. Like a real family. And it dawned on me that I had never had that.

AND WHAT WAS so terrible—I couldn't accept it from them.

I KNOW it's hard to believe, but I couldn't. Some kind of craziness stopped me.

I started acted mean and evil toward them. I hated them because I figured they weren't the right people for me. Or I wasn't the right person for them, for the family. All the stuff they gave me, I threw it at them. Even the picture I loved, I threw it down the stairs. I don't know what came over me, I just went crazy.

They didn't know what was happening. I locked myself in the room, crying.

His mother said she wanted to talk to me. I said I hated her and didn't want to talk to her.

She said, "Ray, I don't understand what's wrong with Ruthie. I thought Ruthie loved us and cared about us."

But she didn't know that I wasn't used to things like that. I finally opened the door and she came in. She sat on the bed.

And I told her the truth, why I did what I did. I told her my childhood.

She listened, and she said, "Ruthie, as long as you're in our house and you're with us, this is the way we are always going to be. And you don't have to be afraid."

It was a hard thing for me to realize. I don't know why it was so hard. I just didn't believe that these people could love me.

I tried to start hugging and kissing like they did. They would tell me they loved me. At night they would tell me good night. In the morning they would tell me good morning. Nobody had ever told me those things.

But I let myself get mixed up into that meanness again. I was mean for no reason. They worked with me as much as they could, but I did it again. I turned on them. I told Ray, "Why are they always doing this? Why do they got to say 'I love you'? I can't hear that so much, Ray.

I got to get out of here. I don't care about any of them."

What was happening to me? It just seemed like it wasn't right for me to be there. And the closer they came to me, the more I pulled away.

But they kept coming, coming, coming.

And one Sunday night, Mrs. Bolton rubbed my head with oil. She told me that she went to church and she prayed for me. She said there was a spirit in me from my childhood, that need to come out—it's been locked up in me so long, and I'm taking it out on them.

And I knew that's what it was.

Slowly, I started enjoying everything. They were taking me places and showing me things, they wouldn't let me be unhappy for a minute. They took me to a place where they make nothing but orange candy. Everything orange, because Florida is the orange state. This store had a big orange tower, and inside you could see in the glass little cabinet stands, all different shapes of orange candy.

One Saturday they took me to Disney World. We got in free because Ray's sisters and brothers worked there. The best thing I saw was It's a Small World—little kids, like puppets, of different colors—Indian, Chinese, Mexican, every kind of kid in the United States. When you go in there, four people ride in a little tub boat, and it moves by itself, and the puppets be singing in different languages. I kept going back in there. I just had to see the kids again. I don't know what it is about children, but I loved them. I had to go in there. And I loved the little African girls best, because they were so pretty. I wonder why they were so pretty in here, but they don't look like that on television. They don't show them like that on television, they show them looking ugly and starving. But they are really pretty. For television they find the ones that look the worst. But they don't look like that in It's a Small World. I used up a whole twenty-four-pack of film taking pictures of It's a Small World.

Oh, and I loved the Saucer. Looks like a teacup, and you ride in it. I wanted to get in that teacup, and I did. It's a big teacup! It just goes around. And my other favorite one was the carousel, because I loved the horses. They remind me of Mr. Buzz old horse that was shot, and Ice Jones shiny-coat horses. But still, It's a Small World was my favorite, because of the children all singing. And they all look happy. There is no sadness in there. If you go in there, you will be smiling the whole time. Everybody got their own language, their own talk, and their own dressing. Even the Ireland kids, they look real good. They look like little leprechauns.

THE BOLTON family would go out to eat all the time. Everybody. We had twenty-three people—Ray's brothers and sisters and the grandkids, so the restaurant always had to connect two other tables with our table. Nobody never argued, nobody said "I don't have no money." When the bill came, everybody just went in their pockets. When Ray and me would put money in, they would give it back. They didn't care what we ordered, they didn't say "Hey, we got a limit." Ray said they been doing like that since they were little kids. His father always take the eleven kids out eating, and people would always wonder how they got the money to buy steak for eleven kids. It's because they worked their butts off in the orange grove.

We went in three cars. They didn't care if you have to sit in somebody's lap, everybody going. We'd be squinched up in there, but everybody got in.

I TOLD RAY'S sisters I was sorry that I said I hated them, I was sorry I threw things at them, and would they forgive me?

And they did.

Every Sunday morning at six o'clock everybody had to be up. Everybody get up, hold hands, say a prayer. We kiss and we hug. At Daddy's house, it had always been, "Get up! Get up, Gal! Do this, do that!" And these people *wanted* to get up that early, six o'clock Sunday morning. Everybody would say a scripture from the Bible, everybody would take turns. After that we would kiss and we would hug, and then we would eat breakfast, we were laughing, we were talking, it was like I was really their sister, she was really my mother. It was so different, so different, so different.

I never told my own family what happened. I didn't think they would believe me. I never told them. Never did.

FOR RAY and me to get married, we had to save the money up, because the Boltons had already spent so much on the wedding I didn't show up for. We had to work in the orange grove to make money, just to plan the wedding all over again.

In the orange grove we would wear the raggiest clothes we could find, and put those bandannas on our head. Ray would always have a sack, put the sack around him. He would climb the tree, shake it, and while all the oranges were falling, I would pick them up and fill up this big giant bin. They pay you twenty-five dollars a bin. It took at least about two hours to fill up one bin. So by the end of the day we would probably fill up four bins and make us a hundred dollars.

But that's how we saved the money to have the wedding that we had. We didn't have a super big wedding, but it was nice. We got married with his sister and her boyfriend, had a double wedding, but it was still at the house, and we came down the stairway with the red carpet.

Ray's people—they are the reason today that

I'm not the person I used to be. The things I had done, I had to get revenge on men, I had to steal, I had to smoke and drink—but at that time, I hadn't met Ray's people.

And the house was always happy. People were always laughing in that house. Laughing all the time. And at our house people were always crying and screaming and beating. In Ray's house people were laughing, we were talking, we were sitting down and drinking coffee. It didn't seem real to me. I felt like I was dreaming. Twelve people? Twelve people in the house, all feeling the same love? I just couldn't figure it out. When only a few people lived at our house, and they had no love. No feelings.

When Daddy used to beat me, I would pray, Lord, don't let me feel the pain. And it was like I felt it, but then I didn't feel it. I felt it, and I didn't feel it. And I said to myself I will never let that man see me tear. Not one tear. And he never did. That's why he called me a tough nigger.

When he said that, I figured I *was* a tough nigger. I had to prove that I was. I made myself to be hard. Towards men. Towards everybody. I learned how to not feel anything at all.

And now the Boltons made me to feel feelings again. They showed me how to do that. You have to wake up, really. I guess at times you think you're living in a dream, and you really need to wake up. And it happened to me so fast, just like waking up. You think, it might be going to take a long time for someone who has had the life I had, done the things I done, to change inside. Not to completely change the way I was and how I acted, because that took me some time, but to change inside. It's like I was waiting for it. Waiting for this family, and when I finally could let myself come in, I was in. They made me feel they were waiting for me, too. All this time.

They took me everywhere. They opened up for me. They gave me something that I always needed, but it wasn't easy for me. Sometimes it seemed like just them doing it made me mad, by making me remember Gal, the little dark child who always wanted a real family. I was mad because it took so long in my life to find that.

I couldn't believe these people. To be so nice, and so understanding. And his mother would cook things for me. She was from Charleston, too, and she would cook food that Charleston people cook, just to make me happy. I just couldn't believe that.

I had said I hated them! Today we talk about it, and they say "Ruthie, you remember when you came down here—but you love us now." And even on the phone now, when we talk, we always say we love each other before we hang up. My people today, they still don't do that. But when my mother-in-law and them write me or call me, they never leave out that word. *Love.*

"I miss you, and I love you." That's what they say. That's the way they are.

His mother, this old lady, still today when you see her, she'll rassle with you on the floor, she'll tickle you, she'll play with you.

It's too late for a person to do that for me now. But if I had never met them, I don't know how I would be today. Because still today, they are the only people that hug me and tell me that they love me, besides Ray and Mrs. Vane.

And my children. They do it all the time. A child, I can understand, they will do it to you. I love them, too, but—I guess I had wanted it from an adult, and I wanted it *already*, to have happened to me when I was little. That is a hard thing to explain—that I want it, but I want it *then*. I want somebody, when I was a kid, to touch me on the leg or the shoulder and say, "Ruthie, how you doing?"

I STAYED down there in Florida for three years. I had my baby, Shana. And all the nurses in the hospital loved her. When I would go for the baby, she wasn't there, and then I would go down to the nurses' station and find the baby with bows in her hair!

And Ray's family loved her. Everybody always loved her, everywhere I took that baby. People always wanted her. I was afraid to let her out of my eyesight. Everywhere we would go, people would say "Oh, man, that's a beautiful baby. If you don't ever want that baby—"

White people said this! It was strange to see, white people wanted my child. A Mexican girl in the store said, "That your baby? That look like a Mexican baby to me."

I said, "No. This baby is *all black*."

But I thought, why would she say that? My mother-in-law was in the store, and I said, "Damn, she might be like Mrs. Millican and figure this not her son's baby." But she knew it was Ray's baby.

But people wanted this baby. Everywhere I went, people would ask me "Is that your baby?" I guess it was because I am dark, and she is a red baby. And the hair is what had people confused. They would say "I never saw such beautiful hair," and they would actually want to comb the baby's hair.

I LOVED the Boltons, but Florida was not the place for me. Or Tolley, Florida, was not. It wasn't where I wanted to raise kids. I missed Charleston, the city life. Tolley was a small country town. Everybody knew everybody in that town. All the mail people know who who is. And the town was full of rednecks. There was a lot of prejudice.

And the restaurants. Conroy's Restaurant, right down the street from Mrs. Bolton house. Usually the Bolton family was the only blacks that would go in there. But one day a black preacher came in. And a white man kept looking at him and looking at him. The black man just kept eating, like nothing was going on. Kept eating.

Mrs. Bolton said, "Why is he looking at him like that?"

I said, "Well, I ain't going to pay it no attention. I'm hungry."

So we kept on eating. The preacher had on blue pants with a red pleated shirt, and he had his hat on the table. The white man got up from his table and came over to the preacher, and he said, "Looking mighty swifty in that outfit there, hunh?"

The preacher kept eating.

The man *slapped* his hand on the table. "You hear what I said?"

Preacher just looked up at him. Kept eating again.

I had to stop eating, because I wanted to know what was going to happen. The white people in there, they just acted like this is normal, this is what's supposed to happen.

He did it again, bammed on the preacher table.

And the preacher stood up.

He was about seven feet tall.

He said, "Look, here. If you do this one more time, I'm going to have to hurt you." He turned around to get back in his seat, and when he did that, the white man grabbed him on the shoulder.

The preacher reach up and just put one hand on the top of the man head, like a claw. That preacher hand was *big*. I will never forget this. He bang that head down on the table. The white man fell back and he bumped his head on another table, and he was *out*.

The police came. And arrested this black man.

I was upset. They put the handcuffs on him. He tried to tell them what happened, and we tried to tell them, but nobody else would tell the truth, and they took the preacher away. I said to myself, "I will never go there again."

But one more time Ray and me went in for breakfast, and we sat there and we sat there. We waited. They just looked at us, they never came to the table. A white couple came in, and before they could even sit down, the girl brought them water, took their order.

I'm turning around, looking, and I said, "Ray, what in the hell is going on here?"

He said, "You'll learn about these people sooner or later."

She finally came, took the order. Another white couple came. We're still sitting there. I said, "Damn, we didn't even get no coffee yet." Two more couples came in, got their coffee and their drinks.

I had tears in my eyes. They finally brought the coffee, and the bitch was cold. Sorry to say that, but it's true.

I took a sip out of it, and I spit it back in the cup. I said, "I'm not going to drink this, Ray.

They probably stick their damn fingers in there, make sure it was good and cold."

I called out. "Excuse me, Miss," I said, "I don't care what you say, I think you are prejudiced. This place is prejudiced. Matter of fact, I do not see one black person working here." I was pissed off. Everybody was looking. Everybody knew I wasn't from there.

And she said, "Ma'am, you are going to pay for that cup of coffee."

"I'm not paying for the coffee. The coffee is ice cold."

Next I know, Tolley police came in. He said, "Ma'am, you are to be barred out of here, and never come again."

"You're damn right. I'm going back to South Carolina. I won't dare come back to this old hick town never in my life."

I told Mrs. Bolton I just can't deal with it. She said, "Ruthie, let me let you know. This is the way it's been way before you came here, and there's nothing we can do."

I said, "But every store I went to, all the shopping areas, not one black person working nowhere? Not one? Not even in Gilbert's!"

Ray's brother Zack said, "They ain't going to hire no black person there."

I said, "Well, we will see about that."

I went there, big grocery store. Gilbert's. I asked to see the manager. His name was Mr. Smoak.

It matters the way you talk to people. I asked

him real nice, was he hiring any cashiers. He said no, he wasn't hiring any cashiers at all, but I could fill the application out. So I filled the application out.

Waited two days. Didn't call.

And I noticed they had a new girl in the store. So I went back there and I asked for Mr. Smoak again.

He said, "You know what, Ruthie? You look like you really want to work here."

I said, "Yes, I do. I'm not from here, I'm from South Carolina. I've never been a place where I didn't see one single black person working." I told him. I told him, in a friendly way, it was time. It was 1985.

He said, "You know anything about a demo?"

"No, what is that?"

He said they got this booth where they advertise, let people have a taste of something, to see if they want it. And they need someone to be in the booth.

I got the job right then. He said, "I'll start you off at five dollars an hour."

And it looked like, all of a sudden, Gilbert's turned over. No more than a month later, there was a black cashier. And then some others. Everybody couldn't believe it. In all these years, I was the first black they ever hired. Somebody like me had to come in from somewhere else, because the black people down there were keeping their mouth shut. They were afraid. I'm not like that, I talk a lot. And I couldn't keep my mouth shut.

But the rest of the town was still too much for me. It's a hurt, it's terrible, when you see that. Those white people thought if you're black, you're poor. And if you're poor, you're going to steal. The *minute* I walked in a store, I actually hadn't closed the door good—"Can I help you?" Well, can I breathe first?—they *charge* at you.

If you were just walking past Conroy's Restaurant, the police are going to ask you what are you doing down here. Yes. And one time, Ray's little brother Julian was riding his bicycle on the sidewalk. This white lady went over the sidewalk, hit his bike and he fell off and hurt his head. She asked him was he all right, and then she gave him a dollar.

I said, "Julian, don't you spend that damn dollar." What we did, we took that dollar, we put it in the Bible. And that dollar is in the Bible today. She paid him off! A dollar! If he was a white boy, she wouldn't do that. She'd call a ambulance. Julian was too young and ignorant to take down a license number or anything. I couldn't believe somebody would use a kid like that. You can't do anybody like that, but a child! That's a sin.

I wanted to come home.

Mrs. Bolton, Ray's sisters and brothers, they didn't want us to leave, but I couldn't get it out of my mind. I told Ray we had to move back.

Finally Mrs. Bolton said all right, but she asked me to do her a favor, and when she said it I went crazy one last time.

She wanted me to leave Shana down there.

And suddenly all I could think of was Mary. Leaving her in that blue house with Mrs. Millican and never getting her back. I started crying and screaming, knowing that I made that mistake with my first daughter.

Ray said, "Ruthie, Mama ain't going to take Shana away from you."

I said, "I'm not going to do it."

She said, "Ray, tell Ruthie the only reason why I ask her that is because once you move from here to Charleston, y'all ain't going to be settled. I just wanted y'all to leave this child here, because ain't no need for this child to be going from house to house. Sarah and Josie, then they can bring the child back to you."

But I thought it was happening all over again. I got all fired up.

"Ray, I am going home. I don't care what else I leave here in your mother house—but she want to keep my kid? Hell, no, it ain't no way. And either you are coming or you're not. I'm going."

Mrs. Bolton tried to calm me down. "Ruthie, I don't really know what happened to you with the first child. But it's not going to happen to you like that again. All I'm asking is one thing. I don't know when I'm going to see my grandchild again—you might never come back. Let Shana stay awhile."

But it was like I was seeing Peach mother again. They don't look alike, but it was like Mrs. Millican talking to me. And what really made me think they wanted to take Shana away from me was that I knew they loved her.

I said, "Ray, I made that mistake once. I am not making it again."

We drove to Charleston that day. Moved into another apartment on Palmetto Avenue. No lights, no utensils, no water. I had to ask the grocery store to give us some food.

Not one week later, they came right to South Carolina to see how we were doing! Ray's mother and Zack and Sarah and Cassandra. They brought the things that we left behind, and other things they thought we could use. Mrs. Bolton sat down and she talked with me. She said when they first met me, they sense the spirit in me, and that I was a child that wasn't loved, and she wanted to show me that they did love me, and they did love my baby. It was not that they wanted to take the baby from me.

She said, "Ruthie, you should never leave a person house with a angry heart. The way you left us, that's been on my conscience. There was no need in talking to you, because I couldn't get nothing in you. You wouldn't listen. I forgive you for cussing me. But all I was saying was, you and Ray are two young people, and I was looking out for that child's safety. You left there with no money, no nothing."

I don't know who grab who first, but it was like when I first met them. I felt the feeling all over again. I knew right then that the lady was not going to do anything to hurt me. If she would come all the way from Florida, she wouldn't do it. So I decided I would let Shana go with her for a couple of months.

She told us that she couldn't call me, because we didn't have a phone, but I could make a collect call on the pay phone and she'll pay for it.

I called them three times that week, and she told me the child was doing fine. She said, "Sarah and Josie will bring the baby back within a month. By that time you and Ray should be settled down with a job and everything." And they did just that, just like she said.

She said that I can trust them. And I have had trust for those people ever since. After that it was finished—there was no more of that.

NOW I SEND all my kids down in the summer, and they send my kids back. They are not trying to keep them. But at the time I thought they were doing the same thing to me Mrs. Millican did.

Every time we go down there now, it's the same way with those people. They have not changed. They do anything in the world for me, anything. They buy my kids things, and they send things—and Daddy never bought my kids nothing. When they write, they always send the kids something. Even when they're out of money, they will find some little thing to send.

When we went to visit them in Florida, I said, "Listen, I don't care what y'all say, these kids don't need any more toys. This time they're not getting anything." But when they came back from the store, Shana had a big Barbie car. My boy had a motorcycle with a boy on it that rolls up and down with the headlights flashing. The other girls, Denise and Nicky, got a dinosaur and the Barbie doll—and they got at home almost every Barbie that there is. And that's what I like, too. I like my kids having toys. To tell you the truth, I like those toys myself. From my family, nobody gives my kids anything. But Ray's people—that's the way they are.

Mrs. Bolton told me that we are coming down there for Christmas. I told her that I don't have the money to come. She said, "Well, baby, you know that Mama don't have the money either—but somehow, if the Lord's willing, y'all will be down here." Talking to me, she calls me baby and herself Mama.

They always ask us to come and want us to come. When we come to Florida, they are so excited! They are so happy! My family was never happy to see me. And me and Cassandra, Ray's sister, we hug and talk. I really love Cassandra. Me and Cassandra we always hold hands. And his brother Zack, he is out to sea now, he's in the service, but he still likes to cook for me. And Julian, Ray's little brother Julian, he always love to hug Ruthie. And down to the grandkids— "Aunt Ruthie, Aunt Ruthie"—they all got to hug me and kiss me.

All of these kids hug and kiss each other. And it kind of gets to me sometimes, because these kids are so little, and it's happening for them. And then I see me, being little like that again, and it didn't happen to me like that. Not at all. I never had all those toys. I never had anyone touch me except to beat me. Sometimes I used to get mad, seeing how these kids are loved. I was jealous.

And still I do think like that, when I'm down there. But I don't let it bother me anymore. I don't get mad. Because I know now that these people do love me, and these people do care. If they didn't, there's no way a person can pretend like that with you. There's no way. And call you on the phone, and always say I love you? Who is going to call you long distance to tell you a lie? So it must be true.

And my kids love their grandmother to death. They write her books. Shana wrote her a little book, and she send it down there. And my kids needed that. It would have been bad if my husband mother were dead, that would have been terrible.

* * *

AND I WOULDN'T change that family for nobody in the world. I wouldn't change them for
nothing. His sisters, we wear each other's
clothes. If they bought a new dress or new
pants, and if I say, "Can I wear that?" they don't
say, "You're not going to get your butt in here."
His mother fixes my hair, puts perms in my
hair. They will go out of their way just to see me
happy. That's just the way that they are, and I'm
glad they are.

Still, in the back of my mind, I think to myself
sometimes, I can't believe that they really mean
it. That's because somehow it's not right. Even
though it's right, but I still think back to that
childhood, with me, when I'm around them. But
they don't know that.

That family changed my life. I came out of a
no-love family, and I fell into a love family.

EVEN WHEN Ray and me were back in
Charleston, I knew I was part of that Florida
house. We had our boy, Ray Junior, and we had
Etta, I named her for Ray's mother but we call
her Nicky, and then we had Denise. We went
through some hard times, but from then on I
was thinking about one thing only, and that was
my kids. Daddy and Florence and them were
not part of our life. Our life was our kids. I still
saw Kitty, she would bring her children to our
place on the weekends, but I didn't think about
the rest of them, Daddy and them. And eventually I wasn't even thinking about dope. If I

hadn't had the kids, I believe I might have kept on smoking, kept on drinking. But children will change you. It's true. Children will change your world.

all the girls I grew up with were pretty girls. They always kept their hair real pretty, they always wore nice clothes. Marie still is pretty, and Carmen, Barbara, Ivy, Francene. But some of the others, when I saw them again, all that prettiness was gone. These were Mount Pleasant girls, but they got up into North Charleston like I did. And North Charleston is completely different from Mount Pleasant. They moved on the project area, and they weren't working. They got pulled into drugs.

To be so healthy when they were younger, they became skinny as a stick now. Judy Bellaire, her eyes were bloodshot. One eye was fully red, and she said that can never change—it's going to always stay red. Their faces were not that pretty brown no more. It's a dull look. A drug will change your skin like that. Your face show whatever drug you're taking. And their arms. From needles. It was terrible.

When I saw Judy she said, "Ruthie, you got anything to drink?" These girls got no children,

never was married, all they do is hang out at
the sweet shop drinking all day. And they were
even in the newspaper, fighting policemen.
Their parents just gave up on them. I felt so
sorry for those girls, because they were smart
and pretty, at one time.

And I was thinking, damn, I got all these
kids, and here we are in North Charleston ourselves. It's not a family place.

I GUESS we had been home about three years
when Kitty came over one day and told me that
Daddy was kind of sick, and he was taking insulin, but he was doing it himself. He was putting the insulin in his leg himself, three times a
day.

A month later, they all came, Kitty, Florence,
Naomi, Sylvie. They said they had to talk to me
about something. I didn't know what it was. I
was stunned that it was all of them.

They asked me, if I wanted to, in order to
save money and don't have to pay rent or anything, would we come and stay with Daddy to
take care of him, because he was getting sicker.
They said it was up to me whether or not I
come over there, but they don't know how I
would feel towards him, from all that I been
through with him before.

Florence had moved from New York to Mis-
sissippi, and she said she wasn't going to do it.
Sylvie, Pam, Evelyn were living in Mississippi,
Naomi was in Georgia, and they all said they

damn sure weren't coming to that house again.
And Kitty said she was tired and fed up with
him, because she have her own family. I had a
family of my own too. But they figured that I
wouldn't have to pay any money out for anything, just to take care of him. Kitty said she will
write the checks each month to pay the bills,
from the money Daddy has in the bank.

Ray said, "I don't know, Ruthie. I don't know
if you can do that."

"I don't know either. But who's going to do it
if I don't? Everybody just want to be away from
him. The man can't hurt me no more, he's sick
and old. And Ray, you know, I didn't tell you
but I kind of miss Hungry Neck." So I decided,
yeah, we're going to go ahead on over there.
Something was pulling me back, like it was
something I had to do.

So we put some of our things in storage and
moved.

When we got over there to Hungry Neck, the
house was a total wreck. I mean a total wreck.
Looked like he had started some remodeling
and quit. Junk everywhere, holes in the walls.
Things were in the sink, like it had been there
for a couple of years. Molded stuff in the refrigerator, and the canned goods in the cabinets
were rusted. You could tell that he wasn't doing
any cleaning. The toilet in the bathroom was
corroded. The house smelled just like stink cigarettes. Like you were walking into a tobacco
field.

And Daddy *was* sick and old. He just sat in a chair all day, didn't say much. At first he didn't hardly know why I was there, who all these children was. I said, "This is going to be okay."

Me and my husband took the last bedroom, and my kids took the twin bedroom, and there was nobody staying in the first bedroom. My grandfather was in the middle bedroom.

When I pull his bed back to clean from behind it, it looked like he had cigarette butts that when he got through smoking cigarettes, instead of him outing the cigarettes, he just threw it behind the bed. You could see all the burn marks on the floor. And all on the wall. I told Ray that I just can't sit here all day long just taking care of Daddy, I need to go find a job. So I did went and found a job, at the Bi-Lo up on Highway 17, and Ray he started working at Cameron Van Lines as a truck driver.

The yard was full of old washing machines, typewriters, old cars—we couldn't even pull our car into the yard, we had to pull on the side of the street. Soon as you walk in the door, there was Sheetrock, plywood, sitting right there against the wall. Paint buckets. Old paintbrushes. In the living room, there was old sheets, old curtains, couple of typewriters, the dust so thick. The dining area was plywood on the floor. The kitchen floor was plywood, no tiles. The old good wooden floors were dull, so dull till they looked black. In the den there was an opening in the wall where Daddy had wanted to put a bar for his liquor and wine. Down the hallway, you could see where they started the Sheetrock, but it was all those two-by-fours still there, they never completed it.

Inside the first bedroom was nothing but papers and junk and old clothes. In the bathroom, no shower curtain, no towel, the walls were filthy dirty. In his room was a old dresser and his bed, and the old chiforobe still sitting in there. In the next bedroom, it was just mattresses on the bed with holes all in it, and the bottom of the mattress had worn off so bad you could see some of it hanging out, all the cotton on the floor. And in the last bedroom, the red old dressers that we had, they were still in there, and the old bed. No curtains. The doors were torn off. The windows were so dirty you couldn't look out. And in the utility room you couldn't even see the washing machine if you wanted to—he had some of every junk you can think of, things that didn't even make sense. Just old things, clothes, some of everything.

He never had a trash can in the house. Didn't have a broom, didn't have a mop. Didn't have a damn dustpan. The front yard had a couple of old trucks, a old big engine lying out there, a couple of washing machines. And in the backyard, God knows—I couldn't even see in the backyard. You had to walk around so many things, I couldn't even let my kids go outside. I was afraid. There were snakes and lizards—I had never seen lizards that big before in my life.

And the grass was so tall. There was water in buckets that looked like it had a shiny skin on top, grease or something.

I said, "We're going to start in the house first."

Had to move all the plywood out, and the Sheetrock. I took it inside the utility room, and I measured the walls, and I cut out the Sheetrock. It wasn't perfect, but I start nailing it in. I nailed it in and I fixed all that. In one room you could see through the wall, where he had started to put a washing machine—you could see outside, and I knew in winter the coldness would be coming in. I got some of the plywood, I measured it, and I cut it out and put it around the pipes, and I nailed it in. I Sheetrocked it up. I got that tape that you put on the Sheetrock, I fixed that up.

All those dirty clothes, old sheets and old clothes that he had laying in the living room, I bagged that up. I threw it out in front for the trash man.

I went and I asked Kitty if she had any money, because I didn't have any money yet, could she get me some tile to go on the floor. She said, "Okay. Let's go to Lowe's. Pick out what you want. And let's go to the place where they have wallpaper on sale. If you want some wallpaper, I'll get it out of Daddy's money. We'll use his credit union card to get money out of the teller. But I can't take out but a certain amount."

I got tiles for the kitchen floor. I got wallpaper for the hallway. Wallpaper for the kitchen. And paint. I wallpapered the hallway and the kitchen. I painted the dining area.

All the cushions in the chairs were black and filthy. I bought some chair cushions to put on top so nobody could see the stains.

My grandmother's old curtains were still in the living room, but in the other rooms he didn't have curtains. He had sheets to the windows, all sheets. As soon as I had a couple of little checks coming from the job, I told Kitty I would buy the curtains myself. I put curtains up.

He had nailed every single window down. You couldn't even up a window. Some of the windows were cracked, stuffed with socks. There were no screens. I told Ray, we need to let some air in this house.

Mrs. Vane must have seen me taking out trash. She came over. "Ooh, Ruthie, who put up this wallpaper? Oh, my God! Who did the floors?"

"I did that."

"Ruthie, I'm getting ready to get me some new carpet in my bedroom, even though those one been there since Downey and I bought the house and even since Downey died. But it's some expensive carpet, and you can have it. You can have the padding, too."

So I measured out the dining-room floor. I put

down the padding, and I put the carpet down on the floor.

That room looked so much better.

I went myself and bought wallpaper for it. Rose, a pretty rose color. And I realized now, that the living room didn't look as good. Once you start doing one part of the house and it start looking good, you can see what the rest needs. I bought rose paint for the living room. The curtains that Grandmama had in there were still good, they were expensive curtains, all I had to do was clean them.

I told Ray we got to either paint these hallways or we got to wallpaper in there too. So I painted the hallway blue. Those old furnitures that Daddy had that wasn't any good, like his old cracked nightstand with no drawers, I threw that out. The table in the den was holding on one leg, he had blocks underneath it. I threw that out. I bought a new table from a yard sale. Only cost me five dollars. With four chairs. A wooden one.

We didn't ask anybody to help us. Slowly but surely, me and Ray lifted those heavy washing machines out of the backyard to the front, by the road. The stack was so high that the trash man put a note on our door and told us that they would come only once a week to collect.

All of a sudden I could see the backyard. I realized the clothesline was still there. I couldn't see it before.

In the utility room there were tools rusted.

Paint in the can that was in there so long, all you had to do was turn it over, and it fell out in one lump. Paint thinner was there, open. He had boxes of nails piled up—we didn't realize that the box was wet, and when we picked it up the whole box came apart and all the nails scattered every whichaway. There were tools in that utility room that Daddy bought that had price tags on. The man never touched them. We still got those tools today.

On the outside of the house, where it was supposed to be white, it was black. We painted that.

We rented a buffer and got the floors buffed real good. But they still looked bad. Real dull. Mrs. Vane said, "Ruthie, get yourself some polyurethane. You put about three or four coats on there, I guarantee you the floor will look new." We did that, and the floors became shiny.

In the den where Daddy had tried to make a bar, you could see through the hole right into the kitchen. He never finished that, so I put edging around it. To make it look like a bar, I put a couple of bar stools in front of it, and a old-West curtain.

The glass door didn't have a curtain, so I bought some curtains and put them up, with a shade. We cleaned the bathroom and I wallpapered it, and now it looked like a new bathroom. New shower curtains, new everything.

Kitty said, "This can't be the same house."

"Yes, it *is* the same house."

She gave me some curtains for the middle bedroom.

It took us about six months to move all the junk out of the backyard. After that I said to Ray, "Look at these trees in the yard. They aren't even growing." I trimmed the branches on the trees, and within three weeks, the tree shoot up high and green. But we needed to do something else in the yard. I decided to start planting, to make the yard look like something.

I planted on both sides of the house and around the back. I planted azaleas, some gladios, some daisies, some salvias, pampas grass, zinnias. I planted everything I could get my hand on to make it look pretty. We bought a gazebo, we put that up, and I made a greenhouse cover for my plants. We bought two picnic tables to set out there. I planted crepe myrtles, plum trees, apple tree, couple of fig trees. I saved my money for all that, and I bought it when K-Mart and Wal-Mart had a special. I planted a bunch of mums in the yard, and I planted a Japanese shrub, and a lot of red-tips on the side of the house. And I planted four rosebushes.

Daddy had some old bricks, so I decided to make a walkway from the front steps to the road, bring it out and turn it so people could know not to drive to the door but go on the side. I bought pine bark and put it in the walkway where I had lined it off with bricks, so it would *look* like a walkway.

Daddy never said thank you. Never said it looked good.

Mr. Larue came over, and him and Daddy was sitting in the den. I was outside, sitting under the oak tree. The glass door was open. Mr. Larue said, "Hey, Fleetwood, your yard sure looking good."

"I ain't done none of that. Gal did that."

Mr. Larue came to the door and said, "Gal, you can come in my yard and do that."

"No, no, no, I got too much work to do here."

"Well, the yard sure looking better. And not only the yard. This house ain't even the same house that it used to be."

Daddy said, "Gal did that, too." But he never said thank you. Never did. Even though he saw the change in the house. He never told me it looked good.

Francene Topp's mother, Miss Regina, walked by. She stopped. She said, "Look like somebody new moved into this house." She had never seen curtains in the house. All she saw was junk in the yard, nobody never cutting the grass, she could not believe that was the same house.

And all the people in the neighborhood was really excited and wanted to know what was happening. Nosy Mrs. Carvey sent her daughter over to see what was happening. Mrs. Vane came. Florence and those came to Charleston to visit, and they were actually screaming when they came in. They were. They could not believe that I had done all that work.

The neighbors were happy that I was there. They didn't want me to leave. My neighbor across the street said now she could see my house from her house. Before, it was trucks and washing machines covering up the house. The house could have been a beautiful house but Daddy never did anything. He would bring junk and throw it on top of junk, but not just carry it way in the backyard—wherever he see a spot, *bam*, it was there.

Mrs. Vane said she used to be embarrassed by Daddy house. Now she start giving me sheets, curtains, material. . . . It seemed like the more I was doing in the house, people would start giving me more things. The Wickers had things that they didn't need, they claimed. Mrs. Vane had things she didn't need, Kitty started giving me things she didn't need. People were just so happy to see me out in the yard and see it was a real yard. Until they would come and say, "Now, when you plant those zinnias, don't plant them too close." I would bring a bush home and they would see me out in the yard standing there trying to figure out where to put it, and they would say "Hey, Ruthie, now when you plant that, where you going to put it at? We need to tell you, see, because we been planting since you were a little girl." They would tell me what to use and what not to use. They were so happy, they were just going on and on. Even the younger ones, people my age, started coming by the house and admiring the yard. When they

came in the house, they said, "Girl, what have
you done? Oh, my God. Gal, when you get
some time could you come and show me how
to do this?"

And I felt good about that.

I really felt good about it when my family,
Kitty and them, liked the house. Because they
knew how it had been. To hear that from them
really felt good, and to hear that they were
happy I was there. They don't care what I do to
the house, it was up to me, because it had never
looked good like that before. They said it looked
like a real house now, like somebody really
lived there, and don't stop doing what I'm
doing.

Everyone said, "This is a brand-new house,
this isn't the same house."

And the same time, they were saying, "This
isn't the same Ruthie." And I knew that I wasn't
the same.

A N D I R E A L L Y *felt* like it was my house. I said
to myself, "Well, this is my house. I can do what
I want to do. I'm going to do it and do it,
whether Daddy thanks me or not."

He never said a word. He look around, and
he see the change. But look like he would do
things in spite, because he knew I'd done the
work. He would out a cigarette on the wall. He
would drop his food on the floor. I gave him
clean ashtrays, but for spite he would use his

glass, put the cigarette in there. He would use his plate, spit in the plate.

I bought four Oriental-looking rugs—put one in the den, one in the hallway, one in the other hall, and one in my daughter room. I bought my other kids a big round rug. I bought new mattresses for the antique beds, those beds was too pretty for the mattress not to be looking good. Daddy had some closet doors that wouldn't open, I opened them—I just put that oil in there. I bought a new lock for the bathroom door. I cleaned the front door and put polyurethane on it, and it looked like a new door, a brand-new spanking door. I cleaned the chandelier up, I put in a new ceiling fan.

I used Daddy's Visa card for some of the things, and he knew that. I put two comforter sets on the card, which I gave Daddy one of those anyway, and I put another set of curtains on the card. I spent about $300 of Daddy's money. The rest we paid for, Ray and me. We bought all the mattresses, about $60 apiece. The gazebo cost $265. Rugs, $65 apiece, fan, $49. I cut corners, I got things on sale. Paint was kind of expensive because I wanted the gloss, that shiny paint, and buffing the floor costed a good bit of money. But Ray was working as a truck driver, and I was working. And we didn't have to pay rent or utilities. It was worth it to us, to have the house looking good.

* * *

I WAS WORRIED that Daddy would start doing the same things to my children that he had done to us. Sure enough, he started calling my boy. "Junior, go get Papa's shoes. Go get Papa's socks, get the lighter and cigarettes, go get a comb and comb Papa's hair."

My little boy said, "Mama, don't let him call me no more."

He started calling my daughter, Shana. "Go sweep that up. Answer that phone for me. Turn the TV on for me, change the channel, stand there and fix the aerial."

One day he grabbed her by the arm. When I walked in I could see her frisking, trying to get away from him. And she was screaming. I could see his hand on her. He had the grip on her. He was helpless in his chair, but he was strong enough to hold that child. Shana wasn't crying, but the tears were in her eyes real thick, and she was trying to get away, and he wouldn't let her go.

I almost went crazy. To see him, putting his hands on her—

"Daddy, turn her loose."

"Well, she been running—"

"*Turn her loose.* You are not going to do the same to her that you did to me. From now on, you want something, you do it yourself. Don't you ever touch her again."

He knew I meant it. From the look in my eyes. My eyes were bigger than big. He knew it. And he never put his hands on them again.

If I had let it go on, he would have beat them. I am sure he would. Ray Junior was scared of him, because of the tone of his voice. And Daddy had told him one time "Ask your mama how I used to beat her."

And I think he grabbed Shana like that because she look just like my grandmama. Just like her. And I know that reminded him of her. I think that's what made him grab her. I don't know if there was a picture in his mind of his wife, but Shana looked just like her.

But Daddy still was sick. His left arm, he couldn't hardly move it, but then when he moved it, it would shake. It would shake any time he tried to move it. So I decided he couldn't do anything to the kids. All he would do was ask me for a cigarette. All the time, cigarette, cigarette. I told him that if he smoke so much, he know the doctor told him that he was probably going to die off of that, but he didn't care.

My kids always brought home sheets of paper from school. I was cleaning up one day, picking up extra papers, and looking around at the house, straightening things, looking at the dining room . . . and all of a sudden I thought of my grandmother. It just hit me, that memory of her. I walked into the living room. I looked at her picture, and I remembered her gold teeth. They weren't fully gold—in the middle part you could still see the teeth, but around the edges was the gold. When I walked back into the dining room and I saw the school papers, it's like something just had me writing. I don't know what it was. I just started writing. That's what happened. I heard Daddy call me, and that just made me madder. And I said to myself, *I'm going to write a book. I'm going to write everything this man done to me and to this family, and killed my grandmother, and killed my mother too.* I blame him for that, because if he hadn't beaten her the way he did, she would never run away from me. I just had to do it. I just start thinking about my grandmother, and I looked at that picture, and I saw that gold on her teeth, and I just started writing.

chapter thirteen

but then daddy started getting worse and worse. He couldn't even hardly walk at all. I had to lift him out of the bed, to take him to the bathroom, but then sometimes he would pee, and pee all over me because I couldn't make it there in time. Ray was going off to work every day, and I noticed Kitty stopped coming by completely. She used to come but since we were there she just stopped coming. When it was time for me to put the insulin into Daddy's arm or his leg, he always get mad because he said I was sticking it in the wrong place or I was hurting him. So I told him to turn his behind over, and I stuck it in his butt. I was scared anyway to put the needle in him because I'm afraid of needles myself, and when I would get the little package of alcohol that you rub on the skin, as I would be rubbing him he would turn around and look at me to see what I'm doing.

I started thinking about the old times and the things he done to me when I was little. I said,

"Well, I'll fix him." I stabbed him with that needle real hard in his rear end.

He said, "Nigger, you ever do that again to me, you going to see heaven or hell." I'll never forget that. I thought it was funny, him saying that. But then I started giving him the insulin in his arm.

I noticed he was getting worse. He could hardly see. He only knew who you were when you got close up on him. And he never ever want to get up and go and take a bath. I had to get a dishpan and pull his drawers and T-shirt off and wash him. When I washed him between his privacy, he would lie there and look at me. I didn't want to touch it anyway, I told Ray from now on he's going to clean that part, I'm not going to clean that part at all.

I took Daddy to the doctor and they told him that they didn't want him to smoke anymore because his condition was getting worse. He cursed the doctor out, he said he was going to do what he want to do, because he is probably going to outlive the doctor.

ONE DAY he said he needed to go to Mississippi.

I said, "What you going to Mississippi for?"

He said he needed to see Beezy and Oscar. Kitty said, "Gal, any time somebody tell you something like that, he must be know he's probably going to die soon."

I said, "Nah, he probably just want to get out of here."

So we called Uncle Oscar, told him that Daddy wanted to come to Mississippi for a couple of weeks. He said, "Yeah, we can come get him, but we don't have any money."

I told Daddy what he said, so Daddy sent him some money to come. When they came, I told them, "Make sure when Daddy take this insulin, give it to him either in his butt, his leg, or his arm. And he must take that insulin three times a day, and you make sure it's on number thirty, no more than that." I said he may run out, but I gave them the prescription to go to any pharmacy to get it.

They took Daddy car back, with Daddy in the car, and two days later we got a phone call from Uncle Oscar.

I said, "Yeah, Uncle Oscar, how Daddy doing?"

"Clovis doing real good. But you know why I call you, we need some money down here. We need about three hundred dollars. Because, you know, it's going to be costing us to take care of Clovis."

"Uncle Oscar, we gave you five hundred dollars, and you just left the day before yesterday."

"All I know is, Clovis said to send three hundred dollars."

I had Daddy's little telecard at the credit union. Went in there. Got the money out. And I wired the money.

Two days later they called back and said they need two hundred more dollars. And I said, "I don't have the money, because I can't go in Daddy account like that." I told Kitty about it and Kitty said she is not going to send any money. So Florence, she was living near Uncle Oscar, she went ahead and gave him a hundred dollars and said for us to reimburse her later.

But after a few days Florence called, and she said, "Gal, y'all need to get Daddy back in South Carolina."

"What's going on?"

"You know I can't stand Uncle Oscar—and I can't stand Daddy either. I haven't been down there to see him since he came down here, but I sent Izzy down there to give them the money. And from what I heard, Daddy stays in his room and he is drinking every single day."

"Florence, you're kidding."

"No, I'm not kidding."

So I called Kitty on the phone, I said, "Kitty, we need to try to get Daddy back here in Charleston. I don't know what's happening."

She said, "Yeah, I think we better do something."

So I called down there and I told them to get Daddy up here to Charleston, I mean *up* to Charleston *now*, or else I will call the law enforcement and have him up here—with or without the car. They can keep the car down there.

So what happened, they came and they brought Daddy back.

I didn't even know who that man was when they came. I knew it was Daddy car. Uncle Oscar was in there, his son Clovis was in there, and Uncle Oscar had his lover in there, some lady—and there was one other person in the backseat. Ray went and opened up the door, and he said, "Ruthie, is that—that's Mr. Fleetwood?"

I said, "That can't be him."

When I looked at him, he was skinnier than a pretzel stick. He was so skinny. He had on a brown shirt and a checker black-and-white pants, and he always wear Stacy Adams shoes, he had on a pair of Stacy Adams. His pants were hanging down off of him with no belt on it, and when I got closer to him, I saw he had on no underwear, no nothing. His breath smelled like I don't know what. He couldn't walk.

I said, "Ray, help me take him in the house."

It was like dragging a dead person. We took him in, and we sat him on his bed. I said, "Daddy, you want some coffee?"

He said yeah, he want some coffee.

I said, "Uncle Oscar, what's wrong with Daddy?"

"Gal, you know how Clovis go. You can't tell Clovis nothing."

So I told my husband to go ahead on and put the coffee on, and he fix some coffee for everybody.

Uncle Oscar was worried about getting Daddy's rifle. Daddy had a rifle in the closet. So I said, "Uncle Oscar, did you give Daddy the insulin three times a day, like you was supposed to?"

"Oh, yeah, he got it."

"Well, I need his medication. Did he have any this morning?"

He said no.

So I grabbed the needle and I stuck it in the insulin to pull it out, me not even paying attention to the bottle, but before I could put the insulin in Daddy arm, the phone rang, and it was Kitty. She was working at South Carolina General Hospital. She said, "Gal, Daddy home?"

I said, "Yeah," I said, "Kitty, you won't believe it, girl. Daddy didn't have no underwear on, his breath smells, look like nobody didn't never comb his hair," I said, "Kitty, he is skinnier than a pretzel."

Kitty said, "Oh, Lord, no."

I said, "Yes, ma'am. I'm going to tell Uncle Oscar and them that they are going to leave this house and we're not going to give them anything." So I told Uncle Oscar, I said, "Uncle Oscar, I'm not trying to be mean, but," I said, "hey, I don't think Daddy been tooken care of, at all."

He said if I didn't like it then I should have had my black ass down there doing it myself. He was mad. He got in Daddy car and drove straight off with his son and his lady friend. I called Kitty and I said, "Kitty, he even took the car!"

Kitty said, "Don't worry about it, when you

get some time and I got some time, we'll go down to Mississippi ourself to pick up the car."

I thought Uncle Oscar and them had left to go to Mississippi. No, they didn't. They went to the store to go buy liquor and beer. And when they came back, Ray had just gotten through giving my granddaddy some coffee, and all of a sudden, I could hear something wasting all over the floor, and I thought he had spilled his coffee. But that wasn't what it was. He was throwing up. He was throwing up bad. I never smelt that smell in my whole life. It was so strong until I threw up. I ran to the glass door, I opened up the door and had to catch my own breath. And Daddy just kept throwing up, kept throwing up.

Ray came outside and he said, "Ruthie, you all right?"

I said, "Don't worry about me, go see what's wrong with Daddy."

Uncle Oscar and them came back, and I said, "Uncle Oscar, what is wrong with Daddy?"

"I don't know what wrong with Clovis. I told you, Clovis head hard."

I said, "This just ain't right." Something told me to look at that bottle of insulin. I grabbed the bottle.

"This is what you been giving him? Look, this is not the right insulin! This insulin is lavender. The insulin we was giving him was like clear water."

I thought, maybe the pharmacy in Mississippi made a mistake.

I said, "I'm going to call Daddy doctor." His doctor name was Dr. Trentum, he works up there at South Carolina General. I called Dr. Trentum, I said, "Dr. Trentum, listen. This is Clovis Fleetwood granddaughter, Ruthie." I said, "Right now Daddy is so sick, I need to bring him to the hospital. I need to bring him right now."

He said there wasn't nothing wrong with Daddy except cigarettes and liquor. He started going on and on and on, so I hung up the phone on him. Called the hospital back, and asked for Kitty's extension. Kitty said, "Don't call the doctor again, you just bring him on here, in the emergency room."

Me and Ray had to try to get Daddy dressed, and put drawers on him, and clothes on him, and then I made sure I make him rinse out his mouth because it smelled so horrible, then we finally got Daddy in the car and I took him to the South Carolina General. Kitty was at the emergency entrance waiting on me. We put him in the wheelchair and took him in.

When they examined Daddy, they said that he was dehydrated. I really didn't know what dehydrated meant. They said he had accumulated more alcohol in his system than he was supposed to have, and all that they could do was give him some pills and the regular insulin.

Kitty started crying and acting crazy. We was there about an hour, hour and a half. When I brought Daddy back home, it was like the bad insulin that they had given him started working on Daddy's mind. He was calling us every name, people name off the wall, people that don't even exist in the family.

I said, "Daddy, you want me to put a cold towel on your head?"

He just looked at me. Then his eyes start rolling back in his head. I got scared.

I said, "Ray, please call Kitty back again. I don't know what's happening." And Daddy brother sat his ass right there. He didn't even try to help me, he didn't try to do anything.

I said, "Uncle Oscar, what did you give Daddy when he was in Mississippi?"

"Well, I can't help it if Clovis want to take a drink."

"You know Daddy was not supposed to drink! You know you cannot drink when you're taking insulin. And where's his clothes? He left here with three pair of Stacy Adams, now he come back here with one Stacy Adam. All those name-brand clothes that he had, he ain't came back with none of them. Some old pants somebody give him."

Uncle Oscar said he didn't have nothing to do with that. He said he was leaving. "Where is that rifle Clovis told me that he got in the closet?"

"Ain't nobody getting this rifle out of this closet."

"Clovis told me he had some antique guns that he got in Japan."

I told him I didn't know where they were. I couldn't talk to Uncle Oscar no more, I was so concerned about Daddy sick, and he was shaking, shaking, shaking, shaking in the bed. My kids was peeping to the door. I told them, "Get on out of here. Get on out of here now." All of a sudden Daddy threw up again, and he threw up all over my shoes.

Ray said, "Ruthie, get out of here. I'll handle this."

Kitty called back and said, "Gal, I'm just going to take the day off. I'm coming over."

So she came over. She said, "I can't believe this is Daddy. Daddy didn't leave like that."

"I know, Kitty. He been throwing up ever since he came. And Dr. Trentum only gave him some pills and some more insulin, but he got to know Daddy need to be admitted in the hospital."

Daddy didn't even know who Kitty was. He was just lying there and his eyes was rolled up in his head. We put another cold rag on his face and we put a cold rag on his neck.

Then he looked like he was coming out of whatever he was in. He said, "Kitty, I can tell you right now. You know what Gal and Ray been doing to me? They been pulling my drawers down and my pants down and they would beat me with a belt every day. They whip me. They beat me."

Kitty turned around and she looked at me. I was stunned.

I said, "Kitty, you know better."

She started crying. "Gal, you mean to tell me, all this time you and Ray been beating Daddy?"

"Kitty, look at him. Daddy, you are *lying*!"

"I ain't lying, nigger. You did it. Y'all beat me last night. Y'all beat me the day before. Y'all beat me the day before that."

I said, "You wasn't even here! We never touched him, Kitty!"

"Gal, I can't believe that y'all come here, live here in Daddy house, don't pay no rent, no light, no water, no food or anything, and you was beating him."

I stood there and I just looked at her. "Kitty, you know good and well I didn't beat Daddy. Any bruise on his body? Daddy, tell her—"

"No, because y'all lock me up in the room and y'all fed me out of a bowl—"

"Kitty, it's a lie!" I thought he was doing the same old thing, trying to divide us.

Kitty said, "Daddy, now I know for a fact Gal ain't never feed you out of a bowl. I know another thing, this is going to be the last time. You ain't never going back to Mississippi no more."

Uncle Oscar and them didn't leave. I figured they were going to go. They didn't go. They said they were going to stay, he wanted to see how his brother come over his sickness. They stayed for about a week. Then next thing I know, me and Ray and our kids went out, and when we came back, the car was gone, Daddy was gone, Uncle Oscar and them was gone.

They took that man back to Mississippi without our permission.

They got there that night. Who calls but Florence. Florence said, "Gal, why y'all let Daddy come back to Mississippi and you know that all he's going to do here is drink?"

"Florence, we just got back here. We been out all day, we didn't know they was going to take him."

I called Kitty and let her know what was going on, so Kitty came all the way from Wambaw back to the house. Next thing I know, we got a call on the line to be a collect call from Clovis Fleetwood.

"Kitty, that's Daddy on the phone right now!"

But when I told the operator yes, I would accept the call, it wasn't Daddy. It was Uncle Oscar. He said that he wanted us to send the deed and the title to Daddy house to give to him, because Daddy told him that he could have the deed and the title to the house. That's when everything went to pieces.

I didn't know what he was talking about. He said that he wanted the deed and title to all the land that Daddy owned in Mississippi, too.

I said, "Kitty, girl, something is going on here. Here, you take the telephone."

Kitty started crying on the phone. She cries too much. I needed someone to figure this thing out. I went in the living room to pick up the telephone to hear what was going on. I could hear Daddy on the other line.

He was saying "Yeah, that's what I said. I need the deed, and I need the title to the house, because I want it to be in the power of Oscar hand."

Kitty said, "Daddy, do you know what you doing? Do you really, really know what you're doing?"

"Look here, I know what I'm doing. I'm not coming back to South Carolina."

That's when I said, "Oh, hell, no. Ain't nobody sending no deed and no title. If Uncle Oscar listening on the other end, I'm going to tell him this, too. He is not getting any deed and title to no house." I said, "Y'all don't even have to bring him back to South Carolina. I will call the law enforcement, and I will be determined. He will come back to South Carolina."

Kitty said, "Gal, we not going to go through all that. Look here, we just going to go ahead on and go to Mississippi. We just going to pick Daddy up, and that's just it."

I said, "No, no, no, Kitty, I'm not going to do all that."

They hung the phone up on us. Then Florence called, and Florence said, "Uncle Oscar knocking on my door, say Daddy want the deed and title for the house."

I said, "He ain't getting no deed and title for the house. What does he want it for? I don't think he knows what he's doing. He already spent up the limit on his Visa card." The bills was coming to the house. All this gas, food, even the jewelry store, over the amount that Daddy was supposed to spend. We got all these bills in the mail.

I said, "Kitty, I don't care what happens anymore."

The next week, they brought Daddy back home. They said they were tired of him. I told Uncle Oscar, "If anybody think they getting deed and title to this house, they tell a lie. That man worked too hard. Why would he give you the deed and title to his house when he got all these kids to leave behind? How you expect him to give you the deed and title?"

"Well, that's what Clovis told me. Matter of fact, I don't even have to listen to you. Clovis done told me to take the car and I could take it back to Mississippi."

"Take the damn car, you can have it. We don't care. Take the car. When we get a chance, we'll come to Mississippi and get it back."

He said he didn't have any money to go back to Mississippi with. You know what I did? I took the car, I full up the car with gas, I had the oil and everything checked. I said, "If you can't make it with this down there, that's too bad. I'm not giving you any extra money."

That afternoon a man came over to the house. Brought fish, shrimp, oysters, some of everything, in coolers. I thought Daddy had it to be bought for us. But Daddy said, "Oscar, when you go, make sure you give Pam, Evelyn, and Florence, make sure you give them their portion of the seafood." Uncle Oscar took everything, and took it all back to Mississippi, and he didn't give them anything. Nothing at all.

Daddy said, "Gal, you know, when y'all feed me, y'all don't have to put my food on the plate. Just go ahead on and put it in a bowl and push it to me and close the door."

I thought he was lying the time before, but now I thought, the man is getting crazy. From all the bad things he done, maybe his conscience is telling him he deserve that—somebody feeding him in a bowl, closing the door on him.

chapter fourteen

w h e n   w e   d r o v e to Mississippi to get the car, I went and visited Aunt Beezy, she was back in her first house. Sat on that old porch where Mr. Slide used to eat his onion. Looked out at that big pasture.

She said, "Gal, you know I got a picture of your mama."

"You—you have a picture? Oh, Aunt Beezy, can I have it please?"

"No, because if I give you that picture, you ain't going to never send it back."

"I'll get a copy, and I'll send it back."

"Okay, I'll let you have it, but you make sure you send me the original back."

When I looked at that picture, I said, "Aunt Beezy, how old was she?"

"I don't know how old she was. Probably the age you were when y'all were down here."

"No, I doubt that. She's older. Maybe she's nine years old." And then I start thinking, I said, "I wonder where's that dress, that she had on." And then I said, "Look like she is at a church, with a Bible in her hand." And then I said, "Dang, she had long hair. That means I'm supposed to have long hair." And I looked at it again, and I said, "My nose isn't like that." I kept looking at it, and I said, "My eyes ain't like that." But her mouth looked like mine, and the shape of her face. And I said, "If I had those shoes and those clothes today, they'd be antique." And I was so excited about that picture, I couldn't wait to get back to Charleston to show it to Ray and Mrs. Vane.

Mrs. Vane said, "Ruthie, you need to get that picture re-done and put it in a frame. That's the only picture you got of your mama." And I said, "I know. I'm going to never let anybody get this picture." I didn't send it back to Mississippi. I still have that picture today.

She looks happy. I was really wondering to myself, was that took in Charleston? I don't know. I really wanted to know, did Daddy took her somewhere to take that picture? Did Grandmama take her somewhere? Who took her? I just don't know. And I wondered, when I was that age did I look like that? I doubt it, because I had buckwheat plaits on my head.

And for the picture to be black-and-white I think is real pretty. Real pretty. I even like the cracks in it. That's the way it was when I got it.

DADDY WAS getting harder to take care of. He said crazy things. When I turned the TV on, he told me turn it off. He said, "Don't give me no

TV. Just lock me up in the room with a little liquor."

I said, "You know you ain't supposed to have none."

I noticed his hands was shaking while he was eating—shaking up and down, up and down, up and down. And the spoon was hitting on the plate.

"Let me feed you, Daddy."

But as I was feeding him, he gave me the evil look. The look I remember, the most evil look in the world. It was how he used to look at me when he beat me.

And I burned him. With the hot soup. I burned him with the hot soup. Instead of putting it in his mouth I threw it in his face.

I had to get out of the room. I had to ask Ray to come in there and finish feeding him.

That night Ray and me lift him up, put him in the tub, and Ray bathe him off. I said, "I don't even want to look at him anymore." Ray dried him, put on his clothes. Everybody went to bed.

In the middle of the night, I hear "Gal! Gal, Gal." I got up.

He said, "Give me a cigarette."

"No, I'm not going to give you no more cigarette."

Every night he kept calling me. If I didn't come, he would wiggle his butt out of that bed until he fall on the floor. When I heard the bam, I said "Oh my God, oh, Ray, come on, please, let's go pick Daddy up."

"Ruthie, if he call you in there one more time tonight, I don't know what I'm going to do to him."

Daddy called me again and again. I said, "This time I'm not budging. I'm not moving."

"Gal! Help! Help, help, Gal, help, help!"

I really didn't know whether to go in there or not. I said the hell with it, I'm not going in there.

"Gal, help, help!"

"Oh, Ray, please go in there and see what's wrong with that man."

He fallen up behind the bed. He was stuck. Ray said, "Mr. Fleetwood, I'm not going to pull you up one more time. If you wiggle your behind out this bed again, you going to have to stay on this floor until we get here in the morning."

Next day, I called Kitty at the hospital. I said, "Kitty, Daddy call us every single night, twenty-four hours a day, constantly, constantly. I am tired of getting up all night long. I got to baby-sit him all day. We have got to find a solution to this. Every time I put the Pamper on him, he pull those suckers off of him and piss and shit in the bed."

I bought some big pins for the Pampers. He pulled those big old pins out. So I went to Bi-Lo, and I start looking in the tape direction. There was this tape that when you try to tear it, it's got threads in it. I said, this is the solution right here. So at nighttime after we bathe him off, we would get that tape, and we would *wrap* it around that Pamper, and he would just look at us.

He said, "If I got to go to the bathroom tonight, you got to take me."

"No, that's why you got some Pampers on. I'm not getting out of bed."

That night he kicking the wall, just kicking the wall.

Ray went in there. "Mr. Fleetwood, what is it you want now?"

"All I want me is a little bit of water."

"I'm going to give you this water, and that's going to be it for the rest of the night." Ray gave him the water. He had to hold the water up to his mouth, because Daddy hand shaking so bad he couldn't drink it.

No more than five minutes. "Gal, help! Help!" This went on and on. My kids woke up. I said, "Daddy what is it that you want?"

"How in the hell you expect me to get up and pee, you got this damn big Pamper on me."

"I'm going to *keep* that Pamper on you." I said, "Ray, come here. Look in that last bedroom. Get me two double sheets. Tie them together." I pulled Daddy into the middle of the bed, and we tied the sheets together and put them underneath the mattress, Ray pulled one side and I grabbed the other side, and we started to tie it over him in the bed.

"You can holler all night that you want. But

you not going to fall on the damn floor no more."

As we were trying to tie the sheet together, the phone ring. It was Kitty. Daddy hollered, "Help, help, they're killing me."

Kitty said, "Gal, what are you doing?"

I said, "Kitty, look here. *You* live here and let Daddy call you all night long. He'll wiggle out the bed, he'll call to use the bathroom—"

"What he want the bathroom for when he got Pampers?"

I said, "Kitty, I'm getting ready right now to tie him enough so that if he squirm to the edge of the bed, he can't fall off."

Kitty said, "I'm on my way."

She was there in fifteen minutes. She said, "Daddy, now you know you can't call Gal all night long. If you don't keep still in this bed—"

Daddy said, "I done tell Gal, if she put that damn sheet on me, she going to see heaven or hell."

Kitty said, "Come on, Gal, let's do it."

We tied the sheet. I thought it was a sad thing to do, but I had no choice. So we tied it across him.

Kitty left. She said, "I don't see how you can handle it."

Next thing I know, "Gal, Gal, please come help me."

He done wiggle so much, the sheet slip out and tangle around his legs. I didn't know what else to do. I said, I'm going to tie his two damn

foot to the post, and I'm going to tie one hand
to the post. And I did it. By myself. Went back
to my room.

He had a nightstand by the bed. I guess he hit
it with his loose hand, he knocked the phone off
the hook, and I don't know how that man did it
but he wiggle out of those sheets again. I heard
BAM. When I went in there I saw blood on the
floor. He had hit his head on the edge of the
nightstand, and it was bleeding. I said to myself, "They are going to really think I been
beating this man."

Daddy got sick worse and worse. It was getting so bad for him now, it was like he was really paralyzed. He couldn't move his own body.
I told Kitty that we needed to take him back to
the hospital.

But Dr. Trentum said Daddy was fine! He said
the only problem is that he is drinking and
smoking. I told the man, Daddy might be smoking but he is not drinking. He said, "Yeah, Mr.
Fleetwood *is* drinking. The best thing I can do is
tell you to put him in a home."

"No, I ain't going to put him in no home."

A couple of days went by. Daddy started
throwing up again. This time it was red. Then it
was brown. I didn't know what to do. I said,
"Kitty, if I bring him in, it ain't going to do no
good. They going to tell me there ain't nothing
wrong with him."

Mr. Wicker down the street came to see us.
He knocked on the door. At the time, Daddy

was throwing up. Mr. Wicker said, "What's wrong with Mr. Fleetwood?"

I said, "Mr. Wicker, I don't know, Daddy been getting worse and worse."

"Did you call the naval hospital?"

"No, sir, I took him to South Carolina General."

He said, "Look here, that man done serve his time, you need to take him to the naval hospital."

So I called the naval hospital. I told them that Daddy is a retired navy man, and he is getting sick and sicker and there is nothing I can do. I gave them the social security number and all these numbers, all that information, and the man asked me why didn't I call them before? And why didn't I bring Daddy to the hospital a long while back if I knew what was going on?

I told him I didn't know!

"Well, bring him on to the hospital right now."

I called Kitty. Kitty came zooming there. We had to bathe Daddy off, wash him, and get him dressed. Mr. Wicker said, "I'm going with y'all." So we got in Kitty's van. We got there within seven minutes. They told us to come through the emergency entrance. When we got there they took a wheelchair out, and they put Daddy in there. All we knew was Daddy head was limping down.

Kitty started that crying. When the doctor examined Daddy, he said, "Are you two the daughters?" and we said yeah.

He said, "I can't believe that you actually let this man sit home all this time and didn't bring him to the emergency room. You could have killed him yourself."

I said, "Listen, we don't have anything to do with this. He been down in Mississippi, he was taking the wrong insulin."

He said yes, they found the wrong stuff still in his body.

I said, "We didn't give it to him."

He said, "We found alcohol in his system."

Kitty said, "Oh, my God."

I said, "We didn't know what was happening. We didn't know what was going on."

Next thing you know, another doctor came in there and examined Daddy. "Why didn't y'all bring him in here before?"

"I'm going to tell you the same I told the other man. We didn't know what was going on. His own doctor said nothing was wrong."

They called Dr. Trentum and requested Daddy's medical records. Dr. Trentum refused to send them. When the third doctor came in he said, "The best thing we can do for Mr. Fleetwood is put him in the X-ray." They wheeled him out and took him there. It was a round circle thing, and he went in, laying on a bed. We sat there for two whole hours. The man came down. He said, "I need you two to come here to me. I'm going to tell you, there is nothing we can do at this moment, except send him down to the Veterans Hospital downtown, because he has pockets of blood splattered all in the brain. It would be different if he had blood in one area, but it's spread so badly, if we try to operate it can kill him."

Kitty said, "Oh, my God, my God."

I started thinking to myself, I knew how he got it. All those nights that he hollered and called me and fall out the bed, he was bumping his head, all this time, and the blood was traveling all over. I didn't tell them that, but I told Kitty.

They told us go ahead on down to the Veterans Hospital and they would bring Daddy down there. When we got there, they already had him in ICU. We had to go meet another doctor. He kept asking what happened. Why didn't we bring Daddy there earlier? Don't we know that he could have died?

All this was on us, and we was lost. We didn't know what to do. We asked them where he was, and they said he was in ICU, they don't know whether to operate or not to operate, because he's got pockets of blood in the head. I said, "Oh, Lord." Another doctor came in. "Can you tell us what happened?"

"I told you. I told them, I told you. I'm not going to tell anyone else."

Kitty said, "Calm down."

"I'm not going to calm down. They act as though we are the cause of this."

The doctor said, "Did you bring the bottle?"

"It's right there."

"Don't you know this can kill him?"

They took us into a room. "Could you tell us how your father got this?" I mean this went on and on and on. It was morning now. We had been there all night.

I said, "I'm ready to go home. I am sorry to have to be hearing what's happened to Daddy, but Kitty, there is nothing we can do. What can we do?"

Four days later they took him out of ICU, and they put him in a regular room. We went there every single day. We called Florence, we called Naomi, we told all them what was happening with Daddy. But they said he done that on his own. He knew he wasn't supposed to be drinking. They are not coming to see him or anything.

"Kitty, what kind of thing is that? They ain't going to even come and see Daddy." We thought they were going to come anyway—but they never came. They didn't even call to see how he was doing.

We'd go there from morning till night. I said, "Kitty, I'm staying away from my own family. I can't even see my own kids. This man done put us through so much hell, do we got to be sitting here every day?"

"Well, Gal, there ain't nobody else. Florence ain't coming. You know Naomi ain't coming, and you know Pam and Evelyn don't give a hoot about him."

I said, "Not even Sylvie. Sylvie's not even coming."

"I know one thing. We can give account for what we did. The Lord above handle all that."

So we stayed there. Stayed there.

The sixth day, I turned the TV on, and Kitty was there making jokes with Daddy to see if he would laugh. She said, "Daddy, how does it feel now that you haven't smoked any cigarettes in quite some time?"

He turned to the side and he looked at me. *"Change that damn channel."*

I looked at him. "You mean to tell me, you on your deathbed, and you still talking trash to me? Kitty, to hell with him. I'm going out the damn door." I was in the hall, and I was crying. I was upset. I said to myself, This damn man, after all this—here he is on death's bed and still acting stupid.

Kitty said, "Gal, don't worry about it. You know Daddy is like that."

"I don't care. Tomorrow you come by yourself. I'm not coming back anymore."

But then I thought—he is going to die. So let his ass die, and I ain't going to treat him bad. I went back in the room and he just looked at me. He looked at me the kill look. The nurses came in to check his temperature and give him his medication. We went and got something to eat.

When we came back in the room he was

asleep. I said, "Kitty, girl, you don't know how glad I am that he's sleeping. I can't stand even the way he look at me."

DADDY WAS in that hospital two weeks. He got worse but there was nothing those people could do for him. They told us to look for a nursing home.

I said, "Oh, Lord, Kitty, I don't want to do that to that man."

"Gal, that's up to you. You want him to come back home?"

"No, no, no, no, no."

We searched and we looked, and we searched and we looked, and we search and we search. The only home we could come up with was out in the country, down there towards Onion Creek. They told us when we found it to let them know and they would take him on over there themselves. They wanted us to take his stuff back home and get the belongings we wanted him to have at the nursing home.

Kitty said, "Gal, do you want to go with me?"

"I may as well. I been with you from this to that, so I may as well."

When we went in there, those people looked crazy. There were people walking down the hall that looked like they were abused people. Kitty started crying again. "Oh, Gal, you think we did the right thing?"

"I don't know. I really don't know. Now I'm scared. What if we put Daddy in here, then something happens, it's going to be on our conscience."

They told us that they put Daddy in a room with another black man, a older man. But this man could get about and walk. As we were walking down the hallway I was peeping in all the people rooms, just to see who was in there. There was a white couple in there, old people. And there was a nurse walking past me, and I said, "Why y'all got this man and lady in there? Why would you have a man in there with a woman?" She said that they were husband and wife, and their kids put them in there together.

Daddy bed was right next to the window, and it was pretty, it was real pretty outside. You could see all the trees. Daddy didn't have a TV, but the closet was big, and the man in the room, he hailed us. But Daddy didn't talk too much. He didn't say anything. He didn't know what was happening.

"Kitty, how long are we going to stay here today?"

"We ain't going to stay long. But we're coming back in the morning."

The next morning she came to the house. We stopped by Eckerd Drug Store. She said, "Let's find Daddy a pair of shades. Let's find him a hat or something like that." We found a cool pair of shades for him, and a little cool little hat.

When we got near the home, we saw this white man walking toward the highway. He end up in the middle of the street. Cars were blow-

ing. He was running away from the place. He
was running away.

The doctors and nurses raced out there to get
him back. But when I saw the way they handled
that man, right then I said, "Oh, Kitty, they going to kill Daddy in here. They going to kill that
man." As they were chasing him, they were
making him more frightened, he was going farther on out. People stopped in the highway.
When they grabbed him, he was fighting them.
And they threw him down, they put their elbow
in his neck. It was rough. And he was a old
man. And I figured, a old person like that, you
can break their bones real quick. And the way
they were dragging him back to that building—
that's what I didn't like, and that's what made
me wonder how they was going to do Daddy.

"Oh, my God, Gal, do you think we—"

"Don't ask that question no more. The man is
here. And I feel free. I can sleep at night, nobody is calling my name. You just don't know
the relief that I feel." But I told Kitty I wasn't
going in until I see what they do to this man in
the street. When they finally got him closer to
the door, that's when we got out the van. The
nurse said to the man, "And *where* were you going?"

"Home." That's all the man said. "Home,
home, home." He had on pajamas. No shoes.

Kitty said, "Come on, Gal. Let's go."

This lady was in the hallway, just twining her
hair, twisting it. You can tell she keep twisting it

so much that she got some bald spots on her head. I said, "Kitty, this place is bad." I said, "Wait a minute, let's go in the cafeteria, and see what they eating in there."

But it looked like they were feeding the people pretty well. When we got closer to where we thought Daddy was at, I said, "Kitty, are we going the wrong direction? Whyn't we go and ask one of the nurses."

When we got there to where the nurses was supposed to be, there was no nurse up there. There was no nurse nowhere to be found. Nowhere.

So we walked around until we did find Daddy's room. When we went in there, they had a strap around Daddy's bed—but he had fallen out the side, and his neck was hung into the strap! He was *hanging*!

Kitty dropped her glasses. "Oh, my God, Gal!"

I said, "Push him up—push him up."

Kitty push him and I pull him. We push and we pull, and we got his neck out, and we got him in the bed. Kitty said, "Oh, God, what are they doing? Oh, Gal, we did the wrong thing."

"Kitty, I don't know. I don't know. I don't see no nurse. I don't see nobody nowhere."

"Oh, Gal, you think that we—"

"*Don't* ask that question again! Just help me. Stop crying. Go get a wheelchair. Let's get him out of this room *now*."

Got the wheelchair. As we was putting Daddy

in the wheelchair, a nurse came in. "What are y'all—"

I said, "Look here. When the last time did anybody come and check on him? We found him strapped up and hanging, he was actually hanging in the bed!"

She told us that they come in there every thirty minutes to check on him.

"Did anybody give him a bath?"

"Yes, somebody gave him a bath."

"Ain't no way. His Pamper was pissed completely up, his bed was wet. It's being paid for. Now, we going to take him outside in the sunlight for a while. When we come back in this building, I want his bed changed. I want to have some clean towels in there. And the stuff that we brought in here the day before, it's gone. Where is it?"

She said that she didn't know. People wander up and down the hallway.

We put Daddy in the wheelchair. We had to lift each leg up. As we got towards the double door that opens up, the sun was real bright. Kitty put the shades on Daddy, real dark shades. And I sat the hat on top of his head.

Me and her both walked around in front of him and we looked at him.

"Kitty, look how cool Daddy is. Daddy, you look cool today, hunh?"

He was just sitting there with his arms folded one on top of the other. He didn't say nothing.

"Kitty, come on, let's go." We run with the

wheelchair, I mean, we was pushing it and running and laughing, to try to make a joke with him. But he never smiled.

Kitty said, "You want to smell that flower over there?"

He didn't say a word.

I reached in my pocket and lit a cigarette. I was smoking it.

Then he knew who I was.

"Gal. Let me have a puff of that."

I said, "No, no, I can't let you have none of this." I blew the smoke in his face. I said, "Mmmm. Tasty, ain't it?"

Kitty said, "Gal, don't do that."

"Kitty, come on, let's go back inside. It's too hot out here." We went back inside. He still sat in the wheelchair.

He looked like a ghost with bones.

I asked the lady was it time to feed him, and we told them that we would do it. The little bit that he did eat, it wasn't much. Mostly they were giving him liquid stuff, because it was hard for him to even swallow.

Kitty said, "Well, Daddy, me and Gal going to go now. We'll come back tomorrow."

"Florence? Florence? That you, Florence?"

Florence wasn't even there. He just start calling her name.

SO WHEN WE got back to the house, we called Florence. "You need to come up here, Daddy is calling your name."

And it was coming close to Christmas, too. So they all came, Florence, Pam, Evelyn, and Sylvie. The next day we all went to see Daddy.

Florence is tough, Florence is a hard person to cry—but when we went in there to see him, she cried. She ran out the room, she couldn't stay. Pam stood there and just looked at him. But the look she gave him was "You deserve to be in here, and I feel no sorrow or pain for you." That was the look that she gave him. They didn't stay in that room no more than five minutes. Me and Kitty stayed in the room.

"Kitty, you saw that? They ain't even stay that long, and dammit, they going back damn tomorrow!"

When we went out in the hall, Florence said, "Y'all know we can't stay because we had already plan to come down for Christmas."

I said, "Florence, y'all shouldn't go, you know."

"Why shouldn't we go?"

"Daddy's on the critical list right now."

"Well, we have to go. But I have a feeling we going to have to turn right back around and come back again because he's going to die."

The nurse came and said it was time for them to give him a sit shower, sitting down in the stall. She said it would take a while, so we said we would come back the following day.

Florence and them went home. Kitty went by herself the next day to see Daddy.

She called me from there. Talking in a weak voice.

"Oh, Gal, it's Daddy. I was walking down the hall and Daddy fall. He collapsed. And all of a sudden they was doing CPR on him, they was pounding his chest. I can't talk, Gal. He's going to die."

"Kitty, what are you saying?"

Kitty husband came on the phone, Luther. "Gal, Mr. Fleetwood has collapsed. They are doing CPR on him. They're pumping him."

I heard the people on the intercom saying, "Get a helicopter, get a helicopter." Before they could put him on the helicopter he fell again, and he died instantly, on the floor, in the hallway.

Kitty was standing right there. She saw all of that. She saw everything. Luther said, "Gal, I got to go because Kitty is trying to bring your daddy back alive. She's saying, 'God, don't take my Daddy.'"

I immediately called Florence in Mississippi.

"Florence—"

"Gal, don't tell me."

"Yes. Daddy is dead."

She cried again, right then on the phone, and we both were sniffing and crying. After I hung up from Florence, I called Naomi in Georgia.

"Naomi, Daddy is dead."

"Gal, no! I don't know what to do. That means I got to get my kids out of school...."

Cass ain't home. . . . but Gal, I'll be there tomorrow."

I called all the relatives, friends, neighbors, and his ex-lovers. It didn't seem real, because I always thought he would outlive us all and never die.

WHEN DADDY was alive, he beat me with his hands, with sticks, with extension cords. He's dead and gone now and he never could say he saw Gal cry.

So why was I crying when he died? I wasn't even his blood, but I still felt that he was Daddy. He was the only one that I had.

chapter fifteen

the next day, everybody was there.
I never knew a funeral would be so hectic. All
the uncles from Baltimore, Maryland, and everybody from everywhere came down. The
house was full of people, so many people we
couldn't sleep, we couldn't rest. Kitty was crying so much her eyes were swollen, you
couldn't see the whites.

But some of the people weren't sad at all.
They looked more happy than anything. All
they was worried about was finding his insurance paper. And looked to me like they were
more interested in them eating than in anything
else.

Kitty and me were trying to get the burial ar-
rangements together, calling the person to get
the casket. Daddy never attended no church, so
we didn't know where we was going to have
the funeral at, even though we grew up right
there in Hungry Neck, one block from Second
Zion. That's the church and Sunday School we
went to, but Daddy never went. We didn't

know what preacher to call, we said golly, we can't call nobody because he never served time in the church. We had to try to find people to sing, the whole works.

Kitty said, "Gal, you write a lot. You write the tribute for the funeral program."

"I can't do that."

"Well, ain't nobody else going to do it."

Somehow we got to talk to the preacher at Second Zion and talked him into having the funeral there. We went looking for a suit for Daddy, try to find the best suit we could find. We didn't try to find the most expensive casket, but the best one that we could get—a casket that was blue, baby blue, with doves flying in the air, with the clouds on it.

I thought, well, now that he is gone, maybe the family will change. I knew from Ray's people what a family was supposed to be, and I thought maybe now since I fixed the house and everything, they will be like sisters to me. Daddy is not here to cause us trouble and pain. I thought we would all be pulling together now.

Pam came into the room Daddy used to sleep in. I heard her fumbling in there.

I said, "Pam, what are you looking for?"

"I might could use some of this stuff that Daddy left in the drawer."

"How can you think about that now, when this man is not even buried yet?"

I wasn't ready for what she said next. I didn't know it was coming. Pam always used to call me in the summer and beg me to let Shana come stay with them. I thought she cared for me, at least enough to want my daughter with her.

But she said, "Hey, I don't know why you worried about it, because he ain't your daddy. You don't even belong here. We all are sisters, and you are invading on us. You are no kin to us. *You don't belong in the house.*"

That was a total surprise to me. And I wasn't tough no more. I started crying. It was like I fell apart.

But she kept on. "You are nothing to us," she said, "and we want you out of the house. And if Daddy left anything for you, I am going to get a lawyer to make sure you don't get a damn penny."

"P-Pam, when Daddy was sick and on the d-dying bed, you didn't even pick the phone up to say how you doing."

She said, "I don't care how you feel about me. I'm his daughter. Florence and Kitty's his daughter. Sylvie's his daughter, Naomi and Evelyn are his. You are nothing."

"My mother was your oldest sister—"

"That don't matter to me at all."

What made it worse, she didn't even know the will yet. But I knew the will, or one part of it anyway, because Kitty said that she had to tell me, she want me to be aware of it. I knew that Daddy had left me out. Everybody else was in the will, but he had left me out completely.

Florence and Pam wanted to get the will to find out what was in there for everybody. Pam just knew that Daddy left the house for her. She said, "If Daddy left this house to me, you and your kids and husband will pack your bags, and you're going to get the hell out of my house. I don't care if I don't be living here. You going to get out of this house."

It was too much for me. Not the money really, even though I needed some. But money was not on my mind. It was the feeling that they didn't want me. Everything just suddenly fell apart. And the house. I hadn't thought about that, I was so busy, I was so tired. I just hadn't thought about it, even though I knew I wasn't in the will, and he was going to have to leave the house to *somebody*.

I don't know where I went that night. I just wandered, I just roamed. Somewhere, I don't remember where, just walking along the roads. In the dark. I could see the lights on in the houses, but I wasn't going nowhere certain. I don't think I even knew whose house was whose.

I was full of anger. I was lost.

I started thinking to myself, "If he left the house to this girl, he is stupid. She never did visit him or help him or anything."

I didn't tell anybody that Pam told me these things.

THEY HAD the body in Mount Pleasant at the funeral home. We all went there to the wake to see him. There were a lot of people coming in and out of there. I told Kitty and them to go ahead on and I would be in later. Because maybe they all thought like Pam, that I wasn't part of the family.

When they all came out, I went in there by myself. I looked in the casket. I looked at him, and I said, "Why did you do this to me? You make me felt like nothing, all over again." I believed he could hear what I'm saying. I was crying when I came out.

Ray saw me crying. He said, "Ruthie, what's wrong, baby? You don't have to cry."

I said, "Nothing."

When I was getting ready to get into Kitty's car, I turned around, I looked at Pam, and I told Kitty, "I can't ride in the car with her."

"Gal, what's going on?"

"I just can't be in the same car." So Ray and me drove to the church alone.

The funeral was ten o'clock that morning. The church was packed. And if Daddy only could see—all his lovers were in there, and these ladies didn't even know it. Each one of them thought the others were just his friends.

After the service we all got into the limo. I didn't want to be in the car with Pam, but she was in there talking like nothing happened.

AT THE military cemetery in Beaufort, the soldiers were all dressed up. The uniforms were blue, they were dark blue, and the buttons on those jackets were red, and the trimmings on the jackets were red, and the hats were white with red trimmings. As the limo went through the gates slowly, men were in lines on each side, with their hands to their caps. Then their feet went up and down in a rhythm, and their arms moved up and down. They looked like toy soldiers, moving, turning. As we got closer to where the casket was at, under a tent thing, and the limousine stopped, a guy would come walking in slow motion, and they would come one by one and escort us out of the car and I was trying to make sure I got myself to the rhythm as they were marching, because as they were moving, I was trying to move the same way. It was just so nice and it was so smooth the way they sat all of us down. And they all stood in a long line with their rifles on their sides. Then a higher rank man came and he was standing right in front of us, because all of us was on the first row. And there were two soldiers, one on one side of the casket and one on the other side of the casket, and they took the flag off of the top. They were folding this flag neatly and folding it slowly. Just folding it, folding it. After one got through folding it, the other one put it in his hand, and he moved his feet around, and he turned, and he walked towards Kitty, and then he turned again, and he sat it in her lap.

Right after that—*bam, bam, bam*—you could hear the bullets. Shells shooting everywhere, three times. Three. And I screamed out.

Then they talked a little bit, and after that there was more rifle shooting. Then they came one by one and escorted us back towards the limos.

But we didn't get in. We stayed out there. We told them that we wasn't going to get in the car. We wanted to see these people move this casket, to put it in the ground, so we would know exactly where it was. All of the headstones were white, all white, and so many out there, we wanted to know exactly where it was going to be, to make sure we could find it later. We watched them put it into the ground. Even after they covered it up, we stayed. The guy that was driving the limo was ready to go, but we weren't ready to go then. We wanted to take a picture.

I said, "Yeah. Just take a picture, for this last time for us, seeing this man." Every one of us took a picture, some by the flowers, some by the headstone.

Then we left.

We were in the limo on the way back to Charleston, about thirty minutes away from the cemetery, and a strange thing happened. It wasn't no sadness and it wasn't no crying—but we just started talking about how Daddy treated us. We talked about that. We said it had happened to him the same way he'd done Grandmama, he suffered like he'd made her suffer, and maybe worse. We said we have all come through a rough, painful, scared life with him.

But Pam was sitting there, she had her arms folded, and she was looking at me. And right then I said to myself, "Daddy is not dead. He is still sitting right over there."

We got tied up in traffic, we were hours and hours, and people waiting on us. When we got back to the house it was still crowded, but not as much. And after all the people left, Pam said, "I'm taking that microwave back. And I'm taking that television. Oh, and those antique beds—"

Kitty said, "Everything that's in here, I think y'all should let Gal keep that in the house."

I didn't give a damn. I said, "You want it, take it." I didn't have anything left in me.

I said, "Kitty, when is the will going to be read?"

"Tuesday, I think."

I said to myself, "Well, I can go with them, I can be in there even though I won't get anything." I guess I was thinking if I can't be part of the family, I can be on the edge of it anyway. So I went with them.

We drove two vans. We drove Naomi's van and we drove Kitty's van, and I didn't have to ride with Pam.

We got to the lawyer office, right there off of Broad Street. I went in with them. Sat down. He had the paper. As he was reading it, he called off everybody's name. But he counted one extra person in there. And then he looked at me, and he asked me who was I.

I told him who I was.

He told me that I had to leave out.

I begged him. I was trying not to cry. "I know my name is not on there," I said, "but all I want to do is just sit here."

And I begged them.

I said, "Kitty, y'all please let me stay in. Just let me stay in."

Pam turned around. She said, "Kitty, I think we should respect Daddy's will, because if he wanted her to have anything he would have her name in the will. And if she sit here and listen to what's going on, we will be disobeying Daddy."

I asked that man again, I said, "Please, just let me stay, because they are just like my sisters."

He said, "Well, it's up to them."

And Kitty said yes, and Sylvie and Florence said yes. But Evelyn and Naomi and Pam said no.

The man said I couldn't stay.

I just went outside. I walked across the street to the store. I walked in there and I got a couple of packs of cigarettes, and I was just smoking, I didn't care, I was walking in the street crying.

I know people were watching me. I didn't care. I just didn't give a damn. I wanted a car to run over me. Kill me right then. I just couldn't understand what was happening.

They were in there for quite a while. When they came out, I was sitting on a cement bench outside. Kitty said, "Gal, you ready to go?"

I just nodded my head, didn't even open my mouth. When I got to the door of the van, Pam said, "Kitty, y'all remember, y'all can't even discuss this with Gal, because she is not in the will."

But she was very upset, because she thought Daddy left her the house, which though he didn't. He left it to Sylvie.

As we were driving, I sat in the last seat in the back by myself. It was so quiet, nobody said nothing. Nobody didn't say a damn word. I had looked up, and I could see Kitty was looking at me in the mirror and I turned my head the other way. I looked back, and Naomi's van was behind us. And Pam was looking dead at me. I wanted to jump out of that van. I wanted to get away from them all.

We all got to the house. It was quiet the whole time, nobody said nothing.

I told them that I'm going out for a while, and I'll be back. Ray said, "Where are you going?" and I said, "Just somewhere." He didn't know what was happening, and I didn't tell him because I didn't want to upset him, too.

I drunk a twelve-pack of beer. When I came back, I stood in the front yard and I looked at the house. I mean, I just looked at that house. And I looked around. And I walked around the back. Florence was coming out the door.

"Gal, are you all right?"

I just bob my head.

"Come go with me in my car."

When we got in her car, she gave me a joint. She said, "I think you need this." I was already high as a kite, but I couldn't tell, and I smoked it. And all of a sudden, she and I just grabbed each other, and we were really crying. We were crying.

She said, "Gal, I am so sorry that Daddy didn't leave you anything. I cannot believe that he didn't leave you nothing at all."

"I can't either, Florence. Nothing. Nothing. Not even leave my kids nothing whatsoever. And he left Kitty kids something, Naomi kids something, Sylvie kids . . ."

She said, "Don't worry about it. The money that we do get, I know I'm going to send you something, and Sylvie will send you something. And you know Kitty going to give you something."

I said, "I'm not looking for nothing from nobody. I don't care. I just don't care."

"I promise you. I'll send you something."

A month or two later they all got lumps of money. All did. Plus the land in Mississippi and some here in Charleston. He never told us he owned all this land and had money too. We never knew nothing about it, we thought that we were poor for real. Eating corn on the cob for months and months, you figure there's no money. He never bought us clothes. And all the time, this man had money. I guess it was in the bank, but I never saw him write a check in his life. He always paid cash.

Sylvie said, "Gal, listen. I'm not coming back to South Carolina. If you and Ray will only pay the taxes on the house, you can stay here as long as you like."

I told her thank you, and that I appreciate that.

FLORENCE CALLED me one day on the job.

"Remember I told you I was going to send you some money? We all got about ten to twelve thousand dollars each."

I said to myself, "It's six of them. If they all give me a thousand dollars, that would be fine."

Florence sent me $200. I had figured it would be more, but I said well, she sent me *something*. Kitty promised me she would give me some money. At the time, my lights got turned out, we had no money. Everything just went, I don't know what happened to me. I believe I drunk the money up, I smoked it up, everything was going crazy.

I asked Kitty was it all right now, could she give me the money that she promised me. She told me she couldn't, because she just paid somebody to brick in her house.

I said, "Well, I'll ask Naomi." I called Naomi, and she said, "Well, I don't know—"

I said to myself, "Lord knows, if I was really a full-blooded sister, and one of them were the niece, I would never do that to them." That's what I was saying to myself. I would never do that to them. Seem like they all got what they wanted, and after that didn't care about me no more. So I never asked them again for one penny, not a dime. I said to myself, in the long run maybe they will see this was wrong. When Daddy died, and it was time to read that will, regardless if I was in the will, I feel that I should have been in the room with them, and it was up to all of them to say *yes, let her come in.*

I STILL do thank Sylvie for letting me stay in the house. She called a few times and said for sure she is not coming back to South Carolina. And I started thinking, I don't have the money, but somehow I want to buy this house from her. Maybe I could work it out with her to pay her a monthly payment, but at the time she said she won't sell it off.

I saved money, thinking some day Sylvie might change her mind. And she did. But she sold it from underneath me without telling me—knowing that I wanted it. She could have said well, I'll ask Gal and see if she want to buy it. But from what I heard she was going to put it on the market down here and not tell me anything, and then Naomi heard about it. She and Cass bought the house from Sylvie.

I never had a chance at it. Didn't even find out Sylvie was going to sell, until it was too late.

Ray said, "Well, Cass, how much did you pay for it? Me and Ruthie might could buy it from you."

Cass said he cannot quote the price to us.

That's what made me think maybe it wasn't much money they paid Sylvie. Me and Ray might could have come up with the money somehow, maybe on a monthly plan, rent-to-own. We needed the house. We didn't have no other place to live, like they all did.

But there was nothing I could do about it.

And after that, life just went on.

And we all went our ways. I'm still here in the house, paying rent to Naomi and Cass. Kitty got a home in Wambaw on two or three acres. Everybody's got land that Daddy left for them. Florence is on two acres of land, home in Mississippi. Sylvie has got land with a trailer on it, but she is building a home. Pam and Evelyn got one or two acres of land in Mississippi, they haven't build a home on it yet but they can any time they want to. Naomi and Cass got a home in Georgia, live in a white section, a rich section. I told them I couldn't afford to pay the $500 a month that they wanted at first. So I have to pay $350, and the month that I'm late and don't have it, they will put me out. After one year they can up the rent or sell the house. I asked them, the money that I'm using to pay them on it now, could I use that as a down payment?

And the answer is no.

IF THEY LET somebody else live here, somebody outside the family, it wouldn't be the Fleetwood house anymore. It just would not be the Fleetwood house. That person might not take care of the house. The neighbors in my neighborhood, half of them are old people, but on my street everybody try to keep their house and yard looking good. I don't want somebody to move in there who is going to play loud music, tear up the house, bother the neighbors. Before that happens I would go out and pull up all my plants—and I would—or pour it down with gas. I can't take down the wallpaper, I can't pull up the tiles I laid. I remodeled a bathroom, I tore open a wall. I did the work. The yard was like a junkyard, old machines and cars and typewriters out there. We cleaned it up, we scrubbed. The neighbors will tell you, the house that Ruthie and her husband live in now, that's not the same house. It's like a new brand-new house all over again.

For a while I even figured I might be able to get the house another way. What I was going to do was pay that tax for seven years, and then I thought I would own that house. You pay tax on a house for so many years, no matter what they say, you own it. That's what I was going to do, and they didn't know. My husband didn't know. I had already paid the tax for three years. But Naomi said, "I don't want you paying tax on the house no more." She probably figured that out.

So today, every time a car pull up in my yard, I'm thinking it's somebody coming to tell me to move out. Naomi might get so heated up, she might run it through Section Eight, let somebody rent it. If I hear a car, and I don't know who it is, I'm worried.

I guess they think they got rid of me ... but I look around, and I see, they are all gone! I am still here in the Fleetwood family, the only one left. The one that they thought would be the worst, the one they thought was nothing, dumb, couldn't talk, wouldn't make it. They think I have nothing.

But they can work up things—I am working on things myself. I am saving my money. I am loving Ray. And I am loving my kids. Maybe it looks like I have nothing, but I have more than anyone knows about.

And I believe there's a lot of people who have had a life worse than me.

chapter sixteen

i know two good things that Daddy did while he was alive. One was, he always made sure we took breakfast, lunch, and supper over to Mr. Buzz. And the other was when he made cookies for us. Daddy used to cook in the Navy, so he knew how to do it, and he made the best cookies in the world. That's the one good thing he did for us. He would get that dough, that flour and everything, and mix it up, and we would see him with the cutter, cutting, and we knew that we was going to get some cookies. He would bake those cookies, and those were the best cookies you've ever had. He was a good baker and an excellent cook.

And I became a good cook. I love to cook—Southern cooking. I'm a country cooker. I always wanted a restaurant of my own, like my Aunt Ida in Baltimore. I cook the best candy yams in the world. And you should taste my lasagna. Other people's lasagna is falling over but mine, when you cut it, it stays. And when I'm cooking, I use fresh vegetables. I don't like canned vegetables. My homemade soup is the best soup you have ever tried.

Every Easter I make bunny cakes. Big ears, long face, bow tie. I make two layers. One layer, I know that's his face. The next round layer, I cut one ear off each side and I take the middle out and that's the bow tie. I seen one in the store, and I said, that looks simple to do. I make three every year—one for me and my kids, one for Mary, and one for Kitty family. And I make the Easter baskets myself, out of aluminum foil paper.

I make the best garlic bread, and okra soup, and—believe it or not—pig feet! Barbecue pig feet. I love pig feet now, but my kids won't eat it. "Mama, no, it look like a foot! Look at that toe!"

I took some to Willie, the black guy on the job, and Carl, the white guy, said, "Ruthie, let me ask you a question. You won't get mad, will you?"

I said, "What is it, Carl?"

He said, "Where is the meat on the pig feet?"

"Carl, I don't really have time to explain it."

He started laughing.

"But listen," I said. "I got about eight pig feet at home, barbecue. It's delicious. You want me to bring you one?"

He said, "Um, I think I'll pass on that."

"Carl, you don't have to look for the meat! Just eat it."

And some day I'm going to have that restaurant. A little one, somewhere around here, maybe off of 17. "Ruthie's Country Cooking." Nothing big, just country-looking, and somebody singing a little country something, peaceful and mellow, and good food for everybody that comes in.

I DO still stutter but none of my kids do. Sometimes when I'm talking a word will jam up in me so bad, and I get mad, because I feel that I can't *turn* it to say it. I know what it is, but I can't say it. And I think oh, just forget it. But Ray will wait, and say, "Ruthie, go ahead on and say it, take your time"—he doesn't laugh at me. My kids know. They say, "Mama, you stutter sometimes."

I say, "So?"

My kids don't know my childhood. They'll ask me, "Mama, where's your mama? How come we never meet your daddy?"

And I say to myself oh, no. But I tell them, "I will tell you about it when you get older." That's what I have to say. What can I tell them? They come up with questions that I got to be ready to answer. Because they're going to ask again. I don't know what I will say.

I did some terrible things in my life. But that's all in the past for me. I teach my kids not to do those things.

My Etta—we call her Nicky—she is so smart, she knows when something is wrong with me. She will say "Mama, what's wrong?" I am probably thinking about my mother; mainly that's it, my mother, or else things that aren't going right. And she'll say "What's wrong?" And Denise will come and lay her head on my lap and look up at me.

On my birthday the kids always buy me something. And Ray, he'll give me a present, flowers, little bottle of wine. He always buys three roses, three different colors. And one thing I bought for myself on my birthday—a real black Barbie doll. And she is beautiful.

My son, Junior, he is crazy about insects. He loves them, he has a collection. I bought him a bug box to catch them in. I bought him a little book. I'm working at the plant nursery now, and the dead bugs that I find on the job, I wrap them up and take them home, and he puts them in his little book, and he puts the word, what it is.

I never had anything like that, no hobby. Hobby! Your *hobby* was to get your ass up, get your work done, that's what your hobby was! And when I was a child, I thought I was dumb. I realized I wasn't dumb when I started writing. I would hide all my papers, because Daddy always wanted to know what I was writing. I would hide all my stuff.

Then as I got a little bit older I would write things and I would show people. "Aw, what book did you copy that out of?" That's what I would get from people. "You too dumb to write that." People say you're dumb, you're stupid, and in your mind you start to wonder. When I was a senior in high school I made a speech, and I said I was going to work towards my goal, and I heard somebody say "What *goal*. That girl don't have no *goal*."

I write my things, just things to be writing. Even when I hear things on the news that happened, it will dawn on me, what I want to say about it. And Nicky writes. Nicky is eight. She's a honor-roll student. She is too smart. And Shana, she is going to be a singer. She is good. And Denise, my baby, is going to be an actress. I can tell. She is a good actress now. I say to myself, she is just like me, when I was that age. I can see me in her. I used to do those same things.

THE BOLTONS still live in Tolley, Florida. They visit us, and we go down there. And I love the Boltons but I still don't like Tolley. All the black people that own land down there, the white people are now circling them. They're moving in close. Coming close, moving in. Pretty soon they'll run them out.

In Hungry Neck, the same thing is happening. White houses all around us now, down on the waterfront. But Hungry Neck people are not running anywhere. They're going to stay. They been here for too long. I found out black people have been living in Hungry Neck for more than a hundred years, since they first became free and figured out they could get together to buy land together, in a group. This was the first place they did that. And been here ever since.

People in Hungry Neck are good to me. My neighbor down the street, Mrs. Hampton, is a teacher, and she charges ten dollars an hour for tutoring. I sent Shana to her. But she knows I don't have much money. She charged me nothing. She told me anytime to send the kids on down. And when I go down to get them, if it's not words she's teaching them, it's math, with money, nickels and dimes on the table to help them count. She'll have letters, all the alphabet cut out.

Mrs. Vane hugs me. She always grabs me and she squeeze me. Or sometimes when she and I is just standing up talking, she will just grab my hand and she'll hold my hand. If I go to the store with her, she'll hold my hand when we walk in the store like that, and that means so much to me.

And Mrs. Vane treats my kids like grandkids. She never goes to church without them. They go with her to Second Zion every Sunday. She don't have a daughter, and she says I'm the daughter that she never had. I like that. Sometimes she even tells people that I am her daughter. And I like it when she does that.

To TELL YOU the truth, I always wanted people to like me. Even when I was a child, I wanted attention. I wanted to be on camera. And Kitty was my photographer. She always listened, she always watched. When I was little I told her I like to sing, and I said, "Kitty, would you please come listen to me sing this song?" She actually sat there and listened to me sing. I knew it was bad, but I said, "Kitty, how do it sound?" and she said, "Sounds pretty good, Gal." She took billions of pictures of me when I was fourteen, fifteen. And later when I was in trouble she bailed me out. Gave me her Christmas savings. And she really love me now, and I love her. Kitty and me can't do without each other.

I always knew, too, that deep down in her heart Florence could be a sweet person. Today she will give you her heart. She will cook you the biggest meal, she will sleep on the couch and let you have her bed. And Naomi is loving and caring. She ask me can she take one of the kids on a trip. When Cass and Naomi came down to visit, even though I knew they had bought the house and I was hurt about that, still I cooked rice, chicken, and string beans, and we all ate, and it was like nothing had happen. Sometimes it's best to smile and be happy. And that's what I did. Ray called me a good actress for that.

But I told him, I'm not mad with anyone. I don't hate anyone. I can't read their minds, I don't know what they could have been thinking. Maybe when Pam was a child in Mississippi, she said, "Why did Daddy leave me here, and took Gal home? Why is Gal getting everything, and she ain't even kin to him?" But if she only knew, I wasn't getting nothing but beaten. I was being beaten for socks. Shoes. Hair. Bump. Any little thing.

And Pam was the baby of the family. Anybody who's the baby of the family know the baby is supposed to get the most in the will. And supposed to get the house. So Daddy's will turned everything around for Pam. Before that, and this is no lie, she was always a nice girl to me. She always wrote, she always send pictures, until the death of Daddy.

But any time Daddy name is mentioned or a thought of him is in somebody's mind, we turn into a different person. We been flip crazy. He has affected us so much, and we probably don't know, and I probably don't know myself, that we really do love each other and want to be close. But the minute we mention certain things about Daddy it knocks a nerve. I know if Daddy was never in the picture, or if he was not the way he was, none of this would have never come about.

He turned this family upside down. Not just for me. For all of us. He left everybody in a way that has them confused, puzzled, don't even know how to talk to each other right. We can't even come together and sit down and say, "Hey, why are we blaming ourselves for something this man done?"

But I think some day we will do that.

* * *

WHAT'S SO EXCITING to me now, when I'm grown-up, is that I've got things with my name on them. My husband tells me this is crazy, but it's not. Every time I would look in the house, it was always their name, and never my name.

When I finally saw a birth certificate with my name on it was July in 1990. I was stunned to get it, because I never had seen it. On the sheet that they gave me, where it says "father" it says "not known or not given" and for "mother" it says Leitha Homer. And me. Ruthie Homer. I like that.

So I got my birth certificate. And I'm supposed to put it in a safe place, but I can't control myself—I have to keep it with me in my pocketbook. I want to be able to see it all the time. Never had one before.

I guess I got a social security number when they first sent those checks when my real mother died. But Daddy took the checks, and the card. I know now that if he had put those checks in the bank for me, then when he died I would have had something. But that's okay. That don't make no difference to me now. What I wanted was the *card*. When I finally got it, I looked at it for about an hour. And I keep that in my pocketbook, too.

I'm still working at the little nursery, over there by the bread bakery. And I love that place. We got any flower you could want, all the roses, and more fruit trees than the world allows. Fig tree, persimmon tree, pear tree, and we got a new tree that look like tiny little apples—they're red, and when you bite them it taste just like a apple. We got the grape trees, we got the plum trees, we have banana trees. We grow strawberries. We have a Chinese area, and it looks just like China, even got a Chinese house. And then by the gazebo we have the pond. During the first part of the spring, tulips come.

I get a 20% discount off of everything I buy. I can go out there, and certain plants will call to me. I mean I really feel it, them calling to me, pulling me. It's true. There's pretty things all over the nursery, but I will just be walking around, walking around, and it's like a certain plant will tell me "I am the one. Nobody else wants me, and I'm going to die if you don't buy me." And I will buy it. And it will live for me if I buy it. They always do. Never die. Never die.

I've learned a lot of things that I never knew was important about plants. I thought it was just throwing it in, just putting it in the hole and that's it. But it's not that. It's just like a human being, if you don't feed it, it won't live. Or don't take care of it, it won't grow. If you don't fertilize or feed it, or give it the right things, it will not grow for you. I think about it like that, too. That's a baby there. It's going to die if I don't take it. That's what I feel about those plants. Not all of them—only the ones that I know that want me, the ones that are talking to me.

On my lunchtime I walk through. I just walk. Walk and talk. Look. And I say, "Yeah, don't

worry, I'll get you, before I get off work." And
what I do, to make sure nobody else don't get it,
I will tag it. Say *Sold*. It's like I got to have it.

Seem like flowers bring happiness to people,
you know, plants. Because it's beautiful. And I
like pretty things. I always did. I always wanted
pretty things, but I couldn't never get them. But
I see that I can get them now. Just got to work
hard and save your money that's all. Even if
you're in debt for the rest of your life, you can
get a few pretty things in your life. Maybe I'm
not going to have it all my life, but at least I can
say I had it.

I've bought some plants that looked like they
were half dead, brown and shriveled. The boss
would say "Ruthie, there's a better one—" and
I would say "No, I want to get this one right
here." And I get it home, and it grows. I have a
touch for plants. They know that I care about
them. And I love that job, at the nursery. The
people I work for, the Cosgroves, they are good
people. They made me the manager there now,
and I work hard.

But after I get off work, once I'm home, I'm
into home. For children. Once I'm there, it's
family on my mind. Those are the little plants. I
don't care what happens outside that door.
Once I'm in.

Still I always know there is one other person
supposed to be here in this house with us. I
think about her all the time. And it's Mary.

I first got back in touch with her when I came

from Florida. They wouldn't let me see her. Mrs. Millican said if I did come I was not going to bring that nigger with me. She meant Ray. She hated him. For no reason, except I wasn't with her son.

They still kept playing that game with me, not letting me see her. So I stopped calling and going over there for a while. If I did call her, they would be listening on the other phone. Or else Mary would be talking to me, and her grandmama is right there by the phone with her, and you could hear the whispers of Mrs. Millican telling Mary what to say to me.

The first day I really got to see her again, she asked me, she said, "Mama, did you know my daddy?"

That really knocked me.

I said, "We were married!" But the Millicans had never told her that. She didn't really even know what a daddy was or what a mama was. And from what I gather, they were telling her bad things about me. But slowly, slowly, they let me come see her. They realized I am not the same person I used to be.

And today, I can go there seven days a week. I can go get her when I want to, it's no problem. Mrs. Millican told me that she's sorry, what she did, and she understand now what I was going through at the time. And she said, far as she was concerned, I'm still her daughter-in-law today, because I am Mary's mother. She even explained to my husband. And now today, Ray can go there and pick Mary up, and there's never any trouble. Something goes wrong in school, Mrs. Millican calls me.

I told Mary there's a secret that I need to tell her, but she has to be a certain age first. She is too young now. And a secret is a secret, I told her, not between me and you and your grandmother, but just me and you. And when she's old enough I will tell her the whole story.

I know I didn't do it right with Mary, when she was a baby. Matter of fact, I myself didn't really understand what a mama was, even after I was one. It took me some time to know. But now I do.

And even though I go there now, and I see her all the time and take her places, I know it's not enough. I thought, *Damn, she might feel the same way I felt with my own mother.* Mary is like me. Most kids when they have never lived with their mother before, they would call you Ruthie. But never has she called me that. It's Mama. Always. She's going just like I was. I knew I should call my mama Leitha, but I couldn't do it. Most people would do it. But she's the same as me. Always Mama.

I said to myself, *When she turns sixteen, she's going to leave them, and she's going to come where she should have been from the beginning.* That's in my heart today. It's just a feeling that I got. And when I see her, she don't even have to tell me, it's like a contact between us. I can just feel that. She wants to say, "Mama, I want to come with you." But she can't. They won't let her come yet. But I see her every chance I get. I'm going to pick her up today. We're going to Show Biz.

And it's just a feeling. I know it's going to happen. She's going to be with me. Mr. and Mrs. Millican, they're in their late sixties. Mary's a teenager, she's fourteen. She's taller than me now.

And I know it will happen. Mary is my hope. I'm going to have her with us.

AFTER DADDY DIED, I went in to clean up his room. I could smell him. His scent was in there for the longest time. And those stains were on the floor where Daddy used to pee going back and forth to the bathroom. But today those stains are gone.

A couple of months later, Ray told me that he saw my grandfather in the living room. But he wasn't scared.

"Ray, are you sure?"

"Yes. I saw him in there."

I did get kind of frightened at first, because nobody was sleeping in Daddy's room. And I had scrubbed that floor so hard, but now for a minute I thought I still saw those stains. And when I walked past his room, it was like I could feel he was in there.

I was sleeping. And in my sleep he came to me. In my dreams. And he told me, too, he said, "Gal, I am so sorry that I didn't leave you anything. Will you forgive me?"

His voice was just as clear as day, as clear as when he would call me, Gal this and Gal that, and I woke up, and I woke my husband up and I told him what Daddy told me—that he was sorry he left me nothing. And I couldn't wait till the next day to call Kitty, and I told Kitty what Daddy told me. Kitty said "No," and I said, "Yes, Kitty, he came and he told me he was sorry."

Kitty said, "Maybe he had to come and tell you that, because maybe that house was supposed to be yours."

From then on, I figured that the house was going to be mine, somehow, no matter what. But I wonder, today, why he came to me. He didn't say a word about how he beat me. But I guess wherever he is, he can see what he did, and what he should have done.

When I look around the house and see all the things that were in there when I was little, it doesn't bother me. The blue chair, the beds, that old chifforobe, some of the plates and the silverwares that say USN, those two end tables and the lamp . . . still there. And all those things are precious to me. Especially that blue chair. I don't let nobody sit in it. That's the chair that he threw me in and my head went through the window. A little bit of the cotton you can see coming out, but I don't want that to be touched. I don't want to get it reupholstered. I want it to stay as it was.

Still there.

The coffee table where he used to beat me, I kept that a long time even though it had a hole in it where Daddy bammed his hand on there one time. But finally it broke, and I threw it away. There was too much I didn't like about that table.

I NEVER did dream about my mother. I didn't have to, she was in my head. And still is today. I still talk to her. I just did it the other day. I said, "Mama, I am writing this book, if you could only see. But it's making me cry. When I was little I never let Daddy see a single tear, not one. Now I'm an adult and I'm crying my eyes out. Just remembering those times."

And I said—for her—"Yeah, I'm watching, baby. I'm watching you. Don't cry, don't worry." And I pretend that she is rubbing my head, saying, "Don't worry, don't worry." It's just a thing that I do. It's imagination. It's not real.

I thought I saw her one day. But it wasn't her. I remember how she looked, and this lady was talking to me, and I kept looking at her. I knew it was all in my mind, I knew it wasn't her, but I was thinking, "Don't you know me? Why aren't you answering? Why aren't you saying nothing? Don't you know it's me? This is Gal, this is Gal, this is Ruthie!" The lady looked just like her. I knew it wasn't her but I wanted this lady to be her. I said to myself, "You know you know me. Tell me, tell me you know me. I'm Gal."

* * *

THE PLANTS that I love the best are the zinnias, the snapdragons, the chrysanthemums—
and mainly the hibiscus, because it opens up
like a bell but it's got a long thing that comes
out of it like a tongue, and hummingbirds can
get nectar out of that. Those are the main ones
that really call me. The zinnias is my other favorite, and one more—sunflower. I really like
sunflower. Because it makes you happy, you
know. And if you plant one, regardless of how
you set it, when the sun is shining, whichever
direction the sun is shining, I swear to God you
might see that flower turn yourself. The face of
the sunflower will turn directly towards the
sun. As the sun moves around, I swear, it
moves. It will move. It follows the sun.

HOME-GOING SERVICES
for the late
MR. CLOVIS FLEETWOOD
at
Second Zion Tabernacle A.M.E. Church
Hungry Neck, South Carolina

——Interment——
NATIONAL CEMETERY
Beaufort, South Carolina

Chief Petty Officer Clovis Fleetwood was born June 7, 1925, in Shootamile, Mississippi. He was the son of the late Isaac and Edna Fleetwood. He was married to the late Ruth Homer.

On Thursday, February 21, 1991, he departed this life.

Chief Petty Officer Fleetwood received his education in Mississippi, served from 1944 to 1966 in the United States Navy, and worked at the Naval Weapons Station for eighteen years until retirement. He received many medals and awards for his service in the U.S. Navy.

Those left to cherish fond memories include: six daughters—Florence Rudd, Sylvia Givens, Evelyn and Pamela Fleetwood of Shootamile, Mississippi, Naomi Merton of Belview, Ga., and Katherine Cupp of Wambaw, S.C., one step-granddaughter, Ruthie Bolton of Hungry Neck, S.C., two brothers, two sisters, four brothers-in-law, three sisters-in-law, four sons-in-law, thirteen grandchildren, and a host of other relatives and friends.

A TRIBUTE, WRITTEN BY ONE OF THE FAMILY
"Father Dreams"
I have always wanted to teach my children to work hard on this earth, to face sickness and strife, stand up for what you feel is right, get up if you fall down, push hard to understand eternal truth, remembering the work you've done speaks for you. Know right from wrong, ask God to lead you on and keep you strong, no matter how narrow the path may be. Honor thy father and thy days will be long. I am leaving them, dear God, to finish my glorious dream, so I ask your guidance, to lead them on with confidence and happiness in their hearts, with an open mind, and remembering the ten commandments, for we all shall go home to the land of paradise one day in rest and peace.

Ruthie Bolton

AFRICAN AMERICAN
STUDIES

☐ **AFRICANS AND THEIR HISTORY by Joseph E. Harris.** A landmark reevaluation of African cultures by a leading black historian. "A major brief summary of the history of Africa."—Elliot P. Skinner, *Columbia Univeristy*   (625560—$4.99)

☐ **THE CLASSIC SLAVE NARRATIVES edited by Henry Louis Gates, Jr.** One of America's foremost experts in black studies, presents a volume of four classic slave narratives that illustrate the real nature of the black experience with the horrors of bondage and servitude.   (627261—$5.99)

☐ **BEFORE FREEDOM edited and with an Introduction by Belinda Hurmence.** The oral history of American slavery in the powerful words of former slaves. Including the two volumes *Before Freedom, When I Can Just Remember* and *My Folks Don't Want Me to Talk About Slavery.* "Eloquent . . . historically valuable."—*Los Angeles Times Book Review*   (627814—$5.99)

☐ **BLACK LIKE ME by John Howard Griffin.** The startling, penetrating, first-hand account of a white man who learned what it is like to live as a black in the South. Winner of the *Saturday Review* Anisfield-Wolf Award.   (163176—$4.99)

☐ **THE SOULS OF BLACK FOLK by W.E.B. DuBois.** A passionate evaluation of the blacks' bitter struggle for survival and self-respect, and a classic in the literature of the civil rights movement. Introduction by Nathan Hare and Alvin F. Poussaint.   (523970—$4.95)

Prices slightly higher in Canada

Recommended Reading from MENTOR and SIGNET